The Domesticated Penis

THE UNIVERSITY OF ALABAMA PRESS | TUSCALOOSA

THE

Domesticated
penis

HOW WOMANHOOD
HAS SHAPED MANHOOD

Loretta A. Cormier & Sharyn R. Jones

The University of Alabama Press
Tuscaloosa, Alabama 35487-0380
uapress.ua.edu

Hardcover edition published 2015.
Paperback edition published 2016.
eBook edition published 2015.

Inquiries about reproducing material from this work should be
addressed to the University of Alabama Press.

Typeface: Scala Pro

Manufactured in the United States of America
Cover image: Iculanibokola, a penis-shaped cannibal fork used
by Fijian chiefs, replica in the Fiji Museum; photo by James P.
Cormier
Cover design: Michele Myatt Quinn

∞
The paper on which this book is printed meets the minimum
requirements of American National Standard for Information
Science–Permanence of Paper for Printed Library Materials,
ANSI Z39.48-1984.

Paperback ISBN: 978-0-8173-5891-4

A previous edition of this book has been catalogued by the
Library of Congress as follows:
    Library of Congress Cataloging-in-Publication Data
    Cormier, Loretta A.
    The domesticated penis : how womanhood has shaped
manhood / Loretta A. Cormier, Sharyn R. Jones.
    pages   cm
    Includes bibliographical references and index.
    ISBN 978-0-8173-1874-1 (hardback) — ISBN 978-0-
8173-8850-8 (ebook) 1. Penis. 2. Penis—Social aspects. 3.
Masculinity. 4. Men—Sexual behavior. 5. Women—History.
6. Sex role—History. 7. Human evolution. 8. Feminist
archaeology. 9. Feminist anthropology. I. Jones, Sharyn R. II.
Title.
    GT498.P45C67 2015
    305.31—dc23   2015014446

Contents

Illustrations

Acknowledgments

Special thanks go to Sherrie Alexander, Lisa Baker, James Cormier, Joan Ferrante, William Landon, Jill Pruett, and Ashley Wilson.

The Domesticated Penis

1

The Human Penis

Why Study the Phallus?

In 1988, *Saturday Night Live* received over 40,000 letters of complaint following a controversial sketch it aired. The late-night comedy show is intended to parody American culture and politics, but one skit had apparently crossed the line of acceptable joking. What caused this enormous outpouring of public outrage? Conan O'Brien had cowritten a comedy routine that used the offensive "p" word 42 times: Penis. The setting was a nude beach and the shtick was to say the taboo word as many times as possible, culminating in the sketch's anthem:

> Penis, penis, penis, penis
> Penis, penis song.
> Penis, penis, penis, penis
> Penis all day long.

Our cultural taboos involving discussion of the penis are likely why it has not been the subject of serious inquiry into human evolution. The human penis is strikingly unusual when compared with those of our primate cousins, but most people are unaware of this because the evolution of the penis is not discussed in science classes or textbooks. We are taught that humans are unique because we are big-brained, bipedal, and culture-bearing, using tools and language. In this book, we explain why the evolution of the penis is also critical to understanding human nature.

Here, we are not intending to tout the superiority of the male of our species by virtue of his penis; rather, we argue that the distinctive features of the human penis arose from what is termed "female choice." In this process, females make choices about which males they find most desirable and selectively mate with them, thereby driving the evolution of male characteristics.

Female choice explains the elaborate feathers of male peacocks,[1] the mating calls of male tree frogs,[2] and we argue, the distinctive physical and behavioral characteristics of the human penis.

The role of female choice has been given insufficient attention in studies of human evolution. More generally, the role of women has been historically undervalued. In depictions of ancient humans in older textbooks and *National Geographic* magazines, it really is about ancient *man* to the general exclusion of women. It is common to see images depicting men bringing home a slain mammoth, inventing tools, or discovering fire, while women, often naked above the waist, tend to serve as background filler for male cultural achievements. Melanie Wiber's *Erect Men/Undulating Women*[3] documents how the history of scientific illustration has perpetuated gender stereotypes in human prehistory. Although the illustrations are created from an artist's imagination, when the same images are repeated, people begin to believe that they are true. In essence, the message is that men create culture and women are the passive recipients of male cultural achievements.

Unfortunately, it is not just older textbooks that perpetuate these stereotypes. The dust jacket of a 2010 Oxford University Press psychology book asserts: "Amongst our ancestors—as with many other species—only the alpha males were able to reproduce, leading them to take more risks and to exhibit more aggressive and protective behaviors than women. Whereas women favor and excel at one-to-one intimate relationships, men compete with one another and build larger organizations and social networks from which culture grows."[4] Too often, the standard story of human evolution and cultural development has not afforded women the same degree of agency as is credited to men.

The above passage belies a fundamental misunderstanding of the term "alpha male" and the role of the alpha male. Research in primatology has clearly demonstrated that alpha males are not the only males who reproduce. More importantly, as we will elaborate further, the alpha male is not so much a genetically differentiated type of male as a role that a number of males in a group may occupy during their lifetimes. Moreover, although an alpha male may very well be the most aggressive and domineering male while he holds that role, females do not always choose these males as mating partners. Evolution is not a merely a process of inherently superior alpha males excluding their inferiors and winning the reward of mating with the females; female choice has also driven human evolution.

Unsubstantiated assertions that men are naturally aggressive, violent, and competitive while women are far more interested in snuggling babies and puppies keep appearing as scientific facts in the literature. Pop cultural formulaics, such as *Men Are from Mars, Women Are from Venus*,[5] are not only insulting to men and women alike but also patently false. One aim of this book is to set the record straight. Female selection is not an alternate view of evolution—it is integral to evolution. In this book, we examine the myriad ways that females have shaped male anatomy and explore aspects of this phenomenon from the insect world to primate societies.

What is so distinctive about the human penis? A number of differences become apparent when we compare the human penis with that of our primate cousins. However, it is not merely a matter of bigger being better. For example, the human penis is smooth and spineless.[6] Chimpanzees and other apes have knobby bristles on the tips of their phalluses, which make them extremely sensitive. Mating happens very quickly for these species, often within a matter of seconds. At some point in our evolutionary history, genetic change led to the loss of penis spines in our human ancestors, requiring males to spend much more time and effort in order to climax. In effect, it made sex *less* pleasurable for men and *more* pleasurable for women.

Fundamentally, the evolution of the penis is about the evolution of human sexuality. Human sexual behavior is not only about mating to produce offspring. Human females are fertile for only a few of days each month, yet they have sex regardless of whether or not they are near ovulation. The purpose of condoms and birth control pills is to allow men and women to have sex while avoiding pregnancy. Human sexual behavior includes oral sex, masturbation, same-sex partners, and sex among the elderly. Human sexuality also has a dark side, including rape, prostitution, and pedophilia.

Examples of all of these behaviors can be found in other animals as well. Dolphins masturbate,[7] some rams prefer other rams to ewes,[8] and penguin females have even been described as prostituting themselves for pebbles for their nests.[9] But humans routinely seek out a wide variety of sexual experiences unrelated to reproduction. Perhaps the only species whose sexual behavior rivals that of humans is the bonobo (*Pan paniscus*), an African ape closely related to the chimpanzee, who engage in a wide variety of sexual behaviors. Arguably, bonobos are even more sex-driven than are humans. According to primatologist Frans de Waal, in zoos, the average bonobo initiates some form of sexualized contact once every hour and a half during the day.[10] De Waal has suggested that sex among bonobos has evolved as a kind of social lubricant to smooth over conflicts and promote a sense of well-being in the group. He describes the bonobo philosophy as "make love, not war." Humans are bono-bo-like because they use sex to express affection and simply for pleasure. In humans, sex is not a merely a grand prize for male aggressiveness, in contrast to what many theorists have suggested.

However, an important question to consider is that if female choice has shaped the penis, how did we get to the point in the late twentieth century where it was offensive to even say the word "penis" on television networks? Certainly there was a time in human history when penises were in full view, with no fig leaves necessary to hide the shame. We give our children neutered Barbie dolls and GI Joes for fear that they will be psychologically traumatized at the sight of human genitalia. Today, Western society could not give more contradictory and mixed messages about sexuality.

We put those same children in grocery store buggies and wheel them past the check-out line magazine racks filled with headlines on how to improve one's sex life. It would be easy to conclude that the only way to true happiness is to have multiple orgasms in rapid succession. But we also give the message that sex is sinful and dangerous, with the potential to literally destroy human society. A Muslim cleric recently claimed that Iran's earthquakes were the result of women dressing too provocatively.[11] Televangelists Pat Robertson, Jerry Falwell, and others have proclaimed that promiscuity, homosexuality, and feminism were the cause of Hurricane Katrina in New Orleans and the 9/11 terrorist attacks.[12] In recent years, some high school students have worn color-coded jelly bracelets to advertise which sex acts they are willing to perform[13] while others have signed abstinence pledges, vowing to stay virginal until marriage.[14] It is not easy to sort out what is natural human sexual behavior from the trappings of culture, because humans are naturally cultural.

Our modern cultural attitudes toward the human penis, and sexuality in general, are not just a quirk of American society. They reflect long-term social changes that occurred in multiple human cultures with the advent of the agricultural revolution. This was truly a watershed event in human cultural history. As we argue, the agricultural revolution initiated multiple cultural changes, including the association of the penis with masculine dominance, superiority, and the ability to acquire resources.

For at least 90 percent of human history we lived as foraging hunter-gatherer-fishers. Most foraging groups are characterized by living nomadically, following animal herds, fishing, and gathering wild plants. Agricultural societies, on the other hand, domesticate plants and animals. With farming, humans began to settle down in one place, planting crops and raising animals where they lived. Archaeologists still debate why this happened. The growth of farming began around 10,000 years ago, following the end of the Late Pleistocene, which ended around 11,700 years ago and saw extinctions of terrestrial megafauna, including species such as mammoths and mastadons that humans hunted. Such extinctions may have derived from either environmental changes or human overhunting.[15] Human population growth is also linked to the proliferation of agriculture, either because agriculture could support larger populations or because large groups of sedentary people could no longer subsist solely on wild environmental resources, or both.[16]

Another characteristic of modern hunter-gatherers is that they are relatively egalitarian, lacking clear authority figures such as chiefs or headmen. Modern hunter-gatherers generally have a greater equality in relationships between men and women than do other types of societies. Many argue that hunting and gathering societies were more peaceful, particularly with respect to organized warfare, but there is considerable debate as to the extent of violence in ancient human history.[17]

Regardless of the origin of agriculture, it is mistake to think of agriculture as a one-time invention that spread around the world. Over a period of several thousand years, most human groups abandoned full-time hunting and gathering and began farming. People began domesticating a wide variety of plants and animals, depending on their needs and what was available in their local environments. For example, Native Americans began domesticating the "three sisters" plants: maize, beans, and squash.[18] In Asia, rice, soybeans, and chickens were domesticated.[19] In the Middle East and Africa, cattle, sheep, and wheat became important domesticates.[20] Human groups became more territorial and competitive with one another for access to resources. The notion of "I own this land" soon became "I own this person." The person owned was sometimes an individual incorporated into slavery, but ownership often entailed a man's claim to a woman. The penis came to be a symbol of male power and superiority and began to take on magical and mystical qualities. We find evidence of this symbolism in the archaeological record, which charts the emergence of a variety of penis cults associated with many agricultural societies.

One example of a penis cult is illustrated with the Egyptian god Min from the fourth millennium BCE, who was referred to as the lord of the penis. He is often depicted holding his large erect penis in one hand and a sheep-herding flail in the other. He was the god of sexuality and fertility and was also associated with domesticated cattle. The following excerpt from a hymn to Min illustrates well the agricultural cult of the penis: "Min, Bull of the Great Phallus . You are the Great Male, the owner of all females. The Bull who is united with those of the sweet love, of beautiful face and of painted eyes. Victorious sovereign among the Gods who inspires fear in the Ennead . . . the goddesses are glad, seeing your perfection." In this book we will describe evidence of penis cults in archaeological sites from early agricultural cultures across the globe. Changes in the way humans perceived the penis were widespread and pervasive. One might even say that since the shift to agricultural ways of life the general Western public perception of the penis has not changed much. Academy Award–winning actress Helen Mirren could have been speaking of the Bull of the Great Phallus when she recently described the film industry as "worshipping at the altar of the 18- to 25-year-old male and his penis."[21]

If dominant cultural ideologies have shifted our ideas about the penis, then how can we know what is natural sexual behavior in humans? It is perhaps a trick question to propose it as such, for in humans, biological evolution and cultural evolution are not neat categories that we can isolate, for human beings are biologically cultural beings. Cross-culturally, although we can document a wide variety of rituals and ideologies associated with sexuality, it has been much more difficult to get a clear picture of potential differences in human sexual behavior.

Unfortunately, much of what has been written about the sexual behavior of people in other cultures includes exotic erotica from dubious sources that still makes its way into college textbooks in psychology, sociology, and anthropology. Supposed cultural evidence from indigenous peoples is used to contrast their so-called primitive sexual behavior with that of modern Western societies. Fantastic claims are made for faraway places where men and women normally have intercourse 10 times a night, where women routinely experience hour-long orgasms, or where men's penises are so long that they have to tie them in a knot to be able to walk.

In this book we attempt to sort the facts from the fiction in representations of the sexuality of indigenous peoples. One example of a fiction that keeps appearing is that the Karamojong of Uganda have penises so long that they have to tie them in knots in order to walk properly. The tale has been repeated so frequently that several noted researchers in evolutionary biology have presented it as a known fact, although they fail to cite the source. Don't believe it. The original source for the tale is a single grainy photoshopped image that apparently originated from a penis enlargement website. The Karamojong example is representative of a pervasive trend, namely, once an erroneous characterization is published in a textbook or scholarly source, the text itself becomes the authority. Misinformation is reproduced in other sources, and unfortunately, some authors do not bother to do their homework and check the validity of the original source. It seems that the more bizarre the story, the more likely it is to be published.

Finally, we address how modern technologies are responsible, directly and indirectly, for alterations in the appearance and functioning of the penis. Surgeries have developed to enlarge the penis, or in sexual reassignment surgery, to remove the male genitalia and create a simulated vulva, clitoris, and vagina in genetic males or to simulate a penis and testicles in genetic females. It should be noted that although the majority of humans are either genetically XX or XY, there are other chromosomal variants. Mechanically and chemically, penis performance can be enhanced through devices such as penis pumps and drugs such as Viagra. By-products of our industrial technologies have created environmental, or exogenous, estrogens that are implicated in altering the reproductive functioning of a number of species. These include female snails developing male sexual organs, intersexed male fish, feminization of male amphibians, and the worldwide decline in human male sperm counts.

Domestication involves human-directed change in the evolution of a species. This is fundamentally a coevolutionary process whereby humans and targeted species, be they plants or animals, become connected via mutualistic and symbiotic relationships. Adaptations occur in the process and humans may or may not intentionally select for features that convey adaptive advantages. The development of agriculture involved the domestication of a variety of plants and animals. In this process, humans changed plant species; the tiny-kernelled ancient maize are now big, sweet ears of corn. We have also changed animal species; wild wolves are now our lap-dog teacup poodles and pony-size Great Danes.

The renowned, early archaeologist V. Gordon Childe argued in his book *Man Makes Himself* (1936) that we humans have domesticated ourselves. More recently, archaeologist Helen Leach has suggested that humans, like domestic animals, have undergone a domestication process that has produced both morphological and behavioral changes.[22] Following the arguments of both Childe and Leach, female choice can, in a sense, be considered a form of "domestication" of the penis, whereby the penis is modified from an organ of reproduction to a form whose size, shape, texture, and staying power are geared toward providing sexual pleasure to women.

Although advice columns are rife with angst-ridden men wondering whether size really matters to women, it does not matter in the way that the Western obsession might suggest. Although we argue that female choice drove the selection of the human penis, the way that size matters relates not to the relatively minor differences among individual men. In early human evolution, what womankind selected for was a very different kind of penis. The changes seen in the human penis (versus those of other species) are part of human biocultural history. That is, sexual selection came to involve not just partnering to reproduce offspring but also selecting for a much broader sexuality that is intimately related to human culture and sociality.

The agricultural revolution involved not only a shift in food-getting technology but also changes to male and female social roles. While hunting and gathering is associated with egalitarianism, where the land belongs to everyone, agriculture is associated with territoriality and property rights that are typically in the hands of males. The penis cults that emerged with the advent of agriculture have analogues in many of the world's cultures today, where the phallus is a symbol of male power and dominance.

If we paint the history of the penis with a very broad brush, we can identify three important benchmarks: female selection of the penis for social sex, the shift to the penis as a symbol of male dominance in the context of agricultural societies, and the elaboration of diverse penis ideologies among the world's cultures. But culture has taken domestication a step further. Cultural change moves far more rapidly than does evolutionary change. Cross-culturally and historically, the penis has been circumcised, subincised, superincised, or removed altogether. It has been pierced, tattooed, and decorated with gourds, bamboo, and codpieces. Modern technologies have made available penile implants, surgical enlargements, and Viagra to improve performance. We even have sexual reassignment surgery whereby penises can be converted into vaginas.

Today, we are entering a fourth phase wherein human culture is capable of altering biology. As such, the domestication of the penis is ongoing. In the following pages, we present an anthropological history of the penis using evidence from human evolution, primatology, archaeology, and cultures from around the world. In the next chapter, we discuss what makes the human penis so unique and how female choice has shaped it.

more aggressive than males are. Praying mantises and some species of spiders engage in sexual cannibalism wherein the females eat the males after mating.[6] Among mammals, it is usually the males who are larger and more aggressive than the females are. Among our ape cousins, considerable variation exists in sexual dimorphism. Gibbon (*Hylobatidae*) males and females are approximately the same size, while gorillas (*Gorilla* spp.) and orangutan (*Pongo* spp.) males are twice the size of the females. Humans, chimpanzees, and bonobos have intermediate body size dimorphism, but humans have greater differences than do chimpanzees or bonobos.

Sexual dimorphism is not limited to differences in body size. Proboscis monkeys (*Nasalis larvatus*), as the name suggests, have sexually dimorphic noses.[7] A male's nose is long and thick and droops below his chin. In many baboons (*Papio* spp.) and macaques (*Macaca* spp.), male canines are twice the size of female canines.[8] Fully adult male orangutans possess large fibrous fatty pads framing their faces, called "cheek flanges." While sexual dimorphism technically refers to morphological differences, physical differences are often accompanied by behavioral differences, and although somewhat oxymoronic, the term "behavioral sexual dimorphism" is appearing in the literature. For example, male orangutans are sexually dimorphic in their throat pouches, which are associated with the behavioral manifestation of loud, roaring "long calls" to advertise their presence.[9]

Intrasexual selection and intersexual selection are not necessarily mutually exclusive. For example, while the large antlers of male deer are used as weapons in male-male competition, it has also been suggested that they evolved due to female choice.[10] Nonetheless, male features such as the ornate plumage of the peacock and the long nose of the proboscis monkey, like the features of the human penis, are unlikely to have any role in Darwin's law of battle. Some have explained female choice in the evolution of such features in terms of costly signaling theory. Here, exaggerated male characteristics may indirectly advertise health or potential fertility and thereby provide a mating advantage, even if the feature poses a handicap to a male.[11] Costly signaling theory has been applied to a number of male characteristics across species, from male deer antlers to risk-taking behavior such as reckless driving in young men.[12]

In some species, the evolutionary pressures on penis selection are matters of geometry. For example, the male horse has a penis that is about 50 centimeters (19.685 inches) long when flacid and that can reach three times that length when erect.[13] But equine bodies have evolved for speed. They are swift and agile of foot but not very flexible otherwise. For equines to mate, a male must maneuver his stiff body from behind and get close enough for his penis to reach the mare's vulva. In the blue whale, the penis is nearly 10 feet long, but their penises are not actually that large relative to their body size.[14] Blue whales can reach 100 feet in length and weigh 200 tons; moreover, they are built for life in the water, being roundish and slippery. National Geographic mating scenes demonstrate copulatory behavior consistent with their shape and aquatic nature; males and females slowly undulate around each other. But not all mating behavior is like the blue whale's pleasant roll in the sea.

In some species, evidence suggests that the penis has evolved under a kind of agonistic sexual selection. Evolutionary biologist Patricia Brennan has made a number of interesting discoveries about the sexual selection of the phallus in ducks and other waterfowl.[15] Male ducks can behave violently toward females when they mate. Ducks, like many birds, form pair-bonds during the mating season. But unlike many avian species, male ducks will attack females, even if they are already pair-bonded with a mate. Brennan found that approximately one-third of duck matings involve males forcing themselves on unwilling females.

The duck penis has also evolved some unusual characteristics. In the mating season, male ducks grow a temporary phallic extension that has a corkscrew shape. When mating season is over, the phallic extension withers and falls off. Although a male duck's penis extension has evolved to facilitate mating, female duck anatomy has evolved to make mating more difficult. The female's oviduct (essentially a vagina) also spirals like the male's phallic extension. But the spiraling occurs in the *opposite* direction to that of the male extension and contains dead-end pockets. This makes screwing, if you will, between male and female ducks much more complicated.

Brennan believes that this mismatch between the shapes of male phalluses and female oviducts has evolved as a form of sexual selection for females to counter assaults by males. The oviduct pockets and spirals allow the female to push back out the sperm of unwanted males. She found that although one-third of duck matings are forced, these forced mating make up only 3 percent of pregnancies. Furthermore, most males in bird species do not possess a penis at all. Instead, males have a cloaca, which is a small vented opening that males press against the female to transfer sperm.

For purposes of both introduction and caveat to the evolution of the human penis, it is important to recognize that human cultural behaviors are not independent of evolutionary change, for culture can affect evolution. Perhaps two of the best documented examples of the coevolution of genes and culture are lactose tolerance and the sickle-cell trait. In both cases, agriculture has affected human evolution. Many people whose ancestors were involved in dairy farming have the genetic polymorphism that allows them to digest milk products as adults.[16] In most mammals, the ability to digest lactose disappears at weaning. A more complex relationship exists between agriculture, mosquitoes, and malaria.[17] Early Neolithic clearing of fields for agriculture in tropical areas of the Old World led to a proliferation of mosquitoes carrying plasmodia that create the disease of falciparum malaria. As a result, some populations evolved with increased frequencies of the sickle-cell trait, which provides some resistance to malaria but also poses other potential health problems. Arguably, the human penis also can be considered a product of biocultural human evolution.

FEMALE SEXUALITY AND THE HUMAN PENIS

Female Sexuality

Little attention has been given in the scientific literature to the extent to which female choice may have a role in the evolution of the phallus. Surprisingly, the fullest exploration of female selection of males whose genitalic structure and movements provide pleasurable stimulation is found in insects, as noted in the work of the entomologist William Eberhard.[18] Beyond insects, Eberhard argues that since male genitalia of all species are seldom used in male-male aggressive interactions, the evolution of the phallus, across species, is more likely influenced by female choice. Specifically, he suggests that the structure and movements of the male genitalia that are stimulating to females encourage females to copulate. As we will describe below, biologist Alan Dixson, in his analysis of nonhuman primate penile anatomy, similarly argues that complex penile morphology is indicative of the selective pressure of female choice.

A few studies of human sexuality involve showing women images of penises and asking which ones they prefer. The results show that women in US, New Zealand, Chinese, and Cameroon populations prefer penises that are average to slightly above average in size over those that are smaller than average.[19] Although these studies suggest that female choice may drive the size of the penis, they are limited to visualization of the penis. Studies that relate female choice to the ability of the penis to sexually stimulate a woman are lacking.[20]

Discussions of human female sexuality and sexual response, whether in the popular or scientific literature, are often narrowly focused on the female orgasm. Philosopher of biology Elizabeth Lloyd recently made this case in her book *The Case of the Female Orgasm: Bias in the Science of Evolution.*[21] Lloyd challenges the presumption of most evolutionary explanations that human female orgasm is directly linked to reproductive success. She posits, based on the available scientific studies, that human female orgasm is highly variable. While some women are capable of multiple orgasms, which are rare among nonadolescent males, others do not experience orgasm with intercourse at all. Lack of orgasm with intercourse is less common in males.

When human female orgasm occurs, physical stimulation either outside of or in addition to intercourse is often involved. Further, Lloyd argues that female orgasm is not directly related to reproductive success. No clear evidence exists to suggest that females who have orgasms are more fertile or more likely to reproduce than females who do not experience orgasm. More broadly, Lloyd argues that orgasm should be considered only a subset of the female sexual response.

Early sex researchers William Masters and Virginia Johnson are at least partially responsible for perpetuating the focus on female orgasm. According to their model, the human sexual response (for both men and women) is characterized by four stages: desire, arousal, orgasm, and resolution.[22] In this context, there has been considerable debate as to whether there are different kinds of female orgasm and whether the G-spot or female ejaculation exist.

Freud described two types of orgasm in women: the mature adult vaginal orgasm and the inferior and immature clitoral orgasm.[23] Emphasis on vaginal orgasm has led to debate concerning the existence of a vaginal G-spot.[24] The G-spot (or Gräfenberg Spot) is named for a German gynecologist who in 1950 described an area of sensitivity in the anterior vagina.[25] Recently, imaging studies have described a neurovascular complex consistent with a G-spot.[26] Similarly, the potential for female ejaculation with orgasm continues to be debated despite its long history of documentation in ancient Asian, Indian, and Western medical texts.[27] Current evidence suggests that female ejaculation is associated with the "female prostate" (Skene's paraurethral glands and ducts), which is located in the wall of the female urethra and has secretory cells that can produce ejaculate.[28]

Ultimately, such debates miss the mark for they fail to consider that human female sexuality may encompass more than just having orgasms. French feminist Luce Irigaray describes the female sexual response as far more varied:

"Fondling the breasts, touching the vulva, spreading the lips, stroking the posterior wall of the vagina, brushing against the mouth of the uterus, and so on . . . to evoke only a few of the most specifically female pleasures. But *woman has sex organs more or less everywhere*. She finds pleasure almost anywhere."[29] One recent study asked an ethnically diverse group of women why they had sex; most respondents identified it as a way to express love and to experience pleasure.[30] Women who do not have orgasms can experience pleasurable genital sensations and other forms of physical and emotional pleasure from sex.[31] Further, women can experience orgasm without genital contact, including from breast stimulation, mental stimulation, and through dreams.[32] More broadly, as cultural beings, sexual desires and experiences are influenced by gender identities, sexual preferences, sexual mores, romantic feelings, culture histories, and religious/spiritual ideologies.

Urologist Helen O'Connell has argued that the quest to find a reproductive explanation for sexual phenomenon fails to recognize female sexual function as distinct from female reproductive function.[33] Although the two cannot be completely disconnected from one another, human females do seek out sexual experiences at times when they cannot conceive. Levin has described human sexual arousal as a "duarchy," serving both the recreational and pleasurable aspects of sex as well as its reproductive function.[34] Evolutionary biologist Randy Thornhill and evolutionary psychologist Steven Gangestad refer to this as "extended female sexuality"[35] while primatologist Richard Wrangham describes it as "communication sex."[36] In fact, when orgasm has been documented in nonhuman primates, it often occurs in female same-sex encounters. Female bonobos both in captivity and in the wild have been observed to engage in genito-genital (GG) rubbing to orgasm, which arguably decreases social tensions and serves as a form of reconciliation.[37] A somewhat similar form of GG rubbing has been observed in common chimpanzees (*Pan troglodytes*) and may serve to strengthen social bonds.[38] Among stumptailed macaques (*Macaca artoides*) female orgasms have been described in female-female sexual interactions as well as female-male copulation.[39] Nonconceptive sexual behavior has also been described for white-faced capuchins (*Cebus capucinus*)[40] and blue monkeys (*Cercopithecus mitis*).[41]

Human sexuality may have much in common with bonobo sexuality. Primatologist Frans de Waal has written most extensively on this subject[42] and suggests that bonobo sexuality is best characterized as "erotic" rather than reproductive. Bonobos use sex for appeasement and reconciliation, to decrease social tensions, to show affection, and clearly, to experience pleasure.

FIGURE 2.1 "Two Female Bonobos GG-Rubbing," 2008, by Rune Olsen, from *The Sex Lives of Animals* exhibition at the Museum of Sex in New York City.

They engage in a broad array of copulatory positions that include female-female and male-male sexual contacts, in addition to male-female encounters. Sexual behavior is generally incorporated into their daily routine and females seek out sexual experiences regardless of whether or not they are in a fertile state. Human females not only seek out sex when they are not ovulating but also use birth control designed specifically to allow females to enjoy sex and prevent ovulation and pregnancy. Although social sex and reproductive sex cannot be completely isolated, for human beings, sex is not merely for reproductive purposes.

We face additional problems in attempting to understand female sexuality, sexual behavior, and sexual response. As Lloyd pointed out, there are methodological problems with the existing research on female sexual behavior and attitudes.[43] She argues that much of the research is based on self-reporting from upper-middle-class white European/American women from sex clinics, who were often there because they were experiencing sexual problems. A second commonly accessed population for university-based psychologist sex researchers are young college students, who are also predominantly white, upper middle class, and easily influenced by cultural stereotypes about norms of behavior in their self-reports.

Sound cross-cultural studies of female (and male) sexuality and sexual behavior are lacking. Instead, we often find ill-informed exotic erotics (see chapter 5). The inattention to female sexual behavior and response in cross-cultural settings may derive from a number of factors.

First, before the 1970s, most ethnographers were male. It is conceivable that they may have had difficulty interacting with women due to being perceived as a sexual threat by the other men in the culture they were studying.[44] Men conducting interviews with women about their sexual responses certainly would have been threatening. Second, many cultures have various taboos associated with human sexuality, which may make female sexual response a difficult topic to explore in depth. Third, Western cultural taboos associated with discussing intimate details of one's sex life may inhibit the predominantly Western ethnographers more than the potential taboos of the culture under study. In any case, a valid comparative cross-cultural survey on the similarities and differences in female sexual response (and male sexual response) does not exist.

The Human Penis

In humans, as in most mammals, the penis serves two main purposes: to deliver sperm and to eliminate urine. Beyond those functional similarities, the human penis is markedly distinct from those of our primate cousins, as well as of other mammals and animals in general. The human penis has a suite of characteristic features: it is spineless and boneless, it is long and thick, and it has a bulbous glans with a coronal ridge. Perhaps most notably, its tremendous staying power compared to that of other primates, with perhaps the exception of the orangutan, also makes it functionally distinct.[45]

Several lines of evidence suggest that the penis is subject to intersexual selection, or female choice. Nonetheless, it is common in the general population and among some scientists to assert that the human penis has evolved exclusively under intrasexual selection, or male-male competition. One

notable example is the physiologist and popular science writer Jared Diamond, who has claimed that the size and shape of the human penis can be
explained only as an expression of male status, competition, and dominance.
In his view, female choice has *no* role in the evolution of the penis. He states,
"the human penis is an organ of display. . . . The display is intended not for
women, but for fellow men."[46] Furthermore, "women tend to report that they
are more turned on by other features of a man, and that the sight of a penis is,
if anything, unattractive. Instead, the ones really fascinated by the penis and
its dimensions are men. In the showers in men's locker rooms, men routinely
size up each other's endowment."[47]

Diamond's statements may ring true in light of contemporary Western stereotypes. A clear cultural norm is for the adult penis to be concealed in public,
particularly from women. Any public exposure of the adult penis is not only
taboo but also a criminally prosecutable offense. Present-day Western societies have come to view the penis as a most impolite topic of conversation. The
word "penis" is still subject to some degree of censorship on US television.
The exceptions lie at two extremes: It is permissible to discuss male genitalia
in an informational or medical context, and penis talk is treated as standard
vulgarity in late-night stand-up comic routines. As such, it is socially acceptable only in formal informational contexts or in joking contexts where acceptable social norms are intentionally violated. In polite company, one should not
discuss the penis, or more broadly, male or female genitalia.

By far, more scientific attention is given to the form of the penis, in
humans and in our primate cousins, than to its function. Whether the unique
features of the human penis are viewed as a venue for male competition or
female choice, the discussion focuses largely on the visual appearance of the
penis (that is, its display) as opposed to its role as a driving force in evolution.
In part, this bias is definitely driven by what is most practical and easily measured. It is far easier to accurately measure penis size and dimensions than to
measure the murkier and harder to quantify variables of male-female sexual
response. The consequence has been that the visual appearance of the penis
is emphasized as a driving evolutionary force. Functionality of the penis has
been sorely neglected in the literature. If the evolution of the penis is under
sexual selection, and specifically, under female choice, then we cannot ignore
long-term evolutionary variables that contribute to female choice. Change has
occurred as a result not simply of *looking* at penises but also of *interacting* with
them. As our ancestral human mothers became increasingly big-brained,

they gained the capacity to remember which males gave them pleasure and which did not, and to make choices accordingly. The human penis has a number of distinctive characteristics. Following the nonhuman animal studies of Eberhard and Dixson, these features likely evolved due to female choice in humans. Specifically, the structure and function of the human penis serve to attract and to sexually stimulate females. Although the role of the penis in reproduction cannot be debated, the fact that human females routinely seek out sexual experiences when they cannot conceive suggests that human sexuality entails broader functions, which include social communication and sexual pleasure.

Perhaps *the* most distinctive characteristic of the human penis in comparison to those of other primates is that it lacks spines. Penile spines, technically termed "vibrissae," involve the same genetic coding that give many animals sensory whiskers on their faces. Vibrissae are a primitive characteristic of the order Primates and occur in many prosimians, monkeys, and apes.[48] Penile vibrassae occur in a variety of animal species such as rodents (*Myodes* spp., *Peromyscus* spp., *Rattus* spp.),[49] felines (*Felis* spp., *Panthera* spp., *Puma* spp.),[50] ducks (*Oxymura* spp.),[51] insects (*Callosobruchus* spp., *Cimex* spp.),[52] crustaceans (*Artemia* spp.),[53] and marine worms (*Kinorynchus* spp.).[54] While these vibrissae are not necessarily a visually prominent feature, they are functionally important in the sexual response of males and females.

Several explanations have been proposed for the purpose of penile spines. These include making mating more pleasurable for males, making mating less pleasurable for females, or serving to facilitate copulation. Like whiskers, penile vibrissae can function as a sensory apparatus that enhances male stimulation when mating. But in some species, vibrissae are tiny sharp spines that make mating uncomfortable for females. One example is found in the seed beetle (*Callosobruchus maculatus*), whose large, sharp penile spines cause significant injury to females during mating. According to the adaptive-harm hypothesis, a male benefits from damaging the female's reproductive tract because doing so makes her reluctant to allow another male to mate with her afterward.[55] Others locate the adaptive benefit of these penile spines in their effectiveness of anchoring the female in mating, with injuriousness being a side effect rather that the trait under selection.[56]

In humans, penile spines have been selected against. Although chimpanzees and many other primates possess them, humans do not.[57] In many species, penile spines appear to function as a tactile apparatus, sensitizing the penis during mating. Behaviorally, this extreme sensitivity of the nonhuman primate penis means that males climax within a matter of seconds. Even among the highly sexualized bonobos, de Waal gives 13 seconds as the average length of an act of male-female copulation.[58] Very recently, the specific genetic change that accounts for the difference between penises in humans and in the great apes has been identified.[59] Humans lost a regulatory gene that codes for production of penile spines in the androgen-receptor (AR) gene. Since the great apes have this gene, it is presumed that the loss occurred after human ancestors and bonobo-chimpanzee ancestors diverged from one another, likely within the last five to eight million years.

The loss of penile spines in humans makes the act of copulating *less* pleasurable for human males. Their smooth and whiskerless penises are far less sensitive than those of primates with penile vibrissae. It takes much more work and effort for human males to climax. But a smooth and spineless penis with greater staying power makes sex more pleasurable for women. Given this fact, it is possible that human whiskerless penises are under intersexual selection; that is, the penis anatomy is the result of human female choice. As such, extended copulations may facilitate female orgasm, or at the very least, prolong the duration of a sexual encounter.

Although we suggest that the evolution of the human penis may be driven more by functional capabilities than by visual assessment, we do not intend to discount the probability that size and shape have a role in advertising potential functionality. In the primate world, the two species that share penile similarities with humans are our closest relatives, the bonobos and the chimpanzees. Bonobos and chimpanzees are two closely related African apes that belong to the same genus, *Pan paniscus* and *Pan troglodytes,* respectively. Human ancestors and chimpanzee/bonobo ancestors are estimated to have diverged approximately five to seven million years ago,[60] and human and chimpanzee deoxyribonucleic-acid (DNA) sequences are at least 96 percent identical.[61] Although some have claimed that humans have the longest penises of the primates,[62] chimpanzee penises are at least as long, if not a little longer than those of humans, ranging from 10 to 18 centimeters in length.[63] However, the chimpanzee penis is smaller in girth, measuring approximately 2–4 centimeters wide at its base and tapering at its tip.[64] According to de Waal, bonobos have the longest penises of the primates.[65]

The fact that the penis is large and highly visible in unclothed males suggests that it may have evolved to be seen. Unlike the penises of great apes, the human penis is permanently visible, even when it is flaccid.[66] The penises of the great apes retract significantly when they are not erect; knuckle-walking also conceals their penises to some extent. Pubic hair does not so much hide the human penis as draw attention to it,[67] much as eyebrows draw attention to the eyes. Although the eyebrows do serve a protective function, namely, helping keep sweat and other debris out of the eyes, they also have an important function in facial communication. In the same way, pubic hair may attract attention to the genitals and enhance one's anatomy.

In numerous species of Old and New World primates, the display of an erect penis is used as a form of social communication.[68] In some species, including bonobos (*Pan paniscus*),[69] chimpanzees (*Pan troglodytes*),[70] orangutans (*Pongo* spp.), [71] squirrel monkeys (*Saimiri sciureus*),[72] and capuchins (*Sapajus apella*),[73] this has been documented as a male invitation to females to mate. Maxine Sheets-Johnstone has suggested that the evolution of bipedalism may be linked to sexual selection in its more ready display of the penis.[74] Interestingly, among male capuchins, it is the subordinate monkeys that use a bipedal stance with an erect penis display to attract females.[75] Given that in a number of primate species, including our closest relatives, the chimpanzees and bonobos, the penis is visually displayed to attract females, penis display also may have been important in female choice for our human ancestors.

Another unique characteristic of the human penis is that it lacks a penis bone, called the "baculum" or the os penis. The baculum is found in many mammal species and in most primates. Biologist Alan Dixson, who is perhaps the leading authority on primate penile anatomy, wryly suggested the initial letters of the five mammalian orders in which the baculum occurs as providing an apt mneumonic: *Primates, Rodentia, Insectivora, Carnivora,* and *Chiroptera*.[76] The baculum provides a degree of constant stiffness to the penis, which can aid a male in penetrating a female when he does not have a full erection.[77] All male species of (nonhuman) apes and Old World monkeys possess a baculum, as do many, but not all, New World monkey species.[78] Unfortunately, we do not have a strong fossil record of the baculum in early primates; however, given its presence in all the great apes, we can assume that humans lost the baculum sometime after the human and chimpanzee/bonobo ancestral divergence.

Explanations as to why humans do not possess a penis bone range widely and wildly. On the wild side, one team of creationist-leaning geneticists suggested that the baculum is the very bone used by God to construct the biblical Eve, rather than Adam's rib.[79] These researchers argue that the scenario explains both why the baculum is absent in humans and corrects the longstanding problem of reconciling the biblical account with anatomical mathematics. That is to say, if Eve was made from Adam's rib, why do men and women today have the same number of ribs? However, this explanation does not account for the variability of the presence or absence of the baculum in New World monkey species. We would have to assume that God chose to create human and spider monkey females and from the males' penis bones (where it is absent in males) but did not do likewise for gorillas and baboons. Surprisingly, this hypothesis was published in a peer-reviewed journal of medical genetics less than 15 years ago.[80]

Evolutionary biologist Richard Dawkins has provided an interesting explanation for the loss of the baculum in his hydraulic hypothesis.[81] By Dawkins's reasoning, without the support of the baculum, the only way that human males can achieve penetration of females is through sufficient "hydraulics" to pump up the penis, meaning that a male must be healthy with sound blood pressure to maintain an erection, suggesting costly signaling theory. In species with penis bones, he argues, males can, in a sense, cheat the evolutionary game by faking hydraulic erections with penis-bone supported erections. He suggests that female selection is the cause for the loss of the baculum, for without it, an erection provides a visual signal of good physical health in a potential mating partner. Moreover, he suggests that erections also provide evidence for sound psychological health, because depression, stress, and anxiety may result in erectile difficulty.

Another way in which the human penis differs with respect to the baculum is that there is a correlation between relative baculum length and duration of copulatory intromission: the longer the baculum, the longer the copulatory duration.[82] For humans, this might seem counterintuitive, for it would suggest that human males, lacking a baculum, should have very rapid copulations in comparison with other primates, when the opposite is true. Evolutionary psychologist Geoffrey Miller suggests that the complete loss of the baculum in humans is linked to female choice for tactile stimulation.[83] He argues that since the human penis becomes erect with blood, rather than with muscle and bone, it is highly flexible, providing a wider range of copulatory positions. Further, since the human penis is more streamlined, intercourse involves whole-body movements, giving females greater general body stimulation. In addition, he suggests that a human male's ability to engage in whole-body copulations suggests costly signaling vigor and health. The tactile stimulation hypothesis is consistent with Irigaray's characterization of the female's entire body as an erogenous sexual organ.

A final characteristic of the human penis that separates it from that of our closest relatives is the shape of its distal end. The human penis possesses a bulbous glans with a coronal ridge. The human glans is surrounded at its base by an umbrella-like ring of tissue that separates the glans from its shaft. Chimpanzees and bonobos have more pointed and tapering penises that lack a true glans.[84] In contrast, woolly monkeys (*Lagothrix*) and woolley spider monkeys (*Brachyteles*) have elongated penises that are distally bulbous.[85] Dixson has attempted to correlate such features with mating systems, as we will describe further below.[86] In brief, he suggests that complex penile morphologies are associated with increased competition in mating (and female choice), while simple morphologies are associated with less competition.

Several researchers have suggested that the human bulbous glans and coronal ridge operate as a "semen displacement device."[87] In this account, the human penis functions like a plunger to remove semen. The assumption is that in our early evolutionary history, females mated with multiple males in succession. Males' repeated thrusting during intercourse functioned to remove the semen of rival males, giving the last male the best chance of fathering children. Psychologists Gordon Gallup and Rebecca Burch followed this hypothesis with an experiment involving artificial penises (e.g., dildos) and cornstarch. They found that the simulated penis with coronal ridge removed 91 percent of simulated semen, compared with 35 percent for dildos without a coronal ridge. In a corollary to this study, college students were given a questionnaire about their sexual behavior.[88] They found that human males reported different copulatory behavior when they believed that a long-term female partner had been unfaithful. When males accused their partners of cheating or when the couple had been separated for a period of time, males described thrusting "deeper, quicker, and more vigorously" than in typical sexual encounters.

Several researchers have criticized this interpretation of human penile morphology, calling it "far-fetched" and "flawed." [89] One problem is that if the penis were acting like a plunger, a man would also be scooping out his own semen, particularly if there was any thrusting after ejaculation. In addition, since a first male's sperm may have had the chance to advance in the vaginal canal, the bulbous head and coronal ridge of the second male's penis might serve to propel a first male's sperm forward, rather than plunging it out. Dixson seems to provide a more plausible explanation, namely, that complex penile morphologies, including those in the distal penile head, are associated with female choice.

HUMAN AND WILD PRIMATE SOCIAL ORGANIZATION

Primate Penises and Systems of Mating

In his book *Primate Sexuality*[90] and in other articles[91] Dixson attempts to correlate patterns in primate penis morphology with social systems. He argues that female choice should create increased selection pressure for the evolution of complex penile morphologies and patterns of copulatory behavior. He compares 130 primate species according to four characteristics in penile morphology and four types of social systems: multimale/multifemale, polygynous, monogamous, and dispersed. In the multimale/multifemale social system, groups are composed of at least several males and several females. Polygynous groups comprise one dominant breeding male and a group of females. Monogamous groups comprise pair-bonded species, and the dispersed social system describes primates who do not form permanent social groups, such as the nocturnal prosimians and the orangutan. The four penile characteristics are penis length, baculum length, complexity of the distal morphology, and the size of penile spines and papilla. Dixson ranks these characteristics on a scale of 1 to 5.

Dixson predicts that polygynous (single male) and monogamous groups (pair-bonded) will have simpler penile morphology due to less competition for mates than multimale/multifemale groups will. He makes his strongest case for penile length. In multimale/multifemale groups, 51 percent of males score a 4–5 in penile length compared with 14 percent of males in polygynous groups and 8 percent in monogamous groups. One might take issue with the species that fall into these categories of social organization. His examples of monogamous species include marmosets (*Callithrix*) and tamarins (*Saguinus*). For some marmosets and tamarins, "polyandry" is a better term than "monogamy," for they are often found in social groups consisting of one female and two males.[92] The dispersed category contains both the orangutans and nocturnal prosimians, who are distantly related and are also behaviorally and ecologically quite different.

In addition, it is uncertain where humans would score within these specific criteria of penile complexity, since humans lack the baculum and penile spines. Nonetheless, when considered as a whole, the numerous distinctive characteristics of the human penis—including its length, girth, bulbous head and coronal ridge, spinelessness, bonelessness, flexibility, and capacity for relatively long-lasting copulation—suggest its relative complexity among primates. As such, it fits well with Dixson's hypothesis that complex genital morphology is associated with female choice.

Are Humans Naturally Monogamous or Polygynous?

A great deal of ink has been spilled in trying to answer the question, are humans naturally monogamous or polygynous? Humans are cultural beings who today exhibit a wide array of social organizations. Perhaps a more important question to ask is why our cultural flexibility tends to be ignored in favor of a rigid either/or model of the way humans are *really* supposed to be. By carefully selecting the evidence, it is easy to construct a scenario to fit just about any moral, political, or philosophical ideology. Some researchers have looked for evidence in the fossil record of our human ancestors, others have looked to analogies with our great ape cousins, and still others have made cross-cultural comparisons. Beyond these biases, perhaps the biggest problem has been the conflation of nonhuman primate mating systems and social structures with human marriage patterns. These are qualitatively different issues. Nonetheless, terms such "polygyny," "monogamy," and "polyandry" are used to describe very different phenomenon in humans than in wild primates.

Our evolutionary relatedness to other primate species is limited in its ability to provide answers to such questions. The closest of our primate relatives, bonobos and chimpanzees, have a multimale/multifemale social structure, but gorillas, who are not far removed from us, are polygynous. Among the other great ape, the orangutans, males and females live largely solitary lives. The gibbons and siamangs, the lesser apes, are largely monogamous. The same patterns of social organization in the nonhuman apes are also found in the more distantly related monkeys. As such, even in wild primates, there is considerable variation in social adaptation.

However, mating patterns in wild primates are largely genetically hardwired. For example, polygyny in nonhuman primates is a social structure that involves a dominant male and several females with whom he mates. Hamadryas baboons (*Papio hamadryas*) form male-headed "harems," with 1 adult male and up to 10 adult females and their offspring.[93] Any primatologist who studies hamadryas baboon populations in the wild will observe a similar pattern of social organization. The term "polygyny" is also applied to human groups that exhibit a *marriage* pattern whereby one male has two or more wives. But, ethnographers who do field studies with human populations may observe polygynous marriage in one group and monogamous and polyandrous patterns in other groups, even though they are all members of the same species.

Although human marriage (and mating) patterns are variable, one might make the case that from foragers to Western industrialized societies, our basic form of social organization appears to be living in multimale/multifemale groups. Hunting and gathering society typically comprises a number of males and females living together and working cooperatively. Layered on to that basic structure is the cultural variable of marriage, so that bands include individuals linked by marriage and kinship alliances. Even if we look to contemporary Western society, a social form that emphasizes the nuclear family, we find that we are not monogamous in the sense that gibbons and siamangs are. The social organization of gibbons and siamangs, for the most part, involves one adult male, one adult female, and their immature offspring. For Western humans, the nuclear family may be the residence pattern, but it is not the broader social pattern. We continuously interact as part of broad communities with large numbers of individuals involved in cooperative and interdependent social relations. No human groups are either monogamous or polyandrous in the same way as wild primates, such as gibbons and Hamadryas baboons, are.

Human marriage patterns differ from primate mating patterns in other important ways. For one, marriage has social and economic functions beyond mating and procreating. In contemporary Western society, the ideal marriage is often seen as one based on deep and long-lasting bonds of romantic love. But cross-culturally (and historically in Western societies), marriage has not been fundamentally about a contract between two individuals but a decision made by kin groups. In this context, marriage is far more about the lasting social bonds created between two families than between individuals. Cross-culturally, marriage may provide the social structure for raising and enculturating children, but it may also be an economic arrangement, with husbands and wives involved in cooperative labor to acquire resources for survival for themselves, extended families, and other members of the social group.

Marriage patterns and mating patterns are also not necessarily synonymous cross-culturally. While the Western term "extra-marital affair" suggests behavior that conflicts with the marriage contract, not all human groups expect sexual exclusivity as a requirement of marriage. One example is the Awá-Guajá hunter-gatherers of the Amazonian rain forest. Like many Amazonian groups, they have the concept of "plural" or "partible paternity."[94] Here, it is believed that a fetus is created from the buildup of male semen. Awá-Guajá women are expected to have frequent sex during their pregnancies. Moreover, it is believed that the amount of semen needed to create a baby is more than one man can produce, so women, on average, have three sexual partners during a pregnancy. All the men who have sex with a woman during her pregnancy are considered to be biological fathers to the child. These biological fathers may or may not include the husband of the woman. However, even if the husband is not a so-called biological father, he is still a social father and is actively involved in caring for all the children of his wife. To a lesser extent, he also helps care for the biological children that resulted from pregnancies of other women with whom he has had sex.

Awá-Guajá have polygynous, monogamous, and polyandrous marriages, although the pattern varies for men and women for several reasons. Girls are married at a very young age, around five or six years old, to much older men. These young girls do not have sex with their husbands, and they move back and forth between their parent's family and their husband's family until they feel comfortable staying with the husband. When they reach sexual maturity, their sexual relationships are with boys closer to their own age. Often, by the time they are teenagers their first husbands have died and they marry again to a man of their choosing. Boys undergo their first marriage around 16 or 17 years of age. In many cases, a boy will marry a much older woman whose previous husband or husbands have died. These marriages are technically monogamous, one man and one woman, but the boys have sexual relationships with girls their own age as well. In one case, a man was married to a young girl and an older woman who were in a grandmother-granddaughter relationship.

The Awá-Guajá also practice polyandrous marriage. These are most often temporary arrangements and, more accurately, a way for a woman to ease into divorce with minimal conflict. If a married woman wants to be married to another man, she simply begins referring to the second man as her husband and gradually begins spending more time in his household (or he in hers). Eventually, she stops referring to her first husband as a husband, and the two are no longer married according to the group. Statistically, the most frequently occurring type of marriage among the Awá-Guajá is polygynous. In part, this is because women marry as young girls (about 10 years earlier than men do) and are married longer because women tend to live longer than men do. But the label "polygyny" elides important information about what is actually occurring culturally in terms of both beliefs and behaviors.

Many researchers have used cross-cultural statistics for the number of documented polygynous societies as evidence that polygyny represents the ancestral condition in human beings. First, it is a leap to assume that because the numbers suggest a high frequency, polygyny must be the default form and norm. Second, it is an even greater leap to assume that human polygynous marriage systems are the same thing as wild primate polygynous mating systems. This is specious reasoning on both counts. Since the mid-twentieth century, some anthropologists have contributed to a database called the Human Relations Area Files (HRAF). This database compiles cultural features from many different cultural contexts that can be statistically analyzed for patterns. In the different cultures for which ethnographic data has been entered, polygyny is by far the most common pattern. But does that information really tell us anything about what is natural for humans? The argument that because polygyny occurs more frequently, it represents the ancestral condition has holes for many reasons. One problem is that the ethnographic evidence does not represent all of human history. Anthropologists have collected ethnographic data on kinship systems since only the late 1800s. We scarcely have a depth of history beyond 150 years. The data collected over the last 150 years do not reflect cultures living under ancient conditions but cultures much affected by the massively disruptive effects of colonization.

Apart from colonial influence, even if we somehow could access a record of human behavior for the last 1,000 years, it would still be biased and would represent only a small sliver of human history. As previously discussed, for the vast majority of human existence, we lived as relatively egalitarian hunter-gatherers. We have approximately an 11,000-year history living in agricultural societies. This form of social life not only introduced domesticated plants and animals but also sparked notions of private property and status differences among individuals in a given society. Such status differences have led to fundamental misconceptions about the meaning of polygyny in the (relatively) modern world. Cross-culturally polygyny is typically a privilege of men who have accumulated sufficient wealth and status to afford multiple wives. These wives are often younger. But what do we call the marriage patterns of the younger men and the young wives? Younger men may eventually gain enough resources to marry multiple wives. Thus, the general male pattern could be termed "eventual polygyny."

Such a designation essentially ignores the life histories of women. In truth, we do not even have a term in anthropology that describes the female pattern. We might call it "serial polyandry" as opposed to the male equivalent "simultaneous polygyny." In polygynous societies, young women are often married off to older husbands. But what happens when their husbands die? They tend to be remarried. Thus, what the polygyny actually describes is a pattern whereby women typically have more than one husband in their lifetimes and men tend to have multiple wives, but only when they are older. Given that, we should seriously question whether polygynous is a valid term for any society. If women's lives are given equal weight as men's lives, then we more accurately have only polygynous/polyandrous societies.

It is also important to bear in mind that while polygyny is indeed the most frequently documented type of marriage pattern across cultures that have been recorded in the last 150 years, the fact that many societies have preferentially practiced monogamy and polyandry means that there is not a standard human practice. Perhaps even more importantly, we should keep in mind that polygyny, polyandry, and monogamy describe only public marriage alliances. Far less is known from the ethnographic record about more private sexual behavior.

The Problem of Paternity

In the sections that follow, we discuss the alpha-male myth and various arguments that explain female sexuality as a means to confuse paternity and ensure a male's care for her offspring. The contention that our early human ancestors were concerned with paternity is problematic given the ethnographic evidence.

Most cultures today place considerable emphasis on establishing identify through ancestry. However, kinship systems do not always emphasize paternity. Cross-culturally the two most common ways of reckoning descent are bilateral descent and unilineal descent. Cultures with bilateral descent believe that children are equally related to their mothers and their fathers. This cultural perception is, of course, genetically correct. However, many of the world's cultures perceive relatedness as unilineal, involving either patrilineal or matrilineal descent. In patrilineal descent, a child is believed to be a blood relative of the father but not the mother. In matrilineal descent, it is the opposite: a child is believed to be a blood relative of the mother but not the father. Historically, in the cultures that have been documented, unilineal descent is a much more common cultural belief than is bilateral descent.

Matrilineal descent is found around the globe but has been a fairly common form of reckoning in Native North America and Melanesia.[95] Only those persons who can be traced through a female link are considered to be true, blood relatives. However, that does not mean that males in these societies have no interest in kinship ties. Men consider themselves to be blood relatives of their sister's children rather than of their wives' children. Because a brother and sister share the same mother, they are considered blood relatives. This same substance of female relatedness passes from a man's sister to her children, but he does not consider himself related to the children of his sexual partner. In a matrilineal society a man's blood kin are his maternal grandmother, his mother and her brothers and sisters, his own brothers and sisters, and the children of his sisters. He does not consider himself to be a biological relative to his father, his father's brothers (paternal uncles), or the children of his wife. In these societies, men invest considerable time and energy in raising their sisters' children.

Early anthropologist Bronislaw Malinowski saw matrilineal society as a clear challenge to Sigmund Freud's Oedipus complex.[96] According to Freud, a son becomes jealous of the sexual relationship that his father has with his mother. This results in tension and competition between the son and the father. Malinowski, in his work in the 1920s among the matrilineal people of the Trobriand Islands in Oceania, found that fathers and sons had no such conflict. However, there was clear conflict between an adolescent boy and his maternal uncle. The mother's brother was the male who had authority over him. The conflict was not about sex but authority.

Related to paternity is the argument that female sexuality is a means to gain male provisioning for women and their offspring. One interesting challenge to that scenario is the "grandmother hypothesis." While human males are fertile throughout most of their adult lives, female fertility eventually ends and women enter menopause, often surviving long after they are able to reproduce. As early as 1957, some hypothesized that a potential adaptive benefit of female menopause was that parental investment could then be directed toward the survival of existing children rather than toward reproducing new offspring.[97]

Anthropologist Kristin Hawkes and colleagues conducted a field study of grandmother provisioning of tubers and other foods for their grandchildren among the Hadza of Tanzania.[98] They observed that humans are the only primates that provision their young after weaning and that human grandmothers often assist mothers in the care of the young. Recently, mathematical support has been found for the grandmother hypothesis.[99] Computer simulations demonstrated that with grandmothering, chimpanzee-like lifespans would evolve in less than 60,000 years to human-like lifespans. Two implications undergird this conclusion. First, a long-lived grandmother's food provisioning would allow her daughter to produce more children at shorter time intervals. Such longevity genes would be passed to the offspring. Second, children who had to compete with near-aged siblings for their mother's attention may have increased their social skills and complexity, possibly affecting brain size and increased capacity for culture in ancestors.

It should be mentioned that, historically and cross-culturally, patrilineal descent is more commonly practiced than matrilineal descent, but even in cultures that practice patrilineal descent, males are not necessarily obsessed with exclusive rights of paternity. As previously described, a number of Amazonian societies have the notion of plural paternity wherein there can be more than one biological father. For example, Awá-Guajá men are not jealous of the male sexual partners of their wives but see it as normal and necessary for their children to have several fathers.[100] Given the variability in cultural ideas about biological relatedness today, we cannot assume that concerns about paternity guided the evolution of human sexual behavior. Moreover, ethnographically the evidence suggests that there are multiple means through which children are cared for, including brother-sister and mother-daughter pairs, as well as male-female pairings.

THE ALPHA-MALE MYTH IN HUMAN EVOLUTION

The alpha-male myth involves a misuse of a wild primate analogy to suggest that human sexuality involves superior males outcompeting other males to gain the reward of mating with females. Undergirding the myth of the alpha male in human evolution is a fundamental misunderstanding of this role in our primate cousins. Often, the alpha-male category is presented as an either/or class of males. This simplification suggests two types of males in any given society: a few genetically superior males destined to become the alpha males and the larger population of genetically inferior males who are nonalpha. The logic then erroneously follows that these superior alpha males secure more female mates, father more children, and pass on their superior genes, all of which suggests that human evolutionary progress is indebted to a small group of select males. Among human cultures, the tacit (and sometimes explicit) argument is that polygynous marriage was the reward for male genetic superiority in the past and remains so in contemporary societies where polygyny is practiced.

The crux of the error involves attempting to overlay a myth of nonhuman primate social behavior onto human cultural systems while failing to grasp that the alpha male is more a social role than a genetic destiny. In primate societies that have alpha males, the alpha-male role is a social role that any number of males may temporarily occupy for varying lengths of time. The factors that facilitate any given male's rise to alpha status are quite complex, driven by group political dynamics, age-related factors, and genetics. It is a mistake to reduce the alpha-male role to merely either/or criteria of genetically superior or inferior males. However, we are not suggesting that the genetic differences among males and females play no role in reproductive success. Rather, the myth of the alpha male seriously distorts the actual complexities of reproductive success.

In chapter 1 we quoted from psychologist Roy Baumeister's 2010 book, *Is There Anything Good about Men?* His work perfectly illustrates the alpha-male myth: "Amongst our ancestors . . . only the alpha males were able to reproduce, leading them to take more risks and to exhibit more aggressive and protective behaviors than women, whose evolutionary strategies require a different set of behaviors. Whereas women favor and excel at one-to-one intimate relationships, men compete with one another and build larger organizations from which culture grows."[101] Although Baumeister's book was published by a reputable academic publisher (Oxford University Press), his opinions were presented as scientific fact. He makes many authoritative statements about human evolution, our prehistoric ancestors, and the nature of culture with almost no reference to any anthropological research (or really to any standard research). The book is filled with stereotypes presented as statements of fact, which are not only disturbingly sexist for men and women alike but also, and more importantly, scientifically uninformed. Examples include the following:

> Culture is more likely to emerge from groups of men than from groups of women . . . The men were still quite willing to share the fruits of their cultural activities with women.[102]
>
> The women's sphere did not produce progress. It stayed pretty much the same, filled with love, care, gossip, household chores, the joys and burdens of children, and the cultivation of intimacy.[103]
>
> The women accumulated and improved the stock of knowledge of some things, such as cooking and perhaps some lore about health and herbal cures. . . . Still these improvements were few and limited, and in the long run they amounted to much less than the progress that was made in the men's sphere.[104]

The book continues in this vein. Further, the area of cooking seems to be diminished because of its association with women, but cooking is extremely important in human history. It involves food collection, food processing technology, food preparation, and the development of domestic tool technologies, all of which are critical to human cultural evolution.

In Joan Gero and Margaret Conkey's edited volume *Engendering Archaeology*,[105] the point is made that there is no reason to assume that tools were either made by or exclusively used by men. Even for activities traditionally considered in the women's sphere circa 1950, such as cooking, processing food, and sewing clothes, tools would have been not only made for but also essential to these purposes. Gero and Conkey's work is not arguing a male versus female version of tool invention but that there is no reason to assume men were the only toolmakers.

The myth of the alpha male often includes the idea that the most aggressive males are the ones who reproduce. But that is not always the case. Primatologist Barbara Smuts's groundbreaking work *Sex and Friendship in Baboons* forever changed the way that we understand the alpha-male role.[106] Baboon society is based on what is termed a "matriline." Baboons live in troops where at adolescence, males leave the troop they were born into and move into another. In chimpanzees and bonobos, it is the females who tend to leave the natal troop at adolescence.[107] Regardless of the sex that immigrates, such movements decrease the likelihood of mating with a close relative.

The core of baboon society is based on mothers and daughters. Young males come into a new troop as strangers. Smuts demonstrated that becoming well-established in a new troop is not exclusively about outcompeting other male olive baboons but involves gaining the favor of the females in the group. Newcomer males are able to gain acceptance into the group not so much through displays of power and aggression but through cultivating positive social relationships with the females. The males make friends with the females, spending long hours grooming them and displaying affection toward their offspring.

Smuts's work demonstrates that the male-dominance model is insufficient to explain behavior in baboons, wherein dominant males do not prevent lower ranking males from mating and females are not passive objects of male competition. Older males who had established friendships could be observed mating in full view of younger, more dominant males. The protective role and close bonds that males developed with the infants of their female friends could not be explained by paternity alone, for in only about half of the friendships was a male the father to the female's child.

In primatology, decades of research from multiple primate species demonstrate that alpha males are most definitely not the only ones that father offspring. Alpha males tend to guard females and try to monopolize them, but mating is not exclusive to alpha males. It should be stressed again that an alpha male is not a type of male but a position that a male temporarily holds in a wild primate troop. A given alpha male may have better access to females today, but that does not mean he will keep the position and have the same privileges tomorrow. No primate stays in the alpha role forever, and in fact in many species, alpha-male takeovers are quite frequent. Even males who have relatively long tenures as alpha male eventually age and become less able to compete. When the alpha-male role involves aggressiveness and competition, males who must always defend their position are at greater risk of injury, which may also limit how long they can keep that status.

Although the alpha-male role in wild primate societies is often used as an analogy for a hypothetical human alpha-male role, many primate species have no such alpha-male position. Examples include female-dominated common squirrel monkey troops (*Saimiri sciureus*).[108] Common squirrel monkeys, like baboons and macaques, form matrilines. However, squirrel monkey society is far more fundamentally female-based than that of baboons or macaques. Squirrel monkey troops may have more than a hundred members, but troop members consist of females and their offspring. Males are driven out of the troop when they reach sexual maturity and often remain on the periphery of the female group. During the mating season, the males go into what is termed the "fatted male state."[109] At this time, males increase their body size and become more aggressive in order to mate with females.

The orangutans also lack a clear alpha male. Adult males and females do not live together. Orangutans are rather unusual among primates, for beyond mothers and young offspring, they do not form a stable social group. Adult males guard a large territory that includes the smaller territories of several female orangutans and their offspring. Males have large throat sacs that they use to bellow out their presence, both to alert females of their location for mating and to ward off potential competing males.

But, younger males have evolved an interesting way of getting around adult male dominance: they go into a state of arrested development, or bimaturism.[110] Orangutan males can potentially reach full adulthood by around age 13, a state marked by characteristic prominent cheek flanges. But many young

SEXUAL PENIS | 35

males do not fully physically mature and instead go into a state of suspended adolescence for 10 years or more. Because they still have the appearance of immaturity, fully developed adult males do not recognize them as a threat; however, they are fertile. Although males in arrested development are able to reach females without interference from fully adult males, females are not attracted to them and they must essentially rape females to mate with them. "Rape" is a loaded term when applied to nonhuman species, but the behavior of the arrested-development male arguably qualifies as rape because females actively resist them by biting and attempting to fend them off. Unlike the previously described duck rape, these forced orangutan matings are just as successful in producing offspring as those of consensual matings.

Many other primate groups, such as the callitrichids, which include the tamarins and marmosets of Central and South America, have no alpha male.[111] Marmosets and tamarins often form polyandrous social groups, consisting of one breeding female and two adult males. Females typically bear twins and the two males take responsibility for the bulk of the care of the offspring. Bonobo society is female-centered, and the highest-ranking members of the groups are elder females.[112] In addition, the focus on alpha males often elides the fact that females also compete with one another and have dominance hierarchies. Among primates who have matrilines, such as the baboons, macaques, and squirrel monkeys, higher ranking females may have better access to mates, better access to food, and higher rates of infant survival, and they often receive more social attention and grooming.[113]

Clearly, there are many different forms of wild primate social organization relative to the roles of males and females. The alpha-male role is both temporary and context dependent. It does not occur in all primate groups and the analogy that has been drawn between the wild primate form of alpha male and human behavior is specious. What observations of wild primate social behavior have revealed is very different from what has been termed "alpha male" behavior as applied to modern humans. A given wild primate alpha male does not necessarily have greater reproductive success than other males, particularly in light of reproductive behavior over the course of life histories.

TRICKY WOMEN IN HUMAN EVOLUTION

When female choice is considered in human evolution, very often scenarios employ a mythological female trickster narrative. Perhaps the most notorious is the notion of female concealed ovulation. This hypothesis has been propounded in a variety of forms, but the basic theme is that human beings are unusual among Old World primates because females conceal outward physical signs of ovulation. In some primate species, when females enter into estrus, around the time of ovulation, their external genitalia swells and reddens. For many mammal species, mating takes place only when the female is in estrus. Human females are sexually receptive regardless of whether or not they are near ovulation.

Concealed ovulation has been described as a cryptic form of female choice. It is worth noting that such terminology—namely, concealed ovulation and cryptic selection—are linguistically loaded and female-marked. Technically, cryptic selection refers to processes that occur within the reproductive tract and that cannot be seen in field studies of sexual behavior. Sperm competition is equally cryptic but rarely designated as such. The use of such qualifiers imply that male-mediated selection processes are normal and natural, whereas female-mediated processes are special cases and are suspect, involving covert strategies that work around the normal rules of selection. There is no scientific reason to qualify female selection with terminology that suggests underhandedness. But female trickiness is a common theme of gender relations in human evolution.

Various scenarios have been given for why women supposedly hid their ovulation. For the most part, these involve tales of female manipulations to confuse men into thinking they were fathers of their children, to force them into monogamous relationships, or to trick them into caring for offspring. Interpretations of female so-called concealed ovulation seem almost to suggest that women somehow willed the changes in their outward signs of fertility in order to both deceive and confuse men. Little considered, at least in the literature of the evolution of human sexuality, is that sexual swellings on par with those of chimpanzees and bonobos are incompatible with human bipedalism. Biological anthropologist Bogusław Pawłowski advanced this hypothesis: human female sexual swellings were lost not to deceive males in sexual selection processes but to facilitate the bipedal gait, a distinctive characteristic of humans among contemporary primates.[114]

The lack of visible signs of estrus is often treated as an unusual characteristic of human females, but that is not the case. Many primates do not have sexual swellings with estrus and many primates and mammals mate at times other than a female's estrus.[115] The notable exceptions, where females do have prominent sexual swellings are chimpanzees,[116] bonobos,[117] baboons,[118] and macaques.[119] But we do not find prominent sexual swellings in the other apes, which include gorillas, orangutans, and gibbons.[120] Many have assumed, by referential modeling, that because chimpanzees and bonobos have sexual swellings, early human females must also have had them in the past.[121] Although sexual swellings are variable among primate species and their absence, rather than their presence, may in fact be the ancestral ape condition (as their absence, or minimal expression, in gorillas, orangutans, and gibbons may suggest), it is seldom considered that prominent sexual swellings may have evolved independently in the ancestor of the genus *Pan*, to which bonobos and chimpanzees belong.[122]

Moreover, in chimpanzees and bonobos, sexual swellings are not an accurate indicator of ovulation. One study described chimpanzees as exhibiting marked sexual swelling for approximately 50 percent of the intermenstrual interval and bonobos for approximately 75 percent of the intermenstrual interval.[123] Primatologist Barbara Smuts has suggested that bonobos could be considered to have concealed ovulation due to their very extended sexual swellings.[124] As such, neither bonobos nor humans exhibit a reliable indicator of when they are fertile.

Nonetheless, concealed ovulation or reproductive crypsis is still used to explain the evolution of human intersexual behavior and is often used to justify the existence of ancient monogamy in humans. Some of the first descriptions of concealed ovulation were influenced by the Man the Hunter conference organized in 1966 at the University of Chicago by anthropologists Richard Lee and Irven DeVore.[125] The proceedings were later published as a book by that title. From this conference, the hunting hypothesis arose, which argued that the key event in recent human evolution was cooperative male hunting. From there, many important human achievements followed, such as increased brain size, toolmaking, and language. Women are passive in this perspective of social evolution.

One of the first scientists to offer an interpretation of concealed ovulation was zoologist and ethnologist Desmond Morris. In his book *The Naked Ape*,[126] Morris expounded on the man-the-hunter scenario by offering what is sometimes referred to as the food-for-sex hypothesis. Here, the premise is that while men cooperate with other men to be effective hunters, women cooperate with men because they want to eat the game meat they have hunted. Here, concealed ovulation evolved to increase male cooperative behavior. If sexual swellings were present, then men would be engaged in intense competition for women and be disinclined to cooperatively hunt. If ovulation is concealed, all women would be perceived as continually available for men, reducing the drive to fight with one another over women. Morris also viewed women as reluctant to have sex. In his view, women relented to male sexual advances as a bargaining chip to force men into monogamous relationships so that they could obtain a steady supply of meat. Little consideration is given to the fact that women also have a sex drive and that women had a role in obtaining food.

Morris's interpretation is built upon a Western 1950s ideal of a white, middle-class nuclear family wherein men are the breadwinners and women stay at home. As mentioned in chapter 1, in depictions of early humans in older textbooks and *National Geographic* magazines, it is common to see male hunters bringing in game meat, inventing tools, or actively participating in some other important cultural achievement while women wander about naked in the background or perhaps kneel by the fire to cook. Anthropologist Melanie Wiber illustrates this dichotomy well in her book *Erect Men/ Undulating Women*, which describes images of women in human evolution.[127] Anthropologists such as Sally Slocum[128] and Adrienne Zilhman[129] soon challenged the man-the-hunter hypothesis on multiple grounds. One criticism was that it was sexist to suggest that men invented culture while women were merely the passive recipients of culture. Also, there has been much research on the important contributions that female gathering of plants and hunting of small game animals made to the food supply. While humans are indeed meat eaters, plant foods are far more important as dietary staples for most of the world's peoples today. In addition, numerous ethnographic studies from around the world have demonstrated that women hunt and fish and do not helplessly depend on men to provide them with meat or other types of food and that men gather.

Slocum also challenged the idea that human sociality is based on male bonding through cooperative hunting. She stressed that it could just as easily be argued that human sociality is based on mother-child bonding, particularly with the extended period of child dependency that evolved in humans. Likewise, the male communication required for hunting cooperatively is not the only explanation for the origin of language; the mother-child bond is arguably just as important, if not more critical. Linguist Steven Pinker makes a slightly different generalization about superior males being responsible for the evolution of language: "Anthropologists have noted that tribal chiefs are often both gifted orators and highly polygynous—a special prod to any imagination that cannot conceive of how linguistic skills could make a Darwinian difference . . . that played key roles in individual reproductive success."[130] The suggestion is that men with verbal skills became leaders, headmen, and polygynists who fathered large numbers of offspring, thus generating even more such linguistically talented males with increased potential for reproductive success. Given that all major events in language acquisition occur in early childhood and that women tend to have greater responsibility for the care of dependent children, it seems odd that females are not afforded any agency in the evolution of language.

Several other interpretations of the concealed-ovulation hypothesis argue that it involves female machinations to confuse paternity or to secure child care. In the scenario entomologist and evolutionary biologist Richard Alexander and his student Katharine Noonan propose,[131] if males cannot visually determine when females are ovulating, then they are unable to determine when or how many times to copulate in order to effect pregnancies in women. Here, if the time of female ovulation were clear, the male strategy would be to move from one female with a sexual swelling to another in order to impregnate as many women as possible. With ovulation concealed, a man can only ensure paternity if he stays with the same woman and continuously mates with her until she shows visible signs of a pregnancy. The benefit for a woman is that prolonged interaction with a male will convince him to pair-bond with her, and then he will continue to provide care for her and her offspring after children are born.

Alexander and Noonan also believed that concealed ovulation was likely to make women more faithful to a single mate. They reasoned that since a woman was not advertising her fertile state, she would be less likely to receive attention from other males. Coauthors Lee Benshoof and evolutionary biologist Randy Thornhill argued the opposite.[132] They essentially agree with the premise of the pregnancy trap, whereby women manipulate men into providing meat and childcare. However, they argue that concealed ovulation makes it easier for women to cuckold their pair-bonded mates by secretly mating with alpha males to secure their superior genetic material. They can, in a sense, have it both ways by deceiving one male into providing care while securing the best genes for their offspring.

An additional problem with the concealed ovulation hypotheses is that it seems to suggest a higher order thinking and strategizing among males and females in the calculating of paternity probabilities. Even with the benefits of modern medicine, Western science has only relatively recently come to understand when women are most fertile. Before 1930, some Western physicians advised women that the best time to get pregnant was when they were menstruating.[133] Yet, the various concealed ovulation hypotheses suggest that our human ancestors somehow knew swollen genitals were a sign of fertility and then became confused when they could not see them. Moreover, it is diffi- cult to believe that our early ancestors understood the relationship between fertility and copulation and between copulation and pregnancy. Copulation is fast, whereas signs of pregnancy develop slowly. It is unlikely that our ancient ancestors were able to, by reasoning, associate a copulatory event with a later developing pregnancy. While there is certainly evidence from many mammals and some primates that the estrous state does enhance the drive to mate for both males and females, that does not mean that they have any cog- nitive understanding that an act of mating now will result in offspring many months later.

DEMONIC MALES

If many scenarios of human evolution have cast females as manipulative and tricky, some cast men in no better light, as violent and villainous. Two recent examples are Randy Thornhill and anthropologist Craig Palmer's *A Natural History of Rape*[134] and Wrangham and Peterson's *Demonic Males*.[135] The latter is a more generic indictment of the human males that suggests that chimpan- zee and human violence is linked to the importance of male hunting in both species.

In *A Natural History of Rape*, Thornhill and Palmer draw on the Trivers's parental investment theory[136] to make the case that rape is a male reproduc- tive strategy that has been selected for through the course of human evolu- tion. Trivers's parental investment theory argues that males and females have evolved different mating strategies. Here, sexual selection involves not only physical differences between the sexes but also behavioral differences. He suggests that females tend to be choosier about their mates while males are more indiscriminate. The logic is that the female investment necessary to raise successful offspring is greater than that of males. At the level of the gamete, eggs are expensive while sperm is rather cheap. Males produce over 100 million sperm a day while female eggs are far fewer and only cyclically available.[137] Humans present perhaps the most extreme case. The minimum investment needed by a man to successfully bring a child into the world is as little as a one-time mating event with a female. For a female, the investment is always far greater. She carries the child for nine months and provides vital nourishment for the child through breastfeeding for the first few years of the child's life. Today, we have infant formulas that can serve as substitutes, but in traditional societies, it is common for a child to be breastfed for five years. Parental investment theory suggests that a male's best chance of reproductive success is to mate with as many females as possible; a female's best chance of reproductive success is to select the male who is most likely to produce a healthy child.

Thornhill and Palmer interpret human male rape in terms of Trivers's parental-investment-strategy hypothesis. They first contextualize their argument by saying that there has been an aversion to the study of rape from a scientific standpoint because it tends to be the subject of feminist political ideology rather than evolutionary biology. Unfortunately, they do not present scientific evidence so much as rather speculative theory, which leads them to make the same mistake that they purport the feminists have made. To effectively argue that rape was biologically selected for because it leads to greater reproductive success, it is necessary to have data on the degree to which rape results in offspring. The authors do not provide that evidence. However, the question about rape is certainly worth asking. As previously described, we do have such evidence in male ducks and other waterfowl that rape females, and arrested-development orangutans. Males of the former are less successful in producing offspring, while males of the latter are equally successful in producing offspring as those who copulate consensually.

Thornhill and Palmer pick and choose ethnographic data to support their argument, simultaneously dismissing cultural explanations that do not support their view and citing either select statistics from modern Western societies or providing gross generalizations about cultures that do. They stress that feminists have been guilty of committing the natural fallacy, that is, not realizing that there is no connection between what is biologically or naturally selected for and what is morally right. The problem is that evolution does not work that way with humans. Humans, like most primates, are intensely social beings. The evolution of empathy and a sense of fair play are increasingly subjects of scholarly research into the higher primates.[138]

In humans, the specifics of sexual morality are highly variable across cultures. Thornhill and Palmer make the blanket statement that rape occurs in all human cultures. Although their ethnographic research is scanty, it can, for the sake of argument, be conceded that this is probably true. Nonetheless, that is not a sufficient argument, for we find that rape is highly variable cross-culturally. When we find such cultural variability, we have to look beyond what might be generically (and genetically) true for the human species to cultural factors that play a role.

South Africa has been called the rape capital of the world. A recent report by the Medical Research Council of South Africa describes a number of disturbing statistics.[139] First, South Africa has one of the highest rates of reported rape in the world, but the rate of actual rape perpetration is not known. In a survey of approximately 1,700 men, 27.6 percent admitted to having raped a woman or girl (4.9 percent within the last year). Nearly half of the men who had raped (46.3 percent) said they had raped more than one woman or girl. Regarding the age of their first rape victim, 26.2 percent of the rape victims were under the age of 14 (72.7 percent were under the age of 19). Men who had HIV were no more likely to rape than those who did not. This last factor is noteworthy, because many have attributed the high rates of rape to the South African folk belief that sex with a virgin can cure HIV/AIDS.[140] The authors of the study, however, attribute the high rates of rape to cultural notions about South African manhood, including marked gender hierarchy and the sexual entitlement of men.

On the other end of the spectrum, we can consider the sexual mores of the Canela of the Amazonia.[141] They have a periodic ritual sex time where men and women engage in sex with multiple partners. The expectation for women (married or not) is that they should have sex with any man who asks. To refuse such a request is considered quite rude and being "stingy with one's genitals." Here, a woman who has sex with a man who she may not desire is not traumatized; rather, it is more a matter of being polite and generous and helping to promote group harmony.

Thornhill and Palmer also base their evolutionary argument on statistics from Western society that suggest that rapists are more likely to rape women who are at their peak of fertility and child-bearing potential. However, cases of rape that do not fit that profile must also be explained. At the time of the writing of this book, serial pedophilia has been in the US news a great deal, with a wide range of perpetrators, from priests to football coaches. Many of the rape and sexual molestation victims are males; but even if female, pedophiles do not target the sexually mature of either sex. We are also just beginning to address the seriousness of the problem of male-male prison rape. Future generations will hold us to task for not treating this subject more seriously. Nonetheless, there can be no reproductive benefit for males who serially rape children or other males. Perhaps what is most important to highlight is that rape is most definitely not a characteristic of human males. While it is disturbing when men do rape, it is quite a stretch to say that they are born to rape, for few ever do.

CONCLUSION

The human penis has a number of distinctive attributes, none of which seem to have an arguable role in direct male-male competition. Rather these characteristics are far more likely to have evolved to attract females by enhancing their sexual pleasure. Compared with that of other primates, the human penis is anatomically oriented to be highly visible and would have been prominently displayed in ancestral humans, who did not cover their bodies in clothing. By analogy, several primate species use penile displays as a form of social communication, specifically to invite females to mate. The human penis is spineless, which greatly attenuates its sensitivity during copulation, which could be considered to reduce male motivation for sex if argued exclusively from a male perspective. However, reduced male sensitivity necessitates a prolonged period of copulation in order for males to climax, which may make such males more appealing to females. For human females, longer copulations with a smooth, nonirritating penis would serve to enhance the pleasure of a sexual encounter. The human penis is boneless and highly flexible. This allows for a wider range of copulatory positions and also requires that male intercourse involve whole body movements, which provides broader tactile stimulation for females during a sex act. Compared with penises of other primates, the human penis is also relatively long, thick, and morphologically complex, with its bulbous head and coronal ridge.

However, a suite of interconnected hypotheses involving alpha males, concealed ovulation, and the exchange of food for sex ignore female agency in human sexuality, except as a deceptive strategy. Males are often depicted as sexually aggressive, while females are depicted as sexually reluctant, as is perhaps best exemplified in the born-to-rape hypothesis. Sociobiologist E. O. Wilson went so far as to call sex an "antisocial force in evolution," stating, "Bonds are formed between individuals in spite of sex and not because of it."[142]

Little consideration is given to the possibility that females actively seek out sexual encounters and choose males with characteristics that provide them with enhanced sexual pleasure. Also typically minimized is the extent to which female sexuality is expressed outside of reproduction. As primatologist Robert Martin pointed out, from an evolutionary perspective, mating behavior when a female is not fertile could even be considered maladaptive.[143] If species mate outside of ovulation, then they run the risk of fertilizing aging eggs and creating potentially unhealthy offspring. But if female sexuality, and human sexuality, is considered more broadly as part of the complex of human social behaviors, then sex for sex's sake is understandable. Among bonobos, de Waal has described sex as a kind of social lubricant that facilitates cooperative behavior among group members. Human female sexuality in all of its forms is similar to that of our bonobo cousins. But where we diverge from bonobos is in the extent to which female choice has shaped the human penis into becoming a much more effective instrument for female sexual pleasure.

3

The Patriarchal Penis

Phallic Cults and the Dawn of Agriculture

How did we get from our ancestral grandmothers influencing the very evolution of the male physiology and physical form to where we are now? It may all have started with the major *cultural* change in human history that anthropologists refer to as the agricultural revolution. In anthropology, we describe the long shift from hunting and gathering to farming with the dramatic term "revolution" because this shift truly was a watershed event that forever changed the fundamental way that human societies operated. Most importantly, with the agricultural revolution came more concrete ideas of ownership. People began to claim ownership not only of the land but also of people. In this context, archaeological evidence suggests that the penis emerged as a common symbol that was associated with ideas of male dominance and male power. By way of background, it is worth considering the theoretical trappings of these critical concepts—the agricultural revolution and human expressions of gender-based hierarchy. There is much debate among anthropologists about the specific social implications of the transition to agriculture, and dichotomous narratives have ensued. In this framework the adoption of an agricultural lifestyle is viewed as a potential cause for the subjugation of women and the emergence of elaborate organized warfare. However, this interpretation is overly simplistic and hinges on stereotypical and narrowly defined notions of male versus female roles in society and similarly myopic either/or ideas about peace versus violence. Many anthropologists have now come to embrace more nuanced and complex interpretations of the past. Undoubtedly, human violence and some forms of social hierarchy existed before the dawn of agriculture. However, the social shifts that came about in this period appeared to enhance social stratification, interpersonal violence, and gender-based hierarchy in many societies. Support for this perspective comes from two lines of evidence: ethnographic analogs of hunter-gatherers and archaeological data including the material culture associated with social stratification and penis cults in agricultural societies.

Humans lived as hunter-gatherers (i.e., foragers) for at least 90 percent of our history. However, only a handful of cultures still maintain a foraging lifestyle. In general, foragers are relatively nonviolent and cooperative peoples with strong ideas about equality among men and women, and among humans in general. Contemporary hunter-gatherers do not have strong notions of individual property rights; rather all members of the culture have access to communal lands, which belong to the group.[1] Foragers move from place to place depending on the seasons and availability of resources, and they hunt game animals, gather wild plants, and often fish and collect marine or riverine foods. The shift to agriculture changed that way of life for most of the world's peoples. As humans increasingly adopted and came to rely upon the practice of intensive agriculture they changed socially, economically, and politically. The archaeological record suggests that over time, and with new social, political, and ecological pressures, foraging groups became larger agricultural societies and people increasingly competed with one another for access to suitable land to farm and other resources. Ideas about ownership of land were perhaps related to ideas about ownership of people. Cross-cultural studies suggest that egalitarian relationships erode as women and other social classes of people are increasingly treated as the property of males. As human societies became more patriarchal, the penis emerged as a symbol of male authority and dominance, taking on magical and mystical or spiritual qualities. Over time many different ancient societies across the globe developed elaborate material culture related to the penis. Depictions of the penis and phallic imagery and symbolism suggest that the penis relates to the supernatural and that this organ possesses special powers. From a functional standpoint, the magical aspects of an object (in this case the penis) suggest that ritual acts and behaviors may compel certain outcomes that direct the supernatural. We find evidence for magical behaviors and beliefs in the archaeological record associated with a wide variety of penis cults from agricultural societies. There are limitations to our knowledge, however. We cannot know from the archaeological evidence alone about the range of ideas held by all members of any given social group. Therefore we interpret beliefs associated with human sexuality and agency in prehistory based on material culture and architecture that is public and/or widespread. We suggest that the powerful ruling classes in stratified agricultural societies evoked daily reminders of dominant ideologies through religious institutions, monumental architecture, artistic traditions, and even common domestic material culture. Through these practices social institutions and ideologies of the ruling classes would have been reproduced and reinforced in many aspects of daily life.

Archaeological evidence for penis cults is pervasive among agricultural societies. These cults can be found among the ancient Egyptians, the Mayans, the Greeks, Romans, and the Indus Valley civilizations, to name some examples. Cross-culturally, penis worship appears to be closely linked to ideas of ownership, and it is associated with societies that rely on domesticated plants and animals. Here we argue that certain symbols, themes, and types of imagery were both widespread and persistent for long periods of human history. We describe a range of examples from archaeological cultures to argue for a connection between the rise of phallic cults and the practice of agriculture. We do not make a case for a single origin of these practices and widespread symbols; rather, we explain that the phallus as a powerful symbol conveyed different meanings in specific cultural contexts. We speculate about some of these meanings based on archaeological and ethnohistoric evidence. In this chapter we also discuss the thermal model for the development of complex clothing and a recent theory that a need for clothing and fabric is related to the rise of agriculture. Importantly, the developments of fitted clothing and agriculture—both major shifts in human history—are related to significant social and cultural changes. We argue that clothing has shaped attitudes about sexuality and about the penis. As the penis becomes less visible (due to covering), in many cultures the phallus over time took on more visible public roles, and it is found archaeologically in a wide range of domestic and ritual contexts. Elements of human anatomy may take on greater social significance and become increasingly powerful symbols when they are hidden from view. In the case of the penis, because this organ separates males from females it is both a clear indicator of one's sex and, as we posit, enmeshed in notions of power and social dominance that were expressed in rituals, art, and architecture.

THE ORIGIN OF CLOTHING AND THE ADVENT OF AGRICULTURE

To understand the development of penis cults, evolving social hierarchies, and sexuality it is necessary to explain some of the fundamental elements relating to anthropological knowledge of agricultural origins. Anthropologists and archaeologists have traditionally assumed that the provision of food and the production of large amounts of it provided the primary motivation for plant domestication and the development of agricultural systems worldwide. However, researchers have recently come to understand that there are major problems with older theories of plant domestication, and some archaeologists have argued that a need for clothing played an important role in the development and adoption of agricultural practices.[2] The first clothes were created and worn at least 70,000 years ago, although some suggest that this technology existed earlier.[3] The early domestication of plants and animals involved a transformation of species that were previously wild multipurpose resources. That is, these species were not the most useful resources for feeding people, and some were even nonconsumable. The earliest domesticated plants included fiber-producers such as flax, hemp, jute, and cotton. Other early domesticates include peppers, gourds, and items that would have been useful feed for animals, such as wheat and sorghum. As archaeologist Ian Gilligan argues, "Farming only began, and subsequently was only adopted readily, in areas where humans were in the habit of wearing clothes."[4] Moreover, he suggests that biologically based cold adaptations among Neanderthals prevented them from developing the technological capacity for creating complex clothing, and thus contributed to their extinction.[5] He states, "In contrast, the greater biological vulnerability of fully modern humans promoted a precocious appearance of behavioral adaptations among some (though not all) groups, visible in the various archaeological markers of modern human behavior."[6] In essence, biologically modern humans have relatively longer limbs and therefore are adapted to greater heat loss; thus, they would have favored an early adoption of fitted clothing for warmth.[7] This fitted clothing would have covered the genitals and protected them from the elements.

In this thermal model for the origin of clothing Gilligan distinguishes between simple clothing, which is loosely draped, and complex clothing, which provides more protection.[8] This discussion points to both social and technological implications associated with understanding Paleolithic human behavior. Unfortunately, no archaeological remains of clothing exist from the earliest periods of complex clothing production, which may have occurred around 50,000–30,000 years ago. The development of complex clothing was necessitated by the extreme environmental fluctuations that characterized the glacial period known as the Marine Isotope Stage 3 (MIS3), which extends from 60,000 to 30,000 years ago.[9] Importantly, anatomically modern humans were preadapted to adopt complex clothing. To put it a different way, because of our physical characteristics that allow for heat loss, modern humans need warm fitted clothes in cold climates. And, importantly, when humans started wearing fitted clothes, males (and females) began to cover their genitals.

Due to the dearth of direct material evidence, archaeologists must extrapolate from technological evidence such as stone tools, which were likely used for creating protective insulated garments through processes of scraping, cutting, piercing, and sewing. Additional proximate evidence comes from depictions of woven garments on the Venus figurines of the Upper Paleolithic (50,000–10,000 years ago).[10] Microremains of skin beetles and moths have also been used to support arguments that humans were processing fur, skin, and cloth.[11] And, finally, a compelling new line of argument comes from a thermal theory of clothing origins, related to changing environments of the Upper Paleolithic, as discussed above. Fitted clothing conceals the penis and genitals. We may never know whether men covered or sheathed their penises prior to the Paleolithic. However, there are many examples of variations in penis sheathing and coverings from cultures that are unrelated to protection from the elements. These examples will be discussed in chapter 4

Why Adopt Agriculture?

The foundations of what we consider to be modern civilization are associated with both plant and animal domestication. For this reason alone, anthropologists have spent a great deal of time and effort debating why human societies turned to the full-time practice of agriculture and shifted away from hunting and gathering lifestyles. Moreover, it is now generally agreed that the quality of life among many preindustrial farming societies was lower than that of foraging societies.[12] Nevertheless, beginning more than 11,000 years ago, many human groups all over the world were in the process of domesticating wild animals and useful plants that lived in their local environments. Contemporary anthropological explanations for the rise of agricultural lifestyles have shifted their focus away from relatively simplistic single-cause theories based on assumptions of rapid geographically restricted plant domestication. Current interpretations of the Neolithic Revolution involve the application of genetic and archaeological data to multicausal explanations that attempt to understand a combination of factors associated with a dependence on agriculture in specific regions of the world.[13] For example, one hypothesis explains the adoption of protofarming as a risk-management strategy.[14] In this formulation, agriculture and a predictable food supply buffered environmental changes that made local resource availability unpredictable. This change was in response to climate shifts around 10,000 years ago when the last glacial period (of the Quaternary) ended and the earth began to warm. In a much more complicated theory, an intensive and diverse web of human-environmental feedbacks are explored as innovations and specializations.[15] In this model, the rise of agriculture is explained by increasing population densities, innovation in productive areas, and communication along networks that results in improved acquisition of information.

There is no simple explanation for the rise of agriculture, and most archaeologists now argue that the process of domesticating plants and animals was long and varied across cultural contexts. Archaeological data suggests that over several thousand years, human engaged in a combination of behaviors including the casual use of wild species, the use of managed species, the development and exploitation of domesticated species, and a great deal of communication; these behaviors resulted, for example, in the spread of farming to Europe from the Near East on multiple occasions.[16] A slow transformation of low-level food production into more intensive full-scale agriculture characterizes this process. From the currently available archaeological data, it is clear that people all over the world decided to domesticate plants and animals on a large scale at various points in prehistory, starting around 11,000–12,000 years ago (and from approximately 10,000–5,000 BCE). Moreover, important generalized outcomes of the process include increases in both population and social stratification.[17] We will come back to the issue of social stratification below.

Domestication involves artificial selection by humans. While natural selection is a very slow process whereby species adapt to the environment, domestication involves human genetic engineering of plants and animals. In truth, all domesticated plants and animals are genetically modified foods. Domestication takes advantage of random mutations in the DNA. When DNA replicates, mistakes are sometimes made in the code, resulting in mutations. Sometimes mutations can be advantageous, but many are harmful. For example, cancer may start off as a coding error, but once the mistake is made it continues to be repeated. Mutations can also occur in the sex chromosomes, resulting in individuals of the same species being genetically slightly different from one another. For example, a female with a genotype of only one X chromosome (X0) will have Turner syndrome (see chapter 7), resulting in sex organs that do not mature at adolescence, sterility, and short stature.

In artificial selection or domestication, humans decide what types of mutations are advantageous to use or build upon. Corn or maize provides a useful illustration of this point. Corn's wild ancestor, teosinte, has small ears with only 5–10 kernels. Domestication occurred when people took the seeds of mutated teosinte plants and selected for plants with more kernels and sweeter kernels.[18] Over time the process changed many generations of plants and resulted in the big ears of corn we have today.

Like domestic plants, domesticated animals have distinctive physical characteristics that humans selected for. Animals' behavioral traits were also manipulated to breed larger or tamer creatures that may produce more food. A mutualistic relationship exists between domestic animals and humans; humans have modified their culture, including their technology and behaviors, to manage, feed, and care for domestic animals. It is important to recognize that maintaining livestock results in more mouths to feed, and the early farmers may have required a food surplus that was motivated by the need to care for their animals (rather than the need to feed their families directly).

Animals have been domesticated for many purposes and their physical characteristics reflect this. Dogs (*Canis familiaris*) are an excellent illustration of the drastic physical variability we can observe in a single domestic species. The Mexican hairless dog, or Xoloitzcuintli (Xolo), provides a useful example of an extreme breed that was selected for specific traits. This dog is produced in standard, miniature, and toy sizes and it is native to pre-Columbian Mexico and South America. It has with a long neck, bat-like ears, and very little hair on its body, which in the tropics may have been a beneficial adaptation. It was used for food (another probable explanation for its hairless condition), hunting, and domestic companionship. Moreover, the Xolo was thought to be sacred by the indigenous people of Mexico, and mythologies make reference to this dog's role in the afterlife. The Xolo looks and behaves very little like its ancestor, the wolf (*Canis lupus*). Humans have taken wild wolves and directed them into many kinds of dog breeds, including chihuahuas, pomeranians, goldendoodles, pit bulls, great danes, and other dog varieties beginning 13,000–15,0000 years before the present.[19] Anthropological and historical examinations of the concept of sacrifice suggest that ideologically and economically this practice is related to the domestication of plants and animals.[20] Some archaeologists even argue that the domestication of animals was motivated by a desire to provide a steady supply of sacrificial victims for rituals.[21]

Agriculture, animal domestication, and human population growth are intricately related. In any given culture context we cannot determine whether the development of agriculture was motivated by the production of fibers for clothing or whether human population growth resulted from a more steady food supply, made possible by agriculture, or a number of other scenarios.

Regardless, when intensive agriculture occurs in human history we often find evidence of many more people living in densely populated settlements. Unlike foragers, who follow herds and collect wild plants as they move from one camp to another, agriculturalists live in villages, towns, and cities, raising plants and animals near their residences. It is likely that widespread ideas of property and ownership began with agriculture. Although contemporary hunter-gatherers do not have a strong sense of territoriality, with the rise of agriculturalists, we see ideologies akin to "this is *my* land," or "this is the land of *my* family." An example of this can be seen in Europe's first farmers, who are thought to have practiced a patrilocal form of kinship wherein differential access to land was based on male hierarchy.[22] This information is derived from burials and strontium isotopic data collected from over 300 early Neolithic human skeletons. A team of researchers found that males had much less geographic variation in their isotopic signatures than females had (that is, females would leave their ancestral lands to marry farmers in places farther away, while men would spend their lifetimes in their homelands). The data also suggests that the sons of farmers inherited preferential access to fertile farmlands and that social inequality increased over time.[23]

Peoples in different regions of the world arrived at ideas about farming independently.[24] Later in time there is also evidence that some farming communities came into contact with each other and moved crops and livestock into new areas. Nevertheless, many general social changes that occurred with the adoption of an agricultural lifestyle are similar across the globe. To generalize, archaeological data show us that in situations where there were more people living in densely populated settlements there was increased competition for land and stronger ideas of ownership. In this setting, it is not difficult to imagine corporative people becoming more violent and engaging in rivalries as they struggled to claim land and other diminishing resources.[25] Over time, ownership of land extended to ideas of ownership of people; it is likely that the dawn of slavery and ideas of ownership over women developed in association with the dawn of agriculture and the elaboration of social hierarchies.[26] Egalitarian relationships eroded and women began to be treated as the property of men, as evidenced from formal public institutions based in patriarchy and male-oriented social structures.[27] As human societies became more hierarchal and patriarchal, the penis emerged as a symbol of public male authority and dominance and took on religious and supernatural qualities. We find this development in a wide variety of penis cults associated with the archaeological record in the Old World and the New World. These cults reveal

a common complex of penis veneration associated with farming and the glorification of male power. It is interesting to note that new interpretations of
archaeological data from Turkish Neolithic sites in the Middle East suggest
that village formation and domestication occurred in a social context wherein
people were absorbed in using the power of wild animals, phallicism, and
the dead to build social institutions.[28] As people became increasingly engaged
with plants and animals in efforts to provision their activities, they became
tied to domestic products and permanently settled lifestyles.

PENIS CULTS

The rise of penis veneration began with the adoption of agriculture. The
penis, being one of the most obvious physical features that separate men and
women, began to symbolize male superiority, dominance, and authority. The
archaeological record provides evidence of penis glorification and adoration,
which we describe here as "penis cults." We posit that penis veneration is typically directly linked to agricultural lifestyles.

As a preface, we provide some background on the nature of archaeology
and archaeological interpretation. The archaeological record is not a historical
record of the world's cultures. It is a record of what researchers have been able
to recover about ancient human history from material culture (artifacts, food
rubbish, architectural remains, etc.) that has been left behind by the people of
the past. Some regions of the world have higher frequencies of evidence than
others. In part, the availability of such evidence has to do with environmental
conditions and the way that data is preserved in the ground over time. Some
of the best-preserved archaeological sites are in desert environments, such as
those found in Egypt and the high, dry deserts of the Andes where the ancient
Inca lived. Both Egyptians and Incan peoples practiced mummification of the
dead, which has provided a wealth of information to archaeologists. Mummification is difficult to achieve without dry conditions that preserve cultural
and biological evidence.

Another cultural feature that provides an important addition to modern
interpretations of the past is a writing system. A durable writing system, or
one that could be preserved over thousands of years, provides insights into
ancient life (such as ideology and political relations) that might be difficult to
reconstruct without this evidence. For example, the cuneiform script of the
ancient Sumerian culture is one of the earliest forms of writing, dating to
around 4000 BCE.[29] Cuneiform has been beautifully preserved on clay tablets

and provides a wealth of information about Sumerian society and culture. These tablets record information such as the names of rulers and gods, the commemoration of important historical events, and the structure of and change in language over 35 centuries. The ancient people of Mesoamerica also carved in stone and wrote a great deal of information on paper; these written works help us understand the ways that the elites lived and some of the beliefs these peoples maintained. These inscriptions describe events that were relevant for the culture at a specific time and place. Information recorded in many ancient cultural writing systems often references the glorification of the accomplishments of kings, warriors, and mythic gods.

Unfortunately, archaeological data is poorly preserved in tropical forest environments. In these hot and humid climates, everything decomposes rapidly. As a result, there is comparatively less material to work with in the prehistoric cultures that lived in the Amazonian or African rain forests. We believe it is important to emphasize that there is a great deal of information about human history that archaeologists cannot recover through survey and excavation. Nonetheless, the information we do have points to a worldwide phenomenon of penis cults associated with agricultural societies. Over and again we see the cultural message: the penis relates to agriculture, and relates to male power.

It is important to note that in our interpretations of the past we are primarily relying on a two-sex, male and female, model of gender relations. However, we know that the cultures of antiquity expressed a wide variety of gender roles and norms that reflected a range of ideas about sexuality and individual identitiy. A great deal of research conducted in recent decades has suggested that the application of this narrow, two-sex model is potentially problematic because it assumes that humans have universally recognized a fundamental opposition between male and female. We assume that this opposition is related to the rise of agriculture and can be identified via phallic imagery. While this is not the only story about sex and gender relations in the past, it is the focus of this text. Below, we explore the overt public phallic imagery recovered from a variety of archaeological settings; these images are more frequently encountered and well documented than other forms of sex-based expressions. This is not to say that women did not have subtle forms of power and expression in other areas. Undoubtedly, more elusive clues about less dominant gender realities of the past exist. Archaeologists are just beginning to explore and understand these via scant remains. Nevertheless, here we seek to understand the dominant overdetermined public messages related to the penis. This understanding is informed by multiple lines of evidence including archaeological remains, written records, and public and monumental imagery dominated by an abundance of masculine and phallic references.

EGYPT

Some of our earliest evidence of penis worship comes from ancient Egypt. Archaeological remains from Egypt are abundant, widespread, and well preserved. Because Egyptians had a writing system, practiced mummification, built monumental architecture, and lived in a dry climate, their prehistory is comparatively well known. Some of Egypt's important early Egyptian phallic gods are Atum and Min.[30] Atum is a creator divinity.[31] In some creation myths, Atum not only made everything but also made himself. His first wife was his fist. By masturbating with his fist-wife, he began the creation of all the other gods and goddesses from his semen. It is no surprise that Egyptian obelisks have been called phallic emblems and creational symbols, "erected in honor of the Creator and his divine attribute."[32] Moreover, the pyramidal shape at the top of the obelisk (*bnbnt*) originated from a drop of Atum's (or the bull's) seed, and it symbolized the phallus (pillar), rebirth, and resurrection.[33] Additional support for this connection is provided by archaeologist Henri Frankfort's argument that pillar and bull are interchangeable in Egyptian imagery.[34]

A second early Egyptian phallic god was Min, who originates from around the fourth century BC. Min was referred to as the lord of the penis.[35] He is often depicted holding his large, erect penis in his left hand and a sheep-herding flail in his right hand. In addition to sheep, Min is associated with the agricultural domesticates of cattle and lettuce. Min is also depicted as a white bull and called the Bull of the Great Phallus. His association with lettuce derives from the ancient Egyptian idea that lettuce was an aphrodisiac.[36] Moreover, the early lettuce plants domesticated by the Egyptians grew in long straight stalks (representing the phallus) and produced a milky sap (representing semen).[37] This agricultural divinity was worshipped in raucous festivals wherein the pharaoh harvested a sheaf of wheat and Min's statue was anointed with a "life giving mixture of bitumen" and burnt ingredients.[38]

Min is the god of fertility and the promoter of abundant life. He is often depicted standing on a pedestal with a sloping front and stairs, which is said to "represent the primordial hill, a symbol of the resurrection."[39] The primordial hill is a sign of divine life that figures in the Egyptian origin myths and was conventionalized as a stairway.[40] According to the myth, in the beginning

FIGURE 3.1 Egyptian obelisk in the Boboli Gardens of the Pitti Palace, the home of the Medici Family in Florence, Italy. The obelisk, complete with a golden ball at the top of a pyramid pointing to the sky, is a classic example of a structure representing the Egyptian phallic creator god, Atum. The pyramidal shape originated from a drop of Atum's semen. The placement of the obelisk along the central axis of these formal sixteenth-century gardens is significant. Additionally, this obelisk resides in a private garden, which is unusual as these structures were typically positioned in public squares.

there was nothing but the primeval water, Nun. The sun god (also known as Atum) emerged from the water, and because he had nowhere to stand, he climbed the primordial hill that also arose from Nun.[41] This act is significant because Atum conquers chaos when he climbs the hill, comes to dominate the world, and "instituted Ma-a-t [the world order] as the order that eternally prevails."[42] Here the mythical actions of the sun god provide a metaphor for the pharaoh's ascent to the throne. Note that the pharaoh is viewed as the son of the sun god.

Min is clearly associated with fertile earth, male superiority, and authority over women. In mythic writings he proclaims to have conquered the lands, and as a foreigner (or a foreign god originating in the south) he claims to be a bull who "astonishes women with his form" and a "husband who impregnates his fair wives with his beauty."[43] Min was complemented by the goddess Hathor, a consort associated with libidinous feminine qualities.[44] This male-female paring is a common theme in Egyptian myth, and most male gods have a female consort and an offspring that accompany them in myths and cosmologies. The females, however, always play a supporting role.

A few thousand years later, in the Middle Kingdom (2055–1650 BCE), Min became fused with the deity Horus, the son of Isis and Osiris.[45] The mythical king-god Osiris was associated with fertility and the annual rebirth of grain.[46] Countless recorded traditions and rituals incorporate phallic symbols in the worship of Osiris (as well as other Egyptian gods). Followers of Osiris worshipped phallic icons in temples and carried them around as charms and talismans.[47] In this cultural setting the majestic power of the penis is evoked through ritual and worship centered on the cyclical natural order of life, including social hierarchy, the divine origin and rights of the king and queen, and the fertility of the land and its people.[48]

Horus is depicted with a sheepherder's flail like Min's, as well as a shepherds' crook (like that found in depictions of Osiris). The crook and flail are both allusions to the fertility and safety of Egypt's herds and crops.[49] In 120 CE, Plutarch tells of how Horus came to be from his god and goddess parents, Osiris and Isis.[50] According to the myth, Osiris was murdered by his brother, Seth, who dismembered his body and scattered his parts across the land.[51] His sister-wife, Isis, tried to gather up all of his parts; the only part she could not retrieve was his penis. Seth had flung it into the water where it was eaten by a fish. So Isis fashioned him a new penis, copulated with Osiris's resurrected form, and conceived Horus.[52] Osiris may be interpreted as the male principle that was symbolized by the form of round bread (also indicative of the sun), while Isis, the female element, was symbolized by wine.[53] The consumption of bread and wine represented regeneration and the union of male and female elements in nature via products of agricultural labors. The myth of Osiris conveys the message that the power of the penis may be evoked through ritual and worship linked to the fertility of the land and the perpetuation of life and social order.

CIVILIZATIONS OF THE MEDITERRANEAN: GREECE AND ROME

Like the Egyptians, the ancient Greeks and Romans practiced rituals of worship that celebrated the connection between agriculture, domestic animals, and human fertility. Undoubtedly, prehistoric ideologies of sex and gender-based symbolism formed the foundations of later ideas in this region and others. For example, a comparative study of gender relations from ancient Italy illustrates that, over time, "bodily symbols of maleness and femaleness were turned to expressing class distinctions" and in particular, weapons became male symbols of masculinity and violence in a social context of intensified agricultural development.[54] Basic symbols of female and male identity have continuity from the end of the Neolithic through the Iron Age (3000–800 BCE, and beyond). These core symbols are adapted by each successive social regime.

Another expression of male identity, fertility, and power can be interpreted from a relic of a penis cult of the Middle Minoan era (beginning in 2200 BCE). This figurine of a male wearing a codpiece was found in the deeply buried layers of an ancient Greek village, Knossos, on Crete.[55] In the Middle Minoan period the people of Knossos built monumental palaces, erected causeways and aqueducts, and engaged in long-distance exchange with Egyptians and Babylonians. The history of phallic worship among the people of the Mediterranean has deep roots indeed, as suggested by archaeological and historical evidence.

Greek phallic gods included the familiar characters Dionysus, Pan, and Hermes, as well as Priapus, who is less well known. Priapus was a minor fertility deity and was the offspring of the goddess of love, Aphrodite, and the god of wine; he is said to have had a perpetual erection.[56] His image is found in various forms on Roman sculptures, coins, and stones, which were used as devotional objects that brought maternal joys, fertility, and virility.[57] Dionysus, also known as Bacchus, was the god of ecstasy and was associated with domesticated figs, ivy, grapes, and wine.[58] In fact, he is said to have introduced

FIGURE 3.2 Priapus, god of fertility, depicted on the wall in the doorway of the House of Vettii at Pompeii.

both grape vines and wine to Athens, an event that is told in the myth of Icarus.[59] These items were quickly incorporated into the Athenian farming system and became iconic culinary staples alongside olives and grain. Dionysus is often depicted with a procession of female consorts and satyrs with erect penises. He was associated with the goat, which provided a favored sacrificial victim in the god's name.[60]

One of the earliest known Dionysus sanctuaries was found on the island of Keos and dates to the Aegean Bronze Age (ca. 3600–600 BCE).[61] This temple is filled with many terracotta statues of women in Minoan dress, hundreds of votives, and wine cups (made in a style characteristic of Dionysus). The female statues are possibly gifts from worshippers to the god or serve "as perpetual witnesses of the god's epiphany."[62] Wooden poles were carried in phallic processions to honor and celebrate Dionysus across Greece. These *phalloi* were painted and sometimes elaborately decorated. They were either carried or moved in carts through the streets.[63] Research suggests that this practice and others, such as making offerings of stone phalluses, began long before the Bronze Age, perhaps as early as the Archaic Period (ca. 800–480 BCE). Later, during the reign of Ptolemy II Philadelphus, a Greek scholar recorded an account of a Dionysian festival in the Egyptian city of Alexandria wherein a 180-foot-long golden phallus crowned with a gold star was paraded through the city.[64]

It has been argued that *phalloi* do not simply symbolize male sexuality but are also representative of the "exuberant, animating force that makes arousal and procreation possible."[65] Classicist Eric Csapo argues that the phallic power of the god Dionysus is expressed not by his hypermasculinity but by the fact that he expresses gender interstructure and ambiguity. At the same time, "The phallus is the symbol of the surging life principle, but also an instrument of possession."[66] According to the Greek understanding, an essential quality of Dionysus is a vital animal impulse; this "divine part of humanity is located in the male seed, which has a lusty vital impulse to be released and take possession of everything, including the possessor."[67] The phallus is zoomorphic, having a will of its own; the *phalloi* of Dionyasiac processions, for example, were thought to be living organisms.[68] These processions occurred every year when both allies and colonies were expected to send *phalloi* as tribute to the god.[69] These wooden *phalloi* were often decorated with a large eye and effects that suggested a head and neck and an individual persona.

In addition to the idea that the penis has its own will and personality, we see a reoccurring relationship between the cult of Dionysus, the glorification of men, and domestic products. Wine is the most obvious point of connection, but in addition to this libation many Dionyasiac ceremonies can be characterized as male-oriented and included other products of agricultural labor such as pigs, goats, and figs. For example, the City of Dionysia hosted annual celebrations that included a wine-soaked revelry and competitions of choruses, comedies, tragedies, and satyrs; the teams were made up of boys and men.[70] Before the performances the theater was purified with the blood of young pigs and wine for the god, who looked on in the form of a statue.

Pan is a figure who, like Dionysus, merges sexuality and domestication; in this case it occurs both literally and figuratively, as Pan is both man and goat. There is some debate among etymologists as to the origin and meaning of his name. His names indicate "grazer" and the term "pān" meaning "all."[71] The all-ness of Pan is an essential characteristic as in Greek mythology he represents universal nature. Pan is the Latin cognate of the term "pastor," which translates as "one who grazes the flocks."[72] He is known as the god of wild places, god of the hunt (like Hermes, another phallic god), and master of animals; he is associated with domestic herd animals.[73] Depending on the myth and cult, he is described as the son of Zeus or Hermes and has many offspring, who in various myths are often referred to as Pan.[74]

Pan frequently carries a thyrus, a staff of giant fennel topped with a pine-cone and wrapped in a wreath of ivy. This imagery combines the symbol of the fertility of the wild forest (the pine cone, or seed of the penis) with the farm (fennel or the penis shaft) in a way that evokes fertility, power, and domestication. Across Greece, temples, sanctuaries, and cave-shrines were dedicated to Pan. Statues and paintings on pottery often display Pan with an erect penis and a flute and accompanied by herds of sheep and goats and a group of nymphs.[75]

Like the ancient Egyptians, the ancient Greeks and Romans carried personal penis charms that the Romans called *fascinus*.[76] The Romans borrowed much of Greek mythology and culture, appropriating phallic imagery and spreading it liberally around the social landscape of towns and cities, such as Pompeii.[77] Roman cities had phallic statues posted at the city gates for protection and worshipped small phallic statues in their homes.[78] Erotic imagery from Pompeii provides some of the best-known examples of sexual symbolism from the Roman world due to the vast number of well-preserved frescos, sculptures, mosaics, and household items.[79] Among the Romans the fertility imagery was incorporated into many houses on walls and frescos. According to the archaeological evidence, small phallic sculptures appear to have been used as household items of worship.[80] In her in-depth analysis of aristocratic households in Pompeii, archaeologist Ann Olga Koloski-Ostrow focused on understanding home decor and the messages that the Roman ruling class conveyed and reinforced with their stylistic choices.[81] The home decor sends strong messages of power and status based on anatomical sex differences and ideas about the oppression and powerlessness of females. Further, the phallus is interpreted as the ultimate symbol of control in this context.[82]

FIGURE 3.3 Bronze statue of the faun (second century BC), in the impluvium, a shallow pool at the center of the household atrium, at the House of the Faun, Pompeii. The faun is a Roman forest god who is associated with the Greek god Pan.

FIGURE 3.4 Phallic house relief and fresco located along one of the main streets in Pompeii. Note the penises on each corner and the large central phallic image inside the house.

FIGURE 3.5 Penis image carved on the street in Pompeii (note the iPhone for scale). These types of carvings directed visitors to the town's brothels.

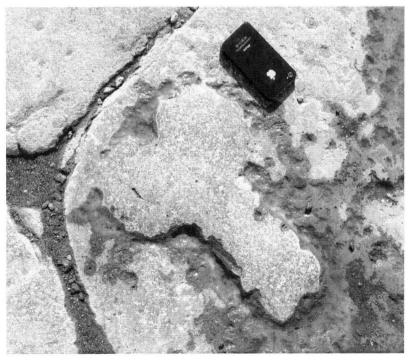

FIGURE 3.6 Fountain depicting the Roman god Neptune in the Boboli Gardens of the Pitti Palace, Florence, Italy. This statue illustrates cultural aesthetics based on male supremacy and aggression and idealized male forms. Note Neptune's trident, which is being thrust down into the clamshell below, a symbol for his consort Salacia, or Venus.

In the cultures of ancient Greece and Rome, male fertility and potency was often depicted in the literal form of the sculpted penis—as depicted in penis charms made of wood, bone, or metal or in statuary. The small *fascinus* were personal items that were carried around and kept in houses where they were involved in rituals of regular domestic worship, while the larger statues were often public. In many classical cultures we find monumental architecture that glorifies male authority. However, the ideology that this imagery represents is critical to our argument. The dominant political and philosophical view of the classical Mediterranean period might be summarized as such: "[They were] committed to a hierarchical belief system and aesthetics based on male supremacy, militarism, and the idealization of the naked male body."[83] Over time, in the Renaissance and beyond, the phallus continued to serve as a symbolic metaphor for male superiority, prowess, and the potential ability to provide sexual pleasure.

FIGURE 3.7 Copy of Michelangelo's David statue at the Piazza della Signoria, in the shadow of the Palazzo Vecchio, which is the heart of this famous square in Florence, Italy.

FIGURE 3.8 Obelisk in Saint Peter's Square at the Vatican in Rome, Italy.

FIGURE 3.9 Renaissance bronze sculpture of Perseus with Medusa's head in the Loggia dei Lanzi of the Piazza della Signoria in Florence, Italy. Benvenuto Cellini's statue of Perseus was commissioned by Duke Cosimo de' Medici around 1545. The statue metaphorically represents the Medici family's strength. However, Cellini used the subject matter to promote himself and Medusa's head in particular to dominate the plaza by symbolically turning the rest of the figures to stone (including the famous copy of the David). Note the hypermasculinity and phallic imagery created by Perseus and his sword.

The Indus Valley Civilizations and Southeast Asia

An abundance of symbolic imagery and associated ideologies that fetishize the penis can be found in the cultural traditions of the Indian subcontinent and the surrounding regions. In the Indus Valley there are abundant archaeological remains from a thriving culture sometimes referred to as the Harappan[84] or the Indus Valley Civilization (its florescence was from 2600 to 1900 BCE and it is located in present-day Pakistan). The Harappan people had roots in the early farming communities of the region that by 7000 BCE had taken up residence in the Indo-Iranian borderlands.[85] This Indus Valley culture flourished over an area larger than that of its contemporary civilizations in Mesopotamia and Egypt. The people of the Harappan culture grew wheat and barley and they kept domestic cattle, sheep, and goats. They engaged in long-distance trade, produced a range of elaborate material culture, and commonly stamped their goods with incised seals.[86] An increase in the frequency of stamp seals in the archaeological record of the Early Indus Period (Early Harappan, 3200–2600 BCE) and the development of a writing system based on a range of signs in these seals appear to suggest the evolution of ownership and control of commodities.[87] This social development would likely have occurred in a context where kinship lines were no longer the main social organizing principle.[88]

One of the most well-known images from these Harappan stamps is referred to as the Lord of the Animals (Shiva Pasupati), which depicts a cross-legged figure with a large erection and clearly illustrated testicles.[89] This yogi is wearing a bullhorn hat and is surrounded by male animals; this deity appears on a range of artifacts, including other stamps, a molded tablet, and ceramic vessels, and is typically accompanied by animals.[90] The bearded figure is believed to be antecedent to the Hindu god Shiva, whose mount is Nandi the great bull, emphasizing his connection with fertility and domestication.[91] Pastoralism was a critical component of the Harappan economy and it is no surprise that Shiva, who first emerged as an important deity in literature (around 1000 BCE) long after the demise of the Indus Valley Civilization, is also associated with domestic cattle. Bulls and cattle were commonly depicted on the stamps and artifacts of the Indus Valley civilization until its disintegration in the early second millennium BCE.[92]

In the past and in modern Hindu religion, Shiva is represented by the lingam, a simple phallic symbol that is typically made of stone. Linga are both personal and public items of worship and they are commonly found

FIGURE 3.10 Harappan seals from the Early Indus Period. These depict cattle and bulls or other domestic animals.

FIGURE 3.11 Elaborate Shiva *linga* carving with head motif in the National Museum of India in New Delhi.

everywhere in India today. These may be small, carried by devotees or worn as a charm, or incorporated into domestic shrines where offerings are made and prayers are said daily. Linga are also found as large permanent installments in temples and public spaces. These items are often covered with flower-and-bead-garland offerings, incense, and candles, and they are involved in many rituals. Linga expresses male creative energy, power, and are often installed in temples in association with the yoni or female symbol (a vulva or womb), representing fertility and the goddess Shakti.[93] Shakti is the consort of Shiva, and while she is powerful, she is clearly subordinate.[94] Linga and yoni are found in Harappan material culture in the form of clay stelae and fire altars.[95] In the *Linga Purana*, one of the 18 major *Puranas* or Hindu religious texts, the origin of linga is explained. According to this text, "The entire world has the phallus as its foundation. All is issued from the lingam. He who desires perfection of the soul must worship the lingam. Fundamental Nature is therefore called phallus. He who possesses the distinctive sign is the supreme being."[96]

FIGURE 3.12 Miniature Shiva *linga* and *yoni* shrine next to a Ganesha statue (the Hindu deity related to wisdom, art, the sciences, and the removal of obstacles in north India.

Both human-made and naturally occurring linga continue to be worshipped by contemporary peoples across Asia. Ceremonies involve the pouring of libations including milk, ghee, sacred water, and other liquids over the lingam to honor Shiva. Some shrines are constructed so that the linga is positioned in the center of a vulva-shaped base (yoni) where the phallus resides. When liquids are poured over the lingam the basin collects these offerings, producing obvious connotations. Elaborate ceremonies accompany the worship of linga and there are many elements involved. For example, the

FIGURE 3.13 Shiva *linga* and *yoni* shrines are still produced in Asia for the tourist trade and for purposes of worship.

worshipper must be purified and bathed in advance. The lingam is bathed in sacred liquids, and offerings of garlands and fruits and other foods are made.[97] Prayers and chants are repeated and the linga is circumambulated many times. The oldest known example of a public lingam that is currently in use is in Gudimally, south India, and dates to around 200 BCE.[98] The yoni-lingam combination is a common and widespread feature of Hindu art.

Hindu myths and legends include a great deal of fertility-based and phallic art and ritual. The Rigveda (or *rgveda*) is an ancient Indian collection of sacred Sanskrit hymns dating to around 1700–1000 BCE.[99] One ritual described in the Rigveda is the horse sacrifice ceremony, known as the Ashvamedha.[100] After the horse is dead, the queen lies with the horse under a blanket for ritual sex, mimicking copulation; then the horse is butchered and eaten. It is said that only a king seeking to acquire power over nearby provinces and prosperity would commission this sacred ceremony and sacrifice.[101] In this ritual we see a connection between male power, sex, symbolic procreation, death, a domestic animal, and control over land and people.

As Hinduism and its associated ideas of philosophy and politics spread from India into Southeast Asia in the first millennium CE, monuments to

FIGURE 3.14 Ancient Shiva *linga* and *yoni* shrine at the Angkor Wat temple complex of Cambodia. These shrines are still actively used by visitors to the temples.

Shiva and linga symbols became common. Hindu temples in Southeast Asia were laid out following Indian Hindu holy texts, and therefore there are many similarities in the sacred architecture of the two regions and its overt fertility symbols.[102] Archaeological research provides a rich body of information on phallus worship and Shiva cults in peninsular South Asia. For example, at second-century CE site of Langkasuka, in Thailand, a bronze statue of a lingam and a stone carving of Nandi, Shiva's mount, have been found.[103] Inscriptions referencing linga and the artifacts themselves have been recovered from sites

FIGURE 3.15 Ancient Shiva *linga* shrine at Bayon temple in Angkor Thom, at the Angkor Wat complex in Cambodia.

FIGURE 3.16 Stone phallus at Shinto shrine. © Jens Tobiska/ Dreamstime.com

Figure 3.17 Carving along the Terrace of the Leper King at Angkor Thom in the Angkor Wat complex in Cambodia. Phallic images such as this one were used to convey the power and strength of the ruling elite.

across Thailand, Vietnam, and Cambodia.[104] At the massive twelfth-century temple complex of Angkor Wat in Cambodia, linga can be found all over and are represented in a range of contexts. This Hindu (and later Buddhist) temple complex was the capital of the powerful Khmer empire. In the context of Angkor Wat, linga are defined as a "phallic emblem, the form in which the god Shiva is generally worshipped. The linga (or Shivalinga) is considered a fiery cosmic pillar, infinite in dimension."[105]

As in India, the nobility elsewhere in Asia used the phallus to symbolize, legitimize, and express power. Cambodian temples to Shiva often have eight linga positioned in a circle around a central linga. The number eight is considered the number of perfection, and there are eight cardinal and subcardinal directions in Hindu tradition. Moreover, linga are the physical embodiment of the mandala form of government; when positioned in a circle, this symbolically expresses a systematic whole of power relations.[106] Similar examples of penis cults are found in numerous Asian cultures, including ancient Japanese Shintoism and the ancient Tibetan Bön religion.

JAPAN

Shinto, an indigenous religion of Japan, is focused primarily on the worship of *kami*, or nature spirits, natural forces, and essences. *Kami* have a wide variety of expression, including animistic beings, human forms, and natural forces such as wind, rain, sunshine, mountains, rivers, and rocks; everything contains *kami*. A literal translation of the term "Shinto" is "the way of the *kami*, or divinities."[107] Shinto originally had no systematic canon, but efforts were made to codify a doctrine in the thirteenth century in response to Buddhist influences in Japan.[108] At this time, distinct schools of practice emerged that provided the foundations for discussions of Shinto as a religion. Shinto practices link the present with the ancestors, or the past. In this cultural context, myths associated with the origin of the universe include phallic symbols. These myths are re-created in phallic rituals and ceremonies.

Farming communities in particular maintained beliefs in both the harmony of the universe and in complementary opposing forces of the world.[109] Agricultural fields were thought to hold generative power to create and sustain seasonal harvests, which in turn supported individuals, families, and farming communities. Phallicism is a form of worship focused on that generative principle. Phallicism is exemplified in the practice of worshiping *dōsojin*, or guardian deities of roads and boundaries.[110] These deities are often represented in the form of a male-female couple of carved stones. The majority of *dōsojin* date to the Edo Period (1603–1868 CE) and beyond, and they are said to represent male and female creator *kami* deities, Izanagi and Izanami among them.[111] Tales of the generative and creative power of the guardian deities abound. Both the consumption of food and the practice of copulation in front of the standing stones resulted in enhanced fertility and pregnancy.[112] In the New Year season, agricultural rites centered on *dōsojin* festivals. The festivities wove together the themes of agricultural bounty and sexual procreation and featured plays and displays that highlighted scenarios of opposition. Men and women (with exposed genitals), young people and the elderly, life and death: all were juxtaposed as ways to visualize and honor the bountiful endowment of the coming seasons and to maintain social order. Kazuo Kasahara explains that these kinds of displays were "intended to ensure a rich harvest for an agricultural society. In fact the primary purpose of all the rites of the Little New Year (January 15), not just those connected with the *dōsojin*, was to ensure agricultural bounty. Thus, the rites displayed many sexual elements, representing generative power, and . . . the bounty of the next harvest."[113]

Seasonal festivals at town and village shrines also incorporate overt phallic imagery. One example is the Kanamara Matsuri (Festival of the Golden Phallus), a celebration occurring each spring at the Kanayama shrine in Kawasaki.[114] This shrine has an enormous phallus in front of it and contains many phallic symbols of different sizes and colors constructed from a variety of materials including stone, wood, and metal. A procession leaves from the temple, following a large banner with a penis on it and a portable shrine containing a giant scarlet phallus.[115] The event includes music, performers, and an array of food and charms fashioned in the shape of the penis. Another Japanese folk festival celebrating the penis and all forms of prosperity and fertility occurs in Komaki City at the Tagata shrine.[116] Celebrations begin in a neighboring village where statues of vaginas are carried through the streets in a series of processions, some lead by men and others by children. The Komaki City penis festival is a much larger affair; wooden and candy penises abound and the main event centers on the parading of a six-foot-long penis sculpture through the streets.

The Kanamara Matsuri and Komaki festivals evoke obvious themes of fertility and sexual potency. Women who seek to become pregnant make payers and offerings to the phalluses. Men with impotency also kiss and seek blessings from the phallus *kami*. As with the *dōsojin* festival, themes of agricultural productivity, sexuality, and the propagation of offspring are central to these springtime celebrations. In contemporary Japanese culture all of these festivals have become pop cultural phenomena and tourist attractions.[117]

Japanese archaeologists have recorded many examples of ancient monumental phalluses as well as small personal penis charms.[118] The uses for these artifacts range from idols of worship to good luck charms. The large stone phalluses are referred to as stone rods, or *raitsui*, meaning thunderbolts.[119] Most of the large stone phalluses are either installed in public places (such as temples) or away from urban areas as stand-alone shrines in the forest, while domestic settings are often littered with homemade paper charms that include phalluses.[120] In Japan the phallic cult is perhaps best understood from the perspective of the duality inherent in the following pairs:

male: female
present: past
ancestors: descendants
planting: harvest
life: death

There are obvious parallels in the penis themes we have reviewed cross-culturally. Agriculture is intimately and inextricably linked with the vital forces of nature. This linkage is emphasized in the varied forms of veneration associated with the penis in agriculture-based societies, including ancient and modern Japan.

THE HIMALAYAS: TIBET, BHUTAN, AND NEPAL

In the Himalayas, the ancient pre-Buddhist Bön religion is still practiced by the people of Tibet and Bhutan. The definitions of Bön in the literature include the following three. First, it is described as an indigenous spiritual tradition that began to be suppressed and/or incorporated into Buddhism in the eighth century, though the earliest documentary evidence on this tradition comes from the ninth and tenth centuries CE.[121] This ancient spiritual tradition has a primary focus on the king, the transition of the soul to the postmortem land of bliss, and associated funerary rituals.[122] These funerary rites, which often involved domestic animals, maintained the welfare and fertility of the living and ensured happiness for the dead.[123]

Namkhai Norbu, a leading authority on Tibetan culture, discusses the role of linga in Bön death rites, explaining that that lingam of various constructions (paper, dough, and drawings) are used in rituals to vanquish negative energy (*gshed*) that is present after death.[124] The lingam are both symbolic representations of the *gshed* and talismans used to defeat it in this practice. At the final stage of the vanquishment rite, the linga is "executed" by a ritual dagger that is used to pierce the phallic symbol.[125] In Bön magical rites of destruction, efforts are made to liberate people oppressed by ignorance and afflicted by negative energies and situations. Specifically, in the rite of destruction the practitioner summons the vital soul (*la*) of the enemy and "unites it with his linga effigy," thus destroying the enemy.[126] Other forms of destructive magic can also be performed. For example, the linga can be buried underground or burned.[127] Themes of destruction and release are also found in Bön symbolism associated with sexual intercourse. It is said that sex represents the union of bliss and emptiness, and the "liberation of destruction."[128]

In the second definition of Bön, scholars describe a religion that dates to the tenth and eleventh centuries in Tibet, at the time Buddhism was reintroduced into the region from India.[129] This version of Bön has a great deal of historical continuity and is still practiced in Tibet. It has both doctrinal and practical parallels with Buddhism and therefore it has often been considered an unorthodox form of Buddhism.[130] Many Tibetans and practitioners of this form of Bön maintain that this religion is pre-Buddhist as exemplified by ideas of religious authority and history, among other distinguishing characteristics.[131] In the third definition, Bön refers to a "vast and amorphous body of popular beliefs, including divination, the cult of local deities, and conceptions of the soul."[132] These traditions are not an essential component of either Buddhism in Tibet or Bön (as described above). Therefore these practices have been referred to as a "nameless religion."[133]

Various forms of Bön are still practiced alongside Buddhism in the Himalayan region, especially in western Tibet.[134] The two religious traditions have become connected in a way that makes distinguishing the specifics of one from the other difficult. Moreover, and most importantly for our discussion of the domestic penis, there is some disagreement among scholars about Bön rituals and whether they involve phallic worship.[135] Some authors and scholars have called Bön an overtly "phallic religion," focused on, for example, both phallus and snake worship.[136] In Tibetan traditions, these symbols represent the creative powers of water and the sun.[137] In the villages of western Tibet it was customary to set up simple phallus stones in wooded areas or by the doors of temples. The ends of these phallic stones would be rubbed with oil or butter as an act of worship. In Buddhist practices associated with a tantric feast, a linga is placed on a shrine and the shrine is then kissed repeatedly, producing an experience of "Great Bliss."[138]

Conversely, some scholars have argued that phallic symbols are not conspicuous. Rather, phalluses crafted from stone, bone, and wood are connected with ancient geomantic practices.[139] Stones erected in farmers' fields and pillars positioned in front of royal tombs that might be interpreted as phallic are in fact described by the inhabitants of Himalayan villages as "navel stones" and "earth pegs."[140] These stones ward off evil, provide protection, and remind onlookers of primal creative energy associated with human nature.[141]

In contemporary Bhutanese, Nepalese, and Tibetan culture, overt phallic signs are realistic representations of the penis and are widespread. These were and are still "painted red and surrounded by a bush of yak-hair" and displayed over the main entry door to houses, especially farm houses in Tibet and Bhutan.[142] Phallic symbols are painted on buildings and above doorways in an effort to bring good luck and drive away evil spirits. Large carved wooden phalluses are hung in the rafters or from the eaves of houses and they are also used in agricultural fields to bring fertility to both the land and the household occupants.[143] The image of a penis may also be used to decorate festival clothing and headdresses for ritual purposes. Modern practices of making offering to phallus stones mirror the linga worship we have discussed previously in connection with Indian and Hindu traditions; these practices are likely related to the incorporation of Hindu gods and ideas into indigenous Himalayan traditions. In contrast to Hindu ideas of the phallus, which celebrate masculine power and domination,[144] in Bhutanese and Tibetan cultures, the phallus has a different meaning. Bhutanese scholars argue that the phallus represents the worldly illusion of desire and reminds men to act with control over the elemental creative force.[145] An unharnessed force can drive men to act in wild and lustful ways, which are uncivilized and corrupting.[146] Tibetan myths also tell of situations wherein demons, gods, and humans are filled with lust and ignorance, resulting in great suffering and harm.[147] The phallus is a central character in these tales.

In contrast to other traditions we have explored, Buddhism lacks some of the obvious polarized oppositions between male and female in its foundational religious ideology. Essentialized notions of gender that ascribe contrasting characteristics to male and female deities project inaccurate ideas on these figures.[148] For example, in the Tibetan Vajrayana tradition, concepts of feminine and masculine are important primarily in terms of ritual and

FIGURE 3.18 Painting depicting penises on the wall of a house and gallery in Bhutan. © Anandoart/Dreamstime.com

meditation. These gender notions are thought to be outside of one's personal identity. That is, they exist in terms of the qualities of a person's experience.[149] To say that something is "masculine" is to refer to qualities of fearless compassion, limitless awareness that provokes enlightened action, and confidence.[150] "Feminine" refers to "limitless, ungraspable, and aware qualities of the ultimate nature of mind; it also refers to the intensely dynamic way in which that awareness undermines concepts, hesitation, and obstacles in the spiritual journeys of female and male Vajrayana practitioners."[151] According to Buddhist tradition, since polarities and extremes represent the endless cycle of suffering, an enlightened view recognizes that oppositional concepts ultimately do not differ from each other.

Nevertheless, from day to day, the lives of ordinary women in Tibet were in fact impacted by polarized ideas of gender and a culture dominated by patriarchy. While women in Tibet had more freedom and social prestige than most women in nearby China or India (especially in terms of trade, herding rights, and domestic management), they were still subordinate to their husbands and fathers and denied full monastic ordination as well as other social freedoms.[152] Once again, we see a culture where women are subject to patriarchy and the phallic symbol holds a position of public and ideological prominence.

FIGURE 3.19 Phallic drinking fountain in front of a house in Nepal. © Valery Shanin/ Dreamstime.com

OCEANIA AND THE NEW WORLD

The horticultural and agricultural peoples of Oceania and the New World have a resounding concern for the seasonal cycles, the sun, and the movement of the cosmos. The sometimes angry and bloodthirsty gods who regulated these important cycles demanded abundant ritual sacrifices. The phallus and its imagery are common in Oceania and in the Americas, where rituals of sacrifice maintained links to creative and procreative processes both cultural and natural. Ritual practices also distinguished humans, especially men, from the animals. Not surprisingly, the physical penis and the symbolic phallus were critical components of myth, ritual, decorative items, and other forms of material culture.

Oceania. Rock art and expressive prehistoric imagery including standing stones, temples, carved idols, and ornamentation from the tropical islands of Oceania display a concern for the penis that their rich oral histories and myths described in detail. The penis and male political power were venerated among many of the pre-European chiefdoms of the tropical Pacific Islands. Given the many thousands of islands in Oceania and the great diversity of cultural groups, we focus here on examples from Polynesia, and the island of Hawai'i in particular, to illustrate the connection between agricultural societies and phallic veneration. There are many similarities between the cultures within the region of Polynesia, as the pre-European inhabitants descended from a group of common ancestors and therefore share an ancestral culture, key aspects of ideology, and many elements of material culture.

In ancient Hawai'i the potent god of war, Ku, is said to preside over all male gods. Ku has many masculine associations and is representative of activities pertaining to and performed by men. Ku, like other deities of ancient Hawai'i, is thought to have myriad bodies and interchangeable body forms, or *kino lau.*[153] *Kino lau* were varied expressions of the gods whose specific characteristics reflected natural manifestations. For example, Ku was associated with the dog, the hawk, game fish, and a species of bird.[154] Ku was expressed in male-associated activities including canoe building, fishing, war, and sorcery.[155] The gods of war's forms often suggest masculinity and fertility. Moreover, the meaning of "Ku" includes "erect," "straight," "to stand," or "to rise."[156] The digging stick that men used for gardening also represented Ku; the stick evoked his straight and firm characteristics as well as his association with penetration. Ku was a source of life. Temples of war were constructed and human sacrifice performed in his honor, and the rituals enacted on such structures evoked life and death, serving to maintain cosmic and social order via the meditation of transitions between destructive and creative power. Ku is paired with the feminine goddess Hina, and together they represent the duality of the sexes that manifests in all natural forms of male and female.[157]

There are four major gods in Hawaiian theology—Kane, Kanaloa, Ku, and Lono—and each is associated with different principle attributes such as colors, cardinal directions, days of the month, natural and inorganic phenomena, plants, animals, seasons, and functions.[158] Ku is said to be the god that "encompasses all the others" in the hierarchy.[159] However, Kane holds a primordial role in creation myths, symbolizes male power of procreation, and is expressed in a variety of form and activities, including spring water, light, dawn, birth, planting, sperm, pigs, and bananas.[160] Kane is the "life giver" and was "addressed as Kane-of-the-water-of-life (Kane-ka-wai-ola). Water (*wai*) was so associated with the idea of bounty that the word for wealth was *waiwai*."[161] This ideology pervades Polynesian religion, and Handy has called the cult of Kane, the lord of life, the "basic cult of the primal procreator of nature and man, out of the union of Sky and Earth."[162] Every young boy, both commoners and those of the chiefly class, went through initiation rites. Handy argues that these rites illustrate the fundamental assumption that every man was a farmer or planter. For example, the dedication to Lono (the god of the harvest and rain), included the subincision of the foreskin, thus consecrating "the boy as a breeder to Kane (male), the procreator."[163] Hawaiian myths speak to conversion from human to god and vice versa, where the rite of subincision distinguishes godly heroes from men. Among the common people, circumcision was performed on boys around the age of seven or eight years; it was believed to enhance pleasure and health, facilitate cohabitation, and make a boy a man, or a breeder of Kane. While the Hawaiian male initiation ceremony involving subincision marked the transition from boyhood to manhood, it also distinguished men from gods and nature from culture, as we will discuss in the following chapters.

Masculine expressions were found in many natural items, phenomena, and actions that one might encounter on a daily basis in ancient Hawai'i. Often overtly masculine items were appropriate sacrificial objects for veneration of the gods. Offerings were a symbol of the deity; therefore, species that were consecrated to a deity were ideally representations of the deity's body or *kino lau*. Ideally, only male animals were sacrificed to one of the four primary gods. Masculine deities were worshipped in the main temples; therefore, all sacrifices in this context, including vegetables, fish, other animals, and even humans, were theoretically masculine.[164] Examples include bananas (said to represent genitals), coconuts (testicles), pigs (their snout was a metaphor for the penis, and they represented both warriors and beastly men), and roosters (also said to represent manhood, chiefs, or warriors).[165] Even the average domestic environment was endowed with gender-specific symbols and imagery. Physical and structural elements of the house represented components of the body and were gendered as well. The house expressed fundamental social oppositions between the sexes; This is indicated, for example, by the names of the ends of the rafters and posts: "the *oa* or rafters equaled in number the front and back posts, and the lower ends were cut all alike into heel and fork, the latter called *kohe* (vagina) as it was to fit the *ule* (penis) of the posts."[166] In this context, as in other cultures we have discussed, building a house was done according to rules that preserved appropriate symbolic relationships, represented its inhabitants, and facilitated the social reproduction of norms and ideologies.

Mesoamerica: Maya and Aztecs

In the Americas, supernatural beings are often associated more abstractly with the growing season and phallicism than some of the overtly phallic deities described from places such as Egypt and Rome. Thanks to the abundant and well-preserved paintings and stone carvings from the ancient peoples of Mesoamerica, an excellent record of ideology and religion exists from which we can explore this relationship. These records suggest that blood sacrifice is connected to agricultural success in the early societies of Mexico and the surrounding areas. The feathered serpent, referred to as Quetzalcoatl by the Nahua ethnic groups, is found in both the ancient Mayan and Aztec cultures of Mesoamerica and represented individualistic political authority.[167] Among the Maya, the feathered serpent is known as the Maize god and is connected with the vision rite, sacrifice, and fertility.[168] For the Aztecs and Toltecs the feathered serpent was related to Venus,[169] the dawn, crafts, warfare, creation, and knowledge.

According to ancient traditions of the Nahua indigenous people of Mexico,[170] the birth of the current human race is the result of the Feathered Serpent-God Quetzalcoatl's trip to the underworld.[171] During this excursion Quetzalcoatl sculpted humankind from the bones of failed human groups of previous epochs. In this indigenous oscillating description of the universe, we find an explanation for the origin of the Maya, Aztecs, and other peoples of the world. After arriving in the underworld, Quetzalcoatl applied blood from an incision in his penis to the bones of the earlier eras of humans, thus imbuing the remains with life.[172] There is a great deal of symbolic continuity in the worship and divine associations of the feathered serpent across space and time in Mesoamerica. For example, we find as early as 900 BCE (at the site of La Venta in the Mexican state of Tabasco) iconographic depictions of such a deity on carved stone slabs at archaeological sites belonging to the oldest civilization in Mesoamerica, the Olmecs.[173]

The artists of ancient Mesoamerica undoubtedly sought to serve a combination of social, religious, and economic functions in the creation of their art.[174] It appears that artistic items were presented to the gods, used as burial offerings, or employed to mark historical events, such as the reign of kings and their conquests. As a result, many virtually perfect, richly decorated artifacts have been recovered from archaeological sites in the region. These artifacts tell a history of kingly competition, warfare, trade, and sacrifice, as well as the less exotic but no less important issues of everyday life. Mesoamerican archaeology provides a wealth of material culture associated with phallic imagery. Recently, some researchers have remarked on the curious lack of in-depth exploration of the meaning of the many stone phallic monuments that litter the northern lowland landscape and archaeological cities of the region.[175] A two-meter-tall phallus within an elite compound at Loltun Cave in the Yucatán provides an impressive example.[176] What may seem to be a lack interest in monumental phallic sculptures and artwork depicting obvious penises may be explained by the Western discomfort with viewing naked bodies, and sexual organs in particular. Moreover, beginning with the sixteenth-century colonial period in the Americas, there has been a long history of unchallenged assumptions about the danger of sexuality and the natural dominance of masculinity.

Carvings from the ancient Mesoamerican civilizations depict ritual piercing of the penis as a fertility and vision rite. When practiced by the ruling elite, ritual bloodletting, as described in the origin story involving Quetzalcoatl, appears to have been a method of legitimizing the social and political position of a ruler's lineage. It was also believed to enhance the well-being of the people in general. These beliefs center on two key aspects of Mayan and Aztec ideology: first, blood represents life, and second, the gods sacrificed parts of their bodies and their blood to create and perpetuate humankind.[177] Both of these aspects are illustrated in the Quetzalcoatl myth. Carvings from the Mayan and Aztec world suggest that social structure was maintained through sacrifices such as the piercing of soft body parts (especially the tongue and penis), but sacrificial offerings would have been a part of more mundane activities as well. The body part from which blood was drawn in bloodletting ceremonies marked the type of outcome sought by the ritual. For example, piercing the penis may have enhanced fertility. These rites were performed in public and atop temples, pyramids, or other platforms where the community could view the bloodletting from the surrounding plazas. The blood produced from the wound was collected and then either burned as an offering to the gods or scattered about. By regularly returning blood and life to the gods, the people of Mesoamerica maintained the social and cosmological order and in the process ensured the satisfaction of the gods and all that they oversee in this world. Interestingly, whether the peoples of ancient Mesoamerica practiced genital mutilations such as incision and circumcision, as many of the peoples of Oceania did, remains unclear.

Sculpture fragments from the Classic period Mayan site of Telantunich in the Yucatán suggest a regional emphasis on depictions of masculine sexuality, especially phallic imagery.[178] Interpretation of this imagery suggests that the ruling elite of the Classic Maya (ca. 250–900 CE) used these symbolic depictions to perpetuate, communicate, and objectify exaggerated masculine concepts and ideals based on values of authority and hierarchies of power.[179] Monumental sculptures depict the elite male figures surrounded by an archway and ancestral and mythical figures while holding a scroll or serpent. The ruling elite figures are also mythical and act as portals, where his status is both connoted by and derived from the figures that appear around him. In the case of the sculptures from Telantunich, the phallus is the object held in the hand of the ruler. The northern lowlands of the Yucatán have produced around 130 stone phalli from a variety of contexts, including many freestanding stone penis statues.[180] The largest sculptures include those at the sites of Chichén Itza and Uxmal. Permanent carved phalli, for example, adorn the so-called House of Phalli at Uxmal.[181] This site also includes a naked figure with a massively enlarged and exaggerated penis, and phalli features such as the discharge ends of drain chutes are built into the architectural setting.[182] In this latter example there is an obvious connection between the phallic symbols and water and perhaps references to generative power.

The south central area of the site of Chichén Itza also contains a temple that has been called a phallic temple or house of phalli.[183] This structure, a two-story structure with many rooms that appears to have been constructed over an extended period of time, is the dominant building in the cluster.[184] It has permanent phallic sculptures that project from the interior walls of five rooms. It is believed to have been a young men's house where all male groups would gather in association with ball-playing, dancing, and training for war. The exterior of the phalli house was surrounded with sculptures and images illustrating musical and dance performances, offerings, and bloodletting. The Maize god figures prominently at this site, and research suggests that blood-letting activities were tied to this deity. These representations of bloodletting and dance occur along the building's upper-level frieze.[185] There are images of Pawahtuns,[186] the patron gods of the Itza Maya rulers of Chichén Itza, riding turtles as they pierce their penises. The narrative of creation was played out on the site of Chichén Itza at the turtle mounds, via dance, and in the imagery sculpted onto the exterior of the buildings. The symbols referenced creation even as they legitimized and reaffirmed the political power of the ruling elite. Moreover, a recently restored façade from the site depicts both a fluid and veg-etation emerging from the penis of a ruler figure, while another illustrates the rain god (Chaac) with liquid flowing from his penis.[187] In this context the phallus is connected with the rain and water cult of Chaac, who was undoubt-edly of great significance in a region where the inhabitants of a seasonally aired environment depended on rain.

Overall, the phallic imagery of the Yucatán fits into Classic Maya iconog-raphy, which is focused on ancestral lineage, kingship, and creation.[188] The overtly realistic phallus depictions commonly found in the Terminal Classic period are explained as a response to regional cultural and political shifts that created cultural anxiety.[189] It has been noted that "overt phallic images served as community symbols that secured Maya religious and ritual practices during this period of drastic change. Phallic imagery served to sanctify sacred ritual space, order the community, and legitimize the authority of the ruling elite."[190] On a more personal level, archaeologist Traci Ardren has argued that the male body is the point of articulation between power and biological sex. That is, among the Maya, "power is naturalized and equated with a biological prerogative to rule."[191] To maintain the widespread ideology of male privilege, overt masculinity was reproduced via habitual daily acts and public remind-ers. This reproduction has been referred to as hegemonic masculinity and is explained as a response to social anxiety.[192] At the time many of the phallic images were created, there is evidence of increasing violence and environmen-tal stress. For example, in the Late and Terminal Classic periods (700–1200 CE) defensive walls were constructed at archaeological sites throughout the regions, there was chronic overpopulation, the death rate increased, people suffered from severe droughts, and artistic works illustrate violent wars and expanding city-states.[193] In this uncertain and changing world, the phallus served as a metaphor for both the origin and source of life.[194] On a social level, iconography and structural features of archaeological sites suggest that men were expected to foster and express hypermasculinity. In addition, they were reminded on a daily basis of their roles as farmers, warriors, and leaders by the phallic imagery that surrounded their cities.

CONCLUSION

Other researchers have argued that phallic imagery is ubiquitous throughout the world and that it is commonly seen in the material culture of the first civilizations, specifically, those of the Indus Valley during the agricultural revolution.[195] Historian Alain Daniélou has argued that phallic imagery became common as early as 13,000 BCE, when phallic representations multiplied in Europe.[196] Some scholars have gone so far as to claim that the world religions have a common origin in phallicism, or the worship of the generative powers of nature as exemplified by the penis.[197] Certainly all humans have the capacity to be inspired by natural phenomena and the mysteries of life and procreation. Nevertheless, it would be almost impossible to assemble evidence supporting a single origin for theological ideas or elements of human culture. This is not the argument we seek to make in this chapter. Rather, we have reviewed a broad range of data from around the globe that illustrates a deep-rooted and pervasive connection between penis cults and agricultural societies. By the nature of this endeavor, a cross-cultural investigation cannot illuminate the diversity of each culture, ethnic group, gender, time, and place. Common cultural expressions, themes, and symbols do not necessarily represent shared belief systems and meanings. However, we argue that many examples of clear patterns relating to phallocentrism emerge from the examination of phallic imagery, material culture, and written records of the past. These lines of evidence suggest an articulation between concepts of domestication, fertility, creation, the legitimacy of rulers, and public expressions of masculine power. In most of the cultures we have reviewed in this chapter, the archaeological and written evidence suggests that material culture emphasized oppositions between the sexes. Ideologies expressed via religious doctrines and rituals were centered on phallic worship and/or incorporated phallic imagery. Those in power in many ancient agricultural societies sought to generate daily reminders of these ideas via religious institutions, monumental architecture, artistic imagery, and more common elements of quotidian material culture. These practices created both history and social institutions. Finally, anxiety about changing social and environmental conditions may have compelled the social reproduction of an ideology of male privilege, as suggested by Ardren[198] and critical theorist Calvin Thomas.[199]

4

The Cultural Penis

Diversity in Phallic Symbolisms

In describing the penis as domesticated, we consider both evolutionary mechanisms that have physically altered the penis as well as cultural ideologies that symbolically alter the way the penis is perceived. As we explored in the last chapter, phallic cults in the archaeological record and beyond describe an association between the rise of higher-density horticulturalists and agriculturalists, deification of the penis, and increased male control over female sexuality. The ethnographic record reveals a much wider diversity in attitudes toward the penis and human sexual behaviors, past and present. In many cultures, the penis is an object of intense interest, particularly in religious rites that manipulate the body and cut the flesh. While much attention is given in the literature to the horrific practice of female genital mutilation, and rightly so, far less attention is given to various forms of male genital mutilation, despite evidence that male genital mutilation has been practiced extensively historically and cross-culturally. In some male initiation practices, such as subincision and some manifestations of the bullroarer complex, female reproductive and procreative functions are imitated, with symbolic and literal penis alterations appropriating female sexuality.

Based on extensive ethnographic evidence, we conclude that it is unlikely that there is any existing culture where the penis does not take on substantial cultural significance in ritual, mythology, and cosmology. The importance ascribed to the penis across cultures is so fundamental, frequent, and pervasive that to document all cultural references to the penis would be tantamount to documenting all references to all known human cultures, past and present. Nonetheless, we do have a few complexes, for lack of a better word, that describe some broad cross-cultural patterns in the way the penis has been treated and conceptualized. These complexes include the bullroarer

Figure 4.1 Bullroarer. © Fpwing/Dreamstime.com

complex, the penis-sheathing complex, the ritual-penis-modification complex, and the magical-castration complex.

The bullroarer complex involves an extremely widespread cultural phenomenon of the association of a simple musical instrument with the male phallus and sacred male initiation rites, which are typically taboo for women. The bullroarer complex is often linked to wind, thunder, and success in the harvest and is reminiscent of the agricultural phallic cults. The penis-sheathing complex describes widely varying cultural practices that paradoxically both hide the penis while drawing attention to the male genital area through exaggerated ornamentation. The ritual-penis-modification complex describes multiple ways in which the penis is cut and transformed, often in association with rites of passage from boyhood to manhood. The magical-castration complex, documented in Malaysia, China, West Africa, and Medieval Europe, involves the belief that the penis has been stolen. Although the penis can still be seen, it is believed to not be actually present because female witches or others with malicious intent have supernaturally removed it. If a common thread runs through these complexes, it is a preoccupation with the penis as a seat of masculinity that results in efforts to secret symbolic penises away from women, exaggerate penile presence through ornamentation, surgically modify the penis to symbolize adult manhood, and manage fears that women and other unsavory persons might seek to steal the penis away.

THE BULLROARER COMPLEX

One of the puzzles for early anthropologists involved explaining the significance of a musical instrument that has been called the "bullroarer." It is a relatively simple instrument, composed of a wooden slat that is whirled around on the end of a cord that generates an extremely loud and pulsating sound.[1] What is unusual about this instrument, and what made it of interest to anthropologists, is that it appears in many cultures around the world and often has similar symbolic meanings. The bullroarer complex involves a biological association with the male phallus, a religious association with male initiation ceremonies, natural associations with thunder, wind, and rain, and ritual taboos on the object for women. As described below, the bullroarer complex appears in Africa, Australia, and Remote Oceania, and among the indigenous peoples of North and South America. It has been described in Dionysian cults in ancient Greece and Rome[2] and has been described as a toy in the British Isles, France, Germany, Poland, and Switzerland, and among European immigrants to the United States.[3]

The archaeological record suggests that the bullroarer complex is quite ancient in human history. Bone, ivory, and stone pendants that appear to be ornamental replicas of the bullroarer have been found in France in deposits dating from 15,000 to 10,000 BCE and in Derbyshire, England, dating from 25,000 to 15,000 BCE.[4] In 1898, the early anthropologist Alfred C. Haddon described it as "perhaps the most ancient, widely spread, and sacred religious symbol in the world."[5]

The enigma of the bullroarer complex has largely faded from the consciousness of contemporary anthropology. However, among the earliest anthropologists, in the late nineteenth and early twentieth centuries, finding an explanation for the bullroarer's widespread occurrence and symbolic similarities across cultures was central to burgeoning theories of cultural phenomenon. Three main perspectives emerged: psychic unity, multiple independent inventions, and cultural diffusion.

Those who attributed the bullroarer to psychic unity offer a somewhat metaphysical explanation for its widespread distribution.[6] The "psychic unity of mankind" was a concept proposed by the German physician and ethnographer Adolf Bastian.[7] He believed that cross-cultural similarities could be explained by the fact that all human beings share identical elementary ideas (*elementargedanken*). This sharedness caused cultures of the world to develop independently along parallel lines because all people inherited a species-specific mental framework. Although these elementary ideas would be modified and shaped to some degree by local cultural contexts and experiences, all human beings possessed a kind of similarity of mind, which led to similarities in cultural features.

Contemporary anthropologists do not put much stock in the existence of such speculative innate characteristics of the so-called human mind that lack any empirical evidence. Nonetheless, the concept of psychic unity has been important in the history of anthropological thought, for it was an early idea that attempted to replace racist explanations of cultural difference. Popular late-nineteenth-century Western thought viewed cultural difference as equivalent to biological difference and thereby evoked a hierarchy of superior and inferior forms of humanity. Some ascribed to the Aristotelian Great Chain of Being, whereby all forms of life fell on a hierarchical continuum from worms to angels; human "races" could also be ranked according to the hierarchy. Others interpreted difference in biblical interpretations of a "fall from grace." Peoples who looked and behaved differently from Europeans were and did so because they had strayed from the teachings of God.

Despite its flaws, the idea of psychic unity represented a small step away from biological racist reductionism because an underlying premise was that all peoples have the same innate potential. One example is in the work of Sir James Frazer, who wrote a massive 12-volume work of comparative mythology, *The Golden Bough*. Here, Frazer describes the use of the bullroarer in harvest rituals by so-called savage people of New Guinea as being of the same nature as ecstatic cult rituals of the Dionysian Mysteries. Psychic unity suggests that the ancient Greeks and New Guinea peoples have similar practices because it is inevitable that the human mind will create similar cultural manifestations. It is also worth noting that the concept of psychic unity influenced Carl Jung's theory of archetypes[8] and the work of the popular mythologist Joseph Campbell.[9] In referencing these two well-known scholars, we do not intend to endorse speculative and metaphysical concept of psychic unity but to point out that it was an approach that was taken very seriously by the scholarly community well into the late twentieth century.

A second explanation of the bullroarer complex is multiple independent origins. Here, there is no necessary geographic proximity or "unity of mind" that leads to the inevitable development of similar culture features; rather, the bullroarer was invented separately in cultures in different parts of the world. Physicist Bo Lawergren suggests that bullroarers may have derived from hunting tools such as the bola and the sling.[10] As such, the bullroarer should not be considered in and of itself a cross-cultural phenomenon but a logical extension of other functional tools, which various cultures independently discovered. Similarly, German ethnologist and archaeologist Leo Frobenius argued that the bullroarer derived from the fish on the hook, that is, the way that a fish would appear if it were dangling from a fishing string.[11]

Cultural anthropologist and former governor of Dutch New Guinea Jan van Baal suggests that the bullroarer may have been independently invented in multiple cultures as a toy.[12] Given that it is a relatively simple implement, consisting merely of a piece of rope or string attached to a piece of flat wood, he suggests that many cultures could easily have constructed similar devices. He also makes the case that because the instrument's sound is so loud and frightening, it came to be used by a community of males to frighten a community of females, and thus became a phallic symbol. What is left unexplained is why, cross-culturally, males should seek to find means to frighten females.

One explanation is that the bullroarer finds its origin in early human beliefs in a supreme being.[13] Although it has an implicit link with psychic unity among the early anthropologists who proposed the idea, it is not directly presented as such and could also be explained by independent invention. Early British ethnologist Robert Ranulph Marett[14] suggests that human fear of the unknown was easily associated with the loud din of the bullroarer, which itself came to be personified as a supernatural being. He calls it a hobgoblin that was used to frighten women, because in his view, women needed to be disciplined and kept in line.

A third explanation is diffusion, which suggests an originating culture that discovered the bullroarer and was responsible for its subsequent spread to other cultures. The early anthropologist Robert Lowie argued in favor of cultural diffusion of the bullroarer as a cultural complex because bullroarer rituals in the Americas, Australia, and Africa all include the characteristic that the bullroarer is taboo for women.[15] Others who proposed monogenesis for the bullroarer were ethnomusicologist Erich von Hornbostel,[16] folklorist Andrew Lang,[17] and anthropologist and Edwin Meyer Loeb.[18]

Early Bristish anthropologist Alfred Haddon,[19] who provides the earliest review of the bullroarer cross-culturally, believes that it was likely a combination of diffusion and multiple independent inventions. He finds the argument for an ancient single origin unlikely. First, although the bullroarer is quite widespread, it is not a cultural universal. And second, since the bullroarer is a very simple instrument, there is no reason to believe it could not have been spontaneously invented by numerous peoples. However, the similarities in the bullroarer complex do suggest some cultural borrowing, and he believes that it is likely quite ancient in some parts of the world. As for the issue of it being taboo for women, like Marett, he sees a link with its loud sound and association with the supernatural. As such, men have used it to exert power over women.

An additional novel explanation for the bullroarer comes from the folklorist Alan Dundes.[20] He has questioned why the bullroarer has been interpreted as a phallic symbol since this interpretation does not adequately explain either its association with wind and thunder or why it is so often taboo for females to see it (for women do need to see penises during sex). He suggests that it has anal symbolism and represents a "flatulent phallus," based on its use in some cultures in ritual homosexuality and reversal myths. For the latter, as will be described below, in the mythology of a number of cultures, the bullroarer first belonged to the women before it was rightfully given to the men. He argues that in ritual male homosexuality, men are behaving as men and that this is the secret that must be kept from women. Thus, it involves males attempting to supplant female procreativity through the symbolic creativity of the anus. Further, he associates the whirling of the bullroarer with a masturbatory motion. The possibility that male initiation rituals, such as bullroarer ceremonies and penis subincision, are used to imitate female fertility and reproduction is taken up by several researchers, as discussed below.

Although the bullroarer is documented in many cultures, it is perhaps most prevalent in those cultures of Australia and Papua New Guinea. The bullroarer is integral to male initiation rituals in many Australian aboriginal groups and is typically, but not always, kept secret from women. Such groups include the Antakirnya,[21] the Arrernte,[22] the Bād,[23] the Diyari,[24] the Gunai,[25] the Kamilaroi,[26] the Karadjeri,[27] the Keeparra,[28] the Mayi-Kulan,[29] the Murinbata,[30] the Narungga,[31] the Walpiri,[32] and the Wurundjeri.[33] Among the Kariyarra,[34] the bullroarer is used in male initiation, but women are allowed to see it. In some groups, such as the Marind-anim and the Trans-Fly Papuans, it is used in homosexual initiation rituals.[35] The sound of the bullroarer is believed to be that of a supernatural being among the Arrernte,[36] the Bād,[37] and the Narungga.[38] In Narungga myth, it is the voices of boys killed by dogs. Among the Diyari, it is believed that were women to see the bullroarer, there would be no snakes or lizards.[39]

Although used in male initiation, the bullroarer is considered female in some groups. Among the Murinbata, the bullroarer is Karwadi (Mother of All, the Old Woman), living in deep waters, who presents herself with the roar of the bullroarer.[40] Ethnomusicologist Stephen Wild describes the bull-roarer as involved in a male initiation ritual among the Walpiri that involves the appropriation of the female nurturing and procreative role.[41] In the Wal-piri *katjiri* ritual, two bullroarers of different sizes are used, representing two sisters. As a part of male initiation, males dip their fingers into a small hole in the ground containing blood, which they taste and is said to be the urine of the two sisters. They then touch their tongues to the tip of the spear, which represents the clitoris and creates a bond of silence between the two sisters and the initiand. The novices undergo a symbolic rebirth involving the womb of the two bullroarer sisters, which is represented by a pit dug in the ground.

Other groups have additional beliefs and rituals associated with the bull-roarer. Among the Ngarinyin, the bullroarer is the name of the Maiangara rainbow serpent.[42] For the Kumbainggar, the sound of the bullroarer is said to be heard at the site of a sacred spot used to cure diarrhea.[43] The Maori of New Zealand also have the bullroarer.[44]

In Papua New Guinea, the bullroarer has been documented as used in male initiation rites, which are typically forbidden to women in groups including the Bariai,[45] the Bena Bena,[46] the Bukaua,[47] the Dugum,[48] the Ila-hita Arapesh,[49] the Kaliai,[50] Koko,[51] the people of Kiwai Island,[52] the Lak,[53] the Marind-anim,[54] and the Ngaing,[55] and the Trans-Fly Papuans.[56] Bariai women are threatened with gang rape if they witness male initiation or see the bull-roarer;[57] Ngaing women, on the other hand, are permitted to see the bull-roarer as long as it is not being whirled.[58] Among the Kiwai, the bullroarer is called a *madubu*, which means "I am a man."[59]

In many Papua New Guinea groups, including the Bukaua,[60] the Ilahita Arapesh,[61] the Kaliai, [62] the Koko,[63] the Lak,[64] and the Mundumagor,[65] the bull-roarer is described as the voice of a supernatural being. Among the Ilahita Arapesh, the sound of the bullroarer is said to be the voice of Lefin, a red-haired spirit dwarf calling out, "I am a great, great man . . . I am a great, great man."[66] Among the Mundugamor, the voice of the bullroarer is female, namely, the sound of the mother of the supernatural crocodile Asin.[67]

Another theme in Papua New Guinea is the association of the bullroarer with either agricultural rites or control over the elements of nature. Among the Ilahita Arapesh, the bullroarer is used to create auditory thunderstorms during dry-season rituals.[68] The bullroarer is also reportedly used to make crops grow among the Mabuiag Island people of the Torres Strait[69] and is associated with yam growing among the Kiwai[70] and the Kwoma.[71] Among the Mer (Murray Island), the bullroarer is associated with rainmaking,[72] and among the Ngaing, with control of the forces of nature.[73] Among the Chambri, bullroarer are swung by men to bring high waters.[74]

The Kiwai also use the bullroarer in agricultural rites, and it figures in two myths, one associated with the origins of agriculture and another with male-female gender-role reversal.[75] The mythical Soido killed his wife, and from her dead body all the vegetables sprouted. Soido collected and ate them, but they passed to his penis. When he withdrew the first time he had sex with a new wife, all the vegetables in his penis were scattered over the field. This was the origin of vegetables. In agricultural rites, the bullroarer is used to encourage the growth of yams. After men and women have intercourse, their secretions are smeared on the bullroarer, which is swung, causing "medicine" to be spread over the field. In another Kiwai myth, the bullroarer was discovered by a woman when a chip of wood flew off a tree she was cutting and made a buzzing sound. In a dream, Maigidubu, an anthropomorphic snake-man, instructed her to give the bullroarer to her husband. Male-female reversals are also found among the Bariai,[76] and the Kaliai.[77] In Kaliai myth, at one time, men had breasts and cared for children while the women had knowledge of the bullroarer. Their cultural hero Kowdok gave the bullroarer to men and gave men's breasts to women.

In two similar myths of the Trans-Fly Papuans and the Marind-anim, the first bullroarer is extracted from a vagina.[78] Among the Trans-Fly people, the cultural hero and originator Tiv'r (or Kambel) hears a whining sound in his pregnant wife's abdomen. He sends a series of birds to extract it. When the wife is stooping down, one bird succeeds and pulls it out. It becomes the first bullroarer and the first child of the mythic originating couple. The Marind-anim have a similar myth. Here, the evil supernatural being Sosum (which is the same name as the bullroarer *sosum*) has sex with a young girl but cannot extract his penis. The girl's mother cuts off his penis and its remains are later extracted from the girl by a stork.

Various Papua New Guinea groups have other rituals or beliefs associated with the bullroarer. The Koko believe that if a bullroarer is broken and a chip strikes a man, when he next goes fighting and hunting, he will be wounded by a spear or a boar's tusks.[79] The Mer use the bullroarer in a ceremony associated with turtle-fishing.[80] Among the Kaliai, the supernatural being Varku is embodied in the bullroarer, whose role is to avenge breaches of custom.[81] In addition, if a Kaliai woman is abused by her husband, the men surround her husband's house and sound the bullroarer to demonstrate their and their ancestors' grief and anger at the mistreatment of a kin member.[82] Among the

Trans-Fly Papuans, the bullroarer is used in war magic; a warrior calls out to enemies, "*Tokujenjeni* (the first bullroarer) is copulating with you."[83]

The bullroarer has been documented in various African cultures, particularly of West and Central Africa. Its use has also been documented in a few African hunter-gatherer groups. Among the Bambuti of Central Ituri, the bullroarer is used in male initiation ceremonies and represents the presence of a supernatural power.[84] It is also used in male initiation ceremonies of the Ju/'hoan.[85] Among a group described as the /Xam (likely Khoisan-speakers) the bullroarer was used to cause bees to swarm and make honey that was collected in leather bags and taken home to the women.[86] German ethnographer Friedrich Ratzel describes the "bushmen" using the bullroarer as a rain charm.[87]

Among African agricultural peoples, the bullroarer has been particularly well-documented among peoples of Nigeria. Among the Yoruba, the bullroarer is used in male initiation ceremonies[88] and women are forbidden to see it, upon threat of death.[89] The bullroarer is the voice of the criminal ancestors' dead, who has the ability to cleanse a village of female witchcraft.[90] Oro, the bullroarer, also figures in the feast of the new yam ceremony.[91] The bullroarer is also associated with the preparation of a magical charm intended to cause harm called *egbe*, made from a phallic-shaped fungus (*Phallales* sp., stinkhorns).[92] Today in Cuba, the bullroarer is used in the Yoruba-influenced orisha cult of Oro.[93] The bullroarer is also used among the Ebira,[94] the Idoma,[95] the Lela,[96] and the Kadera[97] in male ceremonies that are forbidden to women. Among the Ebira, the bullroarer is the voice of the spirit of Grandfather Ori (*Ohikwami Ori*) or Ori Spirit (*Ekiti Ori*).[98] Among the Esan, initiated men use the bullroarer in a ritual procession of land spirits; the penalty for women who observe the ceremony is death.[99]

Use of the bullroarer has been documented in several other African groups. In Western Angola, the bullroarer is used in the male circumcision ceremonies of the Nyaneka-Nkhumbi and the Handa.[100] Among the Dogon of Mali, the bullroarer is used in the *sigi* ceremony, which is held once every 60 years.[101] The bullroarer represents the speech of the dead and is said to utter, "I swallow, I swallow, I swallow men, women, and children, I swallow all." In the Democratic Republic of Congo, the bullroarer is a secret instrument of male initiation and of the circumcision ritual; it is hidden against the wall near the hearth in the mother's house.[102] Among the Tanela of Madagascar, a bamboo bullroarer was described as used by small boys to frighten birds away from fields.[103] In other African groups, including the Bakongo[104] of the

Republic of Congo and Angola, the G/wi[105] bushmen of the Kalahari, and the Babembe[106] of Central Africa, the bullroarer is used as a children's toy.

Among North American indigenous peoples, the bullroarer is best known among southwestern Native Americans. They appear in several prehistoric archaeological sites including Pecos, Verde Valley, Chetro Ketl, and Grasshopper Pueblo.[107] This distribution in southwestern archaeological sites suggests that bullroarers were either part of the Paleo-Indian tool kit or were independently invented in the Americas. Bullroarers were used in male initiation ceremonies and in rituals involving the control of rain, wind, and thunder. Among the Cahto (Kato), Miwok, Pomo, and Yuki, they were used in male initiation ceremonies that excluded women; these items were thought to represent the voice of the dead, spirits, or the Thunder God.[108] Among Hopi men, the bullroarer was used in the snake dance and other rituals to imitate the sound of thunder in order to petition for rain.[109] It was also used by men among the Papago to represent the sound of rain. For the Tohono O'odham (i.e., the Papago), the bullroarer symbolized growing corn, lightening, thunder, clouds, and the sound of rain.[110] Among the Paiute, the bullroarer was used both to bring rain and to bring warm wind to melt the snow.[111] The Laguna and Zuni Pueblo also used the bullroarer to bring wind and rain.[112] The Sinkyone used the bullroarer for starting and stopping the wind.[113] The Cree used it to bring the North Wind.[114] Similarly, the Pomo used the bullroarer to make thunder and stop prolonged rains.[115]

North American indigenous peoples have also used the bullroarer for other functions. Somewhat surprisingly, the bullroarer was documented as used by masked dancers in a female puberty ceremony among the western Apache.[116] It has also been described among the Apache as being made of wood struck by lightening and used as an amulet.[117] Navajo singers associate the bullroarer with the *diyin din'é'* Holy People.[118] Among the Serrano, it was used by the *paha*, the supervisor of tribal ceremonies, to call for silence during their major annual ceremony.[119] Similarly, the Kumeyaay (Diegueño) of the American Southwest and Mexico used the bullroarer to summon the people to ceremonies.[120] Shamans among the Seri of Mexico used the bullroarer to summon the spirits.[121] In several groups, including the Catabwa,[122] the Nisenan (southern Maidu),[123] Rappahannock,[124] and some Inuit peoples,[125] it serves as a children's toy.

Similar patterns in bullroarer use are seen among indigenous peoples in lowland South America (Amazonia). However, in a number of Amazonian cultures, a similar sacred flute cult appears to substitute for the bullroarer complex. The Borôro and Mehinaku of Brazil have separate housing for men and women. The Borôro use the bullroarer for an initiation ceremony in the men's house and women are forbidden to see it.[126] Similarly, the Mehinaku use the bullroarer in a ritual for the spirit Matupa.[127] A carved and painted bullroarer is suspended on 20-foot cords from 10-foot poles. Women are required to stay inside the women's house when the bullroarer is sounded, and they are told that it is the voice of a female-devouring monster. Women are threatened with gang rape if they leave their huts during the ritual. The bullroarer is also used in male initiation ceremonies among the Canela.[128] The Sherente of Brazil use the bullroarer for a ritual involving the summoning of Mars; they do not view the bullroarer as taboo for women.[129]

The noted cultural anthropologist Robert F. Murphy has identified sacred flutes found in a number of Amazonian groups as the functional equivalent of the bullroarer; the phallic symbolism is clearly extended to these tubular wind instruments.[130] According to Murphy, Mundurucú men believe that their power and dominance lie in the possession of the karökö, sacred flutes that are associated with fertility; as such, it gives them power in a role usually relegated to the realm of females. Traditionally, the Mundurucú had separate men's and women's houses. Each men's house held a chamber for the sacred flutes. Women were never allowed to see them, upon penalty of being gang raped by all the men of the village.

Continuity between the bullroarer and sacred flutes are also found in Kamayurá myth and ritual.[131] In Kamayurá myth, bullroarers are used by the twins, the Sun and the Moon, to frighten away women so that only the men can use the flutes. Kamayurá men perform jaqui flute dances in the middle of the village. Women and children are secluded in their houses and forbidden to see either the flutes or the dances. As in other cultures, women are threatened with gang rape by all the men in the village if they break this rule. In myth of the Wakuénai people, women steal the sacred flutes, which the men eventually regain and use in initiation rituals and other sacred ceremonies.[132] Sacred flutes play a somewhat different role among the Piroa.[133] Here, the ruwang, a dark shaman, purports to have stolen sacred flutes from animal homes beneath the earth. Men play the flutes in "increase ceremonies," which maintain the fertility of the land and also represent the men's attainment of a predatory relationship with animals. Women are forbidden to see the flutes, the rationale being to hide from the women the secret of the treacherous way in which the flutes were obtained. The Wanano in the northwest Amazon (Brazil and Colombia) also forbid women to observe the flute ritual.[134]

While the use of the bullroarer is widespread and exhibits similar patterns of use in terms of its phallic symbolism, its association with men, male initiation, the supernatural, and thunder, and its status as forbidden to women, there are exceptions. Alfred Haddon[135] provides multiple references to the bullroarer being used across Europe and in colonial America, but here, it does not appear to have any ritual function. Rather, it appears as a children's toy. Only a few references to the bullroarer in Asia were located. Among the Minangkabau of Sumatra it is made of a piece of skull bone and is used by shamans for dark magic.[136] The Kerinci people of Sumatra are said to have created a bullroarer from the skull of a tiger and used it to capture tigers.[137]

Perhaps one way to view the bullroarer complex is as an extended phenotype, a concept the evolutionary biologist Richard Dawkins introduced in 1982.[138] While the term "genotype" refers to an individual's DNA profile, the term "phenotype" refers more broadly to the relationship between the genotype and the environment. While the phenotype is, in a sense, passive, involving how the environment biologically affects an organism, the extended phenotype is more active, involving ways in which an organism changes its surroundings. Extended phenotypes include bees building hives, beavers building dams, and a wide range of human cultural behaviors. Like monumental architecture in ancient penis cults, the bullroarer may involve a similar male/phallic symbolism representing patriarchy. Its similar form and function in many cultures may derive from its characteristics of having a loud and frightening sound while being made of simple materials such as string and a slat of wood that many cultures might easily discover. Just as it is common for large towering objects to symbolize the dominance of the penis by exaggerating its size, the bullroarer may express a similar dominance by way of sound that became a phallic symbol. But just as not every architectural structure represents a penis, neither does the bullroarer represent a penis in every case. Nonetheless, it appears to have both been discovered independently and also diffused among some cultural areas. Other cultural practices that may be interpreted as extended phenotypes are penis sheathing and penis modification.

THE PENIS SHEATHING COMPLEX

Coverage of the penis can be considered the norm among contemporary human males. The penis is not typically left to hang free and out in the open in its default flaccid state. It is either covered by clothing or sheathed in some manner. As discussed in chapter 3, archaeological evidence suggests that clothing has existed for at least the last 70,000 years. Although clothing has been an important human invention, allowing for migration into colder climates, practices of penis sheathing are not always related to protection from the elements. In some cultures, the penis is sheathed while little else is worn. Minimally, the glans penis is covered. For example, among the Awá-Guajá of the Brazilian Amazon, a man considers himself naked if he does not tie the end of his foreskin with a piece of cord, thereby concealing the glans.[139] In a number of cultures, penis sheaths can be considered a form of male body art. As such, the two primary uses of such devices are contradictory: to conceal the penis or to bring attention to it. Males have been said to employ penis sheaths to either hide the shame of nakedness or to enhance their display of masculinity.

Since clothing items are typically made of perishable materials, the archaeological evidence comes from works of art. Perhaps the earliest evidence of sheathing comes from the Minoans of the Bronze Age of Crete (ca. 2000–1470 BCE), where male figurines are usually depicted nude, except for a codpiece and a belt.[140] Aegean natives (the Keftiu) are depicted wearing codpieces in several eighteenth-dynasty (ca. 1550–1292 BCE) Egyptian tomb pieces.[141] There is also evidence from rock art from earlier prehistory demonstrating similar patterns in present-day Algeria and Zimbabwe, as well as in Egypt.[142]

Archaeologist Peter Ucko, in his comparative study of the practice of penis sheathing, found it to be both widespread and discontinuous.[143] Forms of sheathing occur with sufficient difference in varied parts of the world to suggest that it developed independently in a number of cultures. At the same time, there are sufficient similarities in some regions to suggest diffusion of the practice.

For example, in Amazonia, Ucko found that for the vast majority of peoples who practice sheathing, it involves binding the prepuce over the glans and placing the penis in the erect position under some form of belt. A number of other practices encase the penis in some form of manufactured sheath made from natural materials. Like the Awá-Guajá, in a smaller number of peoples, the foreskin (prepuce) is tied over the glans and the penis is left in its natural position. In New Guinea, as in the Amazon, tying up the penis under a belt is also fairly common, but in widely scattered regions in this area. Manufactured sheaths are common, but their occurrence demonstrates a highland/lowland difference in common natural materials. Highland groups are more likely to employ gourds while lowland groups, which are located closer to the coast, encase the penis in shells. Bamboo, nuts, and nets are also used. In Africa, penis sheathing is largely restricted to vast areas of West Africa but also includes many South African groups and some peoples of the Congo. In Africa, the vast majority of peoples who use penis sheaths manufacture the sheath from local materials.

In the more detailed available ethnographic accounts of sheathing, a number of indigenous peoples describe their use as a means of concealment rather than of display. For example, for the Amazonian Shavante, penis sheathing is a means to control male sexuality.[144] Similarly, for the northern Kayapo, sheathing is intended to restrain rather than emphasize male sexuality.[145] In recent times, the Kayapo have replaced sheathing with Western-style shorts.[146] Among the Kagwihiv, like the Kayapo,[147] a male receives a penis sheath at puberty, and it is considered immodest for an adult man to be seen without one.[148] The Borôro also receive sheaths at male initiation rites.[149]

In New Guinea, ethnographic evidence among the Dani people suggests similar cultural ideologies to Amazonian sheathing.[150] They report that the *holim* (penis gourd) is used for modesty. It also symbolizes male relatedness, for the term "holim" is used to indicate male kinship relatedness. One difference from its use in Amazonia is that the penis gourd both covers the penis and holds it erect at a 45-degree angle. For this reason, the noted anthropologist Ruth Benedict described the New Guinea penis gourd as a form of exhibitionism, similar to the fifteenth-century European codpiece.[151]

The relatively short-lived European phenomenon of the codpiece was seemingly a fashion trend intended for the exhibition and accentuation of the penis, although alternative explanations have also been offered. The codpiece became an important article of male clothing in the Renaissance in late-fifteenth-century and sixteenth-century Europe. Between the fourteenth and sixteenth centuries, the codpiece changed from a simple triangular cloth attached to the front of male trousers to an elaborately decorated and heavily padded accouterment that gave the appearance of an unnaturally large, semierect, and protruding penis.[152] It has been speculated that the double-stitched fly on trousers is a contemporary survival of the old European fashion.[153]

A number of explanations for the development of the codpiece have been given. One is that it originated with armor worn in Medieval times, which was used to protect the genitals during battle.[154] However, it was made far larger than would have been necessary for that practical purpose.[155] One art historian suggests that the reverse was true, with the military attire of metal codpiece and doublet imitating the fashion of the day.[156] Supporting this view is the more general argument that what has been labeled "Medieval" armor falls more accurately in the early modern period, which bridges Medieval times and the Renaissance.[157]

Another explanation derives from the gradual evolution of men's fashion beginning in the fourteenth century. Men wore hose on their legs and covered their torso and pelvic area with tunics and doublets (a jacket or upper-body vest). However, over time, the tunics and doublets shortened, exposing a male's genitals.[158] Late in the reign of King Edward IV of England (1442–1483) both he and church authorities requested that men's clothing cover their "privy members" and buttocks.[159] Consequently, the codpiece is said to have become popular as an accommodation of the requirement to cover the genitals while still allowing the fashion of short doublets and tunics.

Several authors have offered the interesting explanation that the padded codpiece originated with the syphilis epidemic in Europe in 1495.[160] Symptoms included discharge of large volumes of blood and pus from the penis as well as swelling in the inguinal region. Woolen pads and cloth bandages were needed for medical management of syphilis and the padded codpiece suited this purpose. Historian Carole Frick disputes a strictly practical medical function for the codpiece, arguing that it was also attire for young male children.[161] However, he also argues that children's fashion imitated that of adults.

The codpiece may have arisen for a number of reasons. It may have symbolized male authority and aggressiveness, particularly in its association with military armor. It could also have been a fashion trend in response to a king's decree to cover one's genitals. It is also possible that the codpiece came into fashion not only to treat syphilis but also to disguise it. In any event, it began to disappear in Europe with the reign of Henri III of France (1574–1589), whose attire introduced elements imitative of the current female styles of dress.[162]

THE RITUAL PENIS MODIFICATION COMPLEX

Worldwide, 650 million males and 100 million females living today have undergone some form of genital cutting and alteration as children.[163] Far more attention is given to the practice of female genital mutilation (FGM), and, arguably, with very good reason, for female forms of genital alteration are usually much more extensive and result in much more severe health consequences. Nonetheless, it is worth noting that the global frequency for male genital alteration is six times that of female genital alteration. According to an early medical anthropologist Erwin Ackerknecht, next to the fingers, genitalia are the most common target for religious zeal; he finds 14 different methods of male genital mutilation cross-culturally.[164] Male circumcision is arguably the most common form of surgery performed in modern times, and it was extensively practiced in the past.

Circumcision has an ancient history in Egypt. Mummies analyzed through radiography, computerized tomography, and carbon dating show evidence of circumcision perhaps as early as 4000 BCE.[165] The early archaeologist Grafton Elliot Smith also described mummies that had been circumcised prior to 4000 BCE.[166] The earliest depiction of circumcision (or possibly superincision) is seen in a bas-relief on the wall of the temple of Ankh-ma-Hor at Saqqara (fifth dynasty, 2400 BCE).[167] The Greek historian Herodotus (484–420 BCE) describes the practice of circumcision among the Egyptians, Colchians, Ethiopians, Phoenicians, Syrians, and Macrones.[168]

However, the contemporary widespread practice of circumcision of male infants in the Western world is derived more directly from ancient Judaism. The removal of the foreskin was a symbol of the covenant of Jehovah with the descendants of Abraham, as described in Genesis in the Christian Bible and in the Parashat Bereshit of the Torah. Christian and Rabbinic scholars have estimated that the circumcision of Abraham and the males in his family took place around 1713 BCE.[169]

Freud proposed an interesting theory about circumcision. He suggested that the Jewish practice originated later, in the time of Moses.[170] Psychoanalytically, Freud viewed circumcision as a form of symbolic castration. Historically, he suggested that Moses was not Jewish but actually an Egyptian noble and a follower of the pharaoh Amenhotep IV (later Akhenaten) and the cult of Aten. Freud proposed that when Akhenaten died and his cult was overthrown, Moses led the Jewish peoples out of Egypt and converted them to the Aten cult, which required them to accept circumcision.

By the time of the emergence of early Christianity, the now longstanding tradition of circumcision became an issue in attempting to recruit gentiles to the new religion, this is the so-called Galatian controversy.[171] Although the Gospel of Luke indicates that Jesus himself was circumcised, the Apostle Paul, in biblical books including the Acts of the Apostles, I Corinthians, Galatians, Romans, and Philippians, argues that circumcision is not necessary for salvation and in Titus further warns against heeding "Jewish fables." The Seleucid king Antiochus IV Epiphanes (175–165 BCE) outlawed Jewish circumcision.[172] In the largely Christianized Western world, circumcision was rarely practiced in the Middle Ages and the Renaissance, but was revived in nineteenth-century England. References in a few medical publications recommend it as a treatment for phimosis (a condition where the foreskin cannot be retracted over the glans penis, sometimes occurring with gonorrhea at this time).[173]

In the United States, the widespread practice of infant male circumcision has been traced to the orthopedic surgeon Lewis A. Sayre in 1870 as a health care measure.[174] He claimed to have cured paralysis in a five-year-old boy by circumcising him. From that point on, circumcision took on an odd life of its own in Western medical practice and was touted as a panacea for a wide variety of illnesses. In British and American medical journals, circumcision was viewed as an effective treatment for conditions such as epilepsy, bedwetting, night terrors, homosexuality, hydrocephalus, malnutrition, and tuberculosis; but most of all, it was recommended for prevention of masturbation.[175]

A closely related practice is superincision. Its geographic distribution suggests that it developed independently of the Egyptian-Judaic form. In circumcision, the prepuce (foreskin) is cut and removed, exposing the glans. In superincision, a dorsal slit is made into the foreskin so that the prepuce can be retracted; this also serves to expose the glans, so that circumcised and superincised penises have a similar appearance.[176] Although the foreskin is not removed in superincision, the glans is bare as in circumcision. In the literature, superincised penises (such as in Polynesia) are often mistakenly referred to as circumcised.[177] Typically, superincision is associated with a rite of passage from boyhood to adulthood.

In Papua New Guinea, superincision has been practiced among the Bariai,[178] the Kaliai,[179] the Maenge,[180] and the Ngaing.[181] For the Bariai, only firstborn males undergo superincision; it is linked to mortuary rituals, with the blood spilled providing continuity between the ancestral spirits and the contemporary people.[182] Among the Ngaing, it has been described as a post-contact phenomenon demonstrating a commitment to Christianity; both the baptism of Jesus and his crucifixion have been reinterpreted as ritual superincision ceremonies.[183] The Ngaing practice suggests a form of syncretism, wherein a possibly old traditional Papua New Guinean practice has been reinterpreted with Christianization. Superincision has been described in other parts of tropical Oceania, including in Fiji,[184] Mangaia,[185] Marquesa,[186] Samoa,[187] Tahiti,[188] Tikopia,[189] and Tonga.[190] In Southeast Asia it has been practiced among the Cebuano[191] and the Bagobo of the Philippines,[192] the Selako[193] of Borneo, and the Kodi[194] of Sumba. In Africa, it has been described among the Kikuyu[195] and the Maasai.[196]

A third common form of male penile modification is subincision, which has been widely practiced among Australian aborigines and in some parts of New Guinea. While circumcision and superincision are functionally similar in their result of exposing the glans penis through either foreskin removal or retraction, subincision is a quite different practice. Subincision involves slitting open the underside of the penis, sometimes in repeated rituals, until the penis is split from the glans to the root of the scrotum.[197] The early anthropologist Montague Francis Ashley-Montagu suggested that it was practiced by indigenous peoples across three-fourths of the Australian continent.[198]

Subincision is typically practiced in ritual contexts. Much more rarely, it has been used as a medical treatment. One reported example of the medical use of subincision is as a treatment for candirú fish penile invasion in Amazonia.[199] The candirú is a small parasitic catfish that can invade the urethra.[200] Due to umbrella-like spines at its head, it may not be possible to extract the fish by the tail once it enters the penis. In an early cross-cultural survey of subincision, Ashley-Montagu also reports that among Fijians and Tongans of Oceania, it is believed to prevent or cure diseases such as tetanus.[201]

Ashley-Montagu was the first to suggest that male subincision corresponds to female menstruation, both in terms of the effusion of blood in the ritual and of the subincised penis having a similar appearance to the vulva.[202] The same argument was made more recently for the practice among the Kwoma of Papua New Guinea.[203] A more extensive treatment of this subject was made for the Wogeo in the ethnography *The Island of Menstruating Men*.[204] This explanation is reminiscent of some of the arguments for the bullroarer, with respect to male symbolic appropriation of female reproductive capabilities.

THE MAGICAL CASTRATION COMPLEX

Another recurring cultural belief involving the penis that is found in a number of cultures is magical castration, namely, the belief that the penis is either retracting or has disappeared entirely. It is most commonly referred to as "koro." The term "koro" is believed to derive from a Malay term that means "head of a turtle or tortoise."[205] The standard psychiatric diagnostic manual, the *DSM-IV*, defines koro as an episode of sudden and intense anxiety that the penis (or in females, the vulva and nipples) will recede into the body and possibly cause death.[206] Psychiatrist Arabinda Chowdhury distinguishes between two types of koro or koro-like manifestations: primary and secondary.[207] Primary koro is described as a culture-bound syndrome undergirded by cultural beliefs and myths. Here, it can occur as sporadic cases or as an epidemic outbreak in communities. Secondary koro is associated with central nervous system disorders, drug-use, or a primary psychiatric disorder.

Secondary koro or koro-like symptoms have been reported from around the world. Medical causes include brain tumors and pathology[208] and cerebrovascular accident (i.e., stroke).[209] Koro and koro-like symptoms have been associated with heroin and opiate withdrawal in India,[210] alcohol withdrawal associated with Ramadan fasting in Oman,[211] cannabis use in the United States,[212] India,[213] Greece,[214] and amphetamine use in Great Britain.[215] In the United States and Europe, a number of isolated cases have been associated with psychiatric disturbances including major depression, panic disorder, agoraphobia, and varied psychoses.[216] In the Middle East, it has been associated with phobias of AIDS and other conditions.[217]

Koro as a culture-bound syndrome is most commonly reported in cultures of southern China and Southeast Asia. One of the earliest references is found in the ancient Chinese medical textbook *Huangdi Neiching* (Yellow Emperor's Classic of Internal Medicine), which was written around 200–300 BCE.[218] In China, it occurs as sporadic cases, but several epidemic cases have been reported in the Guandgong area.[219] One of the largest occurred between November 1984 and May 1985; it involved approximately 2,000 cases. The underlying cultural belief is that yin ghosts of the dead, often disguised as foxes, have no penises and therefore seek out the yang element and collect penises in order to bring them back to life.

An epidemic koro-like syndrome involving accusations of penis stealing has also been reported in a number of West African nations.[220] Here, the underlying belief is associated with witchcraft or sorcery, whereby malicious others are able to steal one's penis. Psychiatrist Sunny Ilechukwu associates such outbreaks in Nigeria with economic depression, with women and strangers being the ones most likely to be accused of penis snatching.[221] Unlike the cases in Asia, wherein the culprit is a ghost, West African cases have resulted in mob violence against an accused penis thief. Between 1997 and 2003, 56 cases and 28 deaths were reported in the news in Ghana, Cameroon, Cote D'Ivoire, Senegal, Nigeria, and Gambia from angry crowds beating a person suspected of penis theft.[222]

A similar crime of penis stealing occurred in Medieval Europe during the Inquisition. Smith traces the origins to the *Malleus Malificarum* ("Hammer of Witches," 1487), a manual written by the Dominican inquisitor Heinrich Kramer to guide rooting out suspected witches.[223] The source of all witchcraft is carnal lust, which in females is described as insatiable. These witches steal penises and keep them alive in bird's nests. Some women accused of this crime were burned at the stake. Folklorist Moira Smith attributes many of the bird metaphors for the penis including "pecker," "cock," and the masturbation euphemism, "choke the chicken," to these ideas.

CROSS CULTURAL DIVERSITY OF PENIS SYMBOLISMS

We have discussed recurring patterns in cultural behaviors and beliefs involving the penis. But it is important also to stress that cultural meanings attributed to the penis can vary widely. It is impossible to explore all of the cross-cultural broad range of meanings and symbolic associations in relation to the penis. However, the cases described below illustrate how the penis is variably culturally contextualized, and they confirm that it has been incorporated into myths, art, and iconography since the Paleolithic period of human history. Phallic imagery often exists in domains of abstraction, which are intended for use in caricature, mockery, or jest. In some cultures barbarians are described as having large penises.[224] Penis charms may be used as protection from evil, as fertility enhancing objects, or as expressions of power, as discussed in chapter 3. Phallic images and talismans include double phalluses or penises depicted with eyes, legs, or wings. Our discussion illustrates that while contemporary Western cultures often emphasize the size of a penis, this culture-specific ideal should not be attributed as a human universal of masculinity. There is a wide range of expressions, esthetics, meanings, and contexts in which phallic imagery occurs cross-culturally.

Among the Matsigenka of the Peruvian Amazon, small penises are more desirable than large ones.[225] Demons with large penises figure heavily in Matsigenka mythology and folklore. However, such large penises are viewed as an undesirable expression of sexual aggression, linked to generally malevolent intentions. Mothers bathe newborn boys in an infusion of an orchid species with small bulbs so that their sons will grow up to have appropriately sized (meaning small) penises and become good men. The animal metaphor for hypersexuality among the Matsigenka and many Amazonian cultures is the deer. In Amazonian traditions deer are somewhat analogous to the seductive sirens (mermaids or winged maidens) of Greek and Mediterranean mythology that lured sailors to shipwreck. Among the Matsigenka, deer appear in either male or female form. They seduce humans into sexual encounters, which ultimately lead to catastrophe.

FIGURE 4.2 Phallic cornerstone marker in front of a church in Rome, Italy. Phallic symbolism is widespread in many modern cultures.

The ancient Greeks, who habitually displayed their genitals, also preferred small penises, but for different reasons.[226] Cultural aesthetics in Greek sculpture frequently depict muscular men with delicate penises. Aristotle claimed that small penises were preferred and more fertile, because the seed that had a shorter distance to travel maintained its vitality. Large penises were depicted as belonging to mythical satyrs or barbarians.

FIGURE 4.3 Cerne Abbas giant chalk figure in Dorset, England. ©Allenjeffery/ Dreamstime.com

One ithyphallic monument in Dorset, England, is the well-known yet mysterious Cerne Abbas giant, which measures 180 feet tall and likely dates to the seventeenth century. This figure was created by carving into the hillside and filling the cut with chalk. The giant, who holds a large club in one hand and has a cloak over his other arm, appears naked and with an erection (the penis and testicles measure 36 feet long). Above the giant is an Iron Age earthwork, but most experts agree that the giant postdates this feature. The Cerne Abbas man is located on a National Trust site and is a major tourist attraction. Some interpret the figure as a parody of Oliver Cromwell, dating to the seventeenth century; as Hercules, with associations to the Romano-British Age; or as having a Celtic origin, when chalk figures were constructed on hillsides in the British Isles.[227]

Both Neolithic and Romano-British (CE 43–410) sites in the United Kingdom have produced a range of artifacts that depict phalluses or serve as phallic objects, ornaments, or carvings. These have often been interpreted as items promoting fertility and strength or simply as objects of humor. A ceramic sherd from Cambridgeshire depicts "a man ejaculating while running toward a naked woman who is holding a huge phallus in one hand and pointing toward her genitals with the other."[228] Some of the phallic images display the penis with legs or wings. Phallic images are recorded from carvings on bridges and the walls of buildings and defensive structures. Historian Ronald Hutton suggests that this imagery provided protection, power, and "a reinforced ability to stand."[229]

Old Stone Age (ca. 13,000–11,000 BCE) rock art from the British Isles and northern Europe displays a variety of expressions of human sexuality and genitalia. While human figures constitute only approximately 3 percent of all the recorded art in this region, these works provide some insights into the ideologies of the past.[230] Some of the male figures have accentuated penises and others combine parts of male bodies with the forms of other creatures, such as horses, wolves, or felines. A variety of Neolithic monumental archaeological sites, especially tombs, in northwestern Europe have produced many phallic objects. These carvings of chalk often occur in ritual deposits located in ditches where they are accompanied by pairs of chalk balls that clearly suggest testicles. A curious figurine has stirred some debate about its meaning; this is a carved wooden object with breasts and a large erect phallus dating to around 3800 BCE.[231] This figure has been interpreted as a hermaphrodite. Other figurines with questionable gender attributes have been recovered from the Celtic bog and gravel bed sites of the British Isles that date to the Iron Age (ca. 1000 BCE to 500 CE).[232] These include carved oak figurines that have holes in the genital areas, which represents either a vulva or a place where a removable phallus would have been inserted.

Concentric circular ditch enclosures with causeways from the middle Neolithic (ca. 3800 BCE) are interpreted as ritual structures containing tombs and are typical of this time period in northwestern Europe (especially in southern England and the Midlands). Some of these sites contain ramparts, which suggest defensive features, but most also have human bone deposits in the ditches and pit-cache features containing deposits of ritual objects.[233] At the site of Windmill Hill in Wiltshire, United Kingdom, there is a grave that was left open initially and later filled in after the flesh of the deceased man had eroded from the skeleton. The ditches at this site contain skeletons of pigs and goats, oxen skulls, flint, local and imported pottery, antler picks, stone disks, and a variety of objects made from chalk including cups, plaques, balls, and chalk phalluses. The causewayed enclosure sites appear to have been used seasonally, perhaps as gathering places, and their appearance in the archaeological record corresponds with social changes including an increase in population and farming. Similar types of phallic objects have also been found at later period henge sites, including the so-called superhenge at Mount Pleasant in Dorset, United Kingdom, dating to around 2100 BCE.[234] The ritual deposits at this site contained wild and domestic animal bones, human bones, chalk balls and phalluses, other objects made of chalk, pottery, tools, and drums. Given the antiquity of these archaeological discoveries, it is difficult to interpret their meaning. Nevertheless, it is clear that the agricultural Neolithic societies of northwestern Europe frequently incorporated phallic imagery into their ritual deposits and public gathering places.

A more recent understanding of the role of a phallic symbol in a traditional setting comes from Clifford Geertz's classic anthropological piece "Deep Play: Notes on the Balinese Cockfight." In this ethnography Geertz demonstrates that men in Bali psychologically identify with "cocks," which symbolize masculinity.[235] The double sense of the rooster, or cock, in Bali is similar to the Western joking meaning. But the term "cock" does not translate only as "penis" in Bali; it also means "warrior," "hero," and "lady-killer." When Balinese men pit rooster against rooster, more than a betting game is going on. Before a cockfight, owners suck the heads of the roosters to stimulate the birds to fight, which also symbolically simulates the act of fellatio. The cockfight, then, is a symbolic male competition to express dominance and masculinity.

Conclusion

In this chapter we have reviewed a wide range of cultural customs associated with the penis and have argued that these customs might be explained from the perspective of the extended phenotype. That is, patriarchy is often expressed through these widely used symbols or themes. We have explored ethnographic and ethnohistoric data on phallicism, ritual, and religion. It is no surprise that the penis has received a great deal of attention in many cultures. It has played a central role in myths, rituals, and rites of passage. We have attempted to dispel some of the misconceptions about indigenous practices and to illuminate beliefs that motivate behavior wherever possible. As a symbol, the penis is widespread. The interplay or tension between maleness and femaleness is another theme that permeates this discussion. Finally, the traditional modes of genital modification described here are fundamentally practices that domesticate the penis.

Our review of the bullroarer complex illustrates cultural patterns of masculine associations, male initiation, nature symbols, and female prohibitions. The bullroarer complex appears in traditions that have both temporal depth and wide geographic range. We do not know the extent to which this interesting item of material culture diffused throughout or was invented independently in different parts of the world. Nevertheless, it is intriguing that in some myths the bullroarer was considered a female object before it became associated with men and masculinity. The bullroarer was frequently used to mark male initiation rites and memorialize important events. Again, in the case of both the bullroarer and sacred flutes, we see a tension between masculine and feminine and an emphasis on the supernatural, sacred, and taboo. As an extended phenotype, this complex may be understood as an expression of patriarchy and male procreative power.

Penis sheathing and penis modification are both widespread practices that can be examined cross-culturally as forms of an extended phenotype. These practices have deep roots in many cultures, having been customary for millennia. The male body, and specifically the penis, is manipulated in rites of genital mutilation that include circumcision, superincision, and subincision. These rites involve cutting the flesh, thereby symbolically carrying young males from a state of boyhood to a state of manhood. The acts clearly impart masculine qualities, yet they change the penis in a way that might also be viewed as a form of domestication, culturalization, or even feminization (especially in the case of the subincised penis, which looks somewhat like a vulva). Castration is another practice that feminizes the male in an obvious manner. Some of these practices are performed to mimic menstruation, and the rituals surrounding them evoke ideas of patriarchy, fertility, transition, the sacred, and the venerable.

An ideology of bodily manipulation is also expressed in psychological responses to fears of losing the penis or losing control of it. Variations on magical castration, or koro, are found in many cultures. These instances of penis theft and loss suggest an underlying anxiety related to masculinity or perhaps to male privilege and patriarchy. As in our discussion of phallic imagery from the archaeological record, we suggest that expressions of overt masculinity may be responses to stress and uncertainty. Imagery and rituals may serve as reminders of important events and the dominant role males are expected to perform in a given society.

5

The Erotic-Exotic Penis

Phallic Facts and Fictions

Anthropologists George Marcus and Michael Fischer wrote that one promise of anthropology "has been to serve as a form of cultural critique for ourselves. In using portraits of other cultural patterns to reflect self-critically on our own ways, anthropology disrupts common sense and makes us reexamine our taken-for-granted assumptions."[1] When anthropology is at its best, it affords an opportunity in encounters with other cultures to challenge our beliefs and open our minds to the possibilities of different ways of thinking and interacting. When anthropology is at its worst, as is the subject of the postmodern critique, we do not see but project our own beliefs and biases onto other cultures.

There is perhaps no topic where cultural bias comes so glaringly into play as human sexuality. In anthropologists Daniel Davis and R. G. Whitten's review of the cross-cultural study of human sexuality, they note a number of issues that have historically made the topic of sexuality problematic.[2] Earlier anthropologists tended to focus on the "erotic and exotic," and few researchers have since attempted to follow up on the validity of these studies. Historically, a number of Western biases have come into play, including categorizing some sexual behaviors as natural and correct and others as unnatural and potentially dangerous. Western bias is also at play in the tendency to focus on issues that are of concern to Western society, such as premarital sex, adolescent sexuality, or homosexuality. Ethically, some anthropologists have been reluctant to broach the topic of sexual behavior due to concerns with respecting the privacy of informants. In addition, much of sex research has relied heavily on secondary sources from the Human Relations Area Files (HRAF), which are problematic for reasons to be discussed in this chapter.

Anthropologist Carol Vance has expressed similar concerns.[3] She describes the prevailing view in anthropology as having been that sexuality is not a legitimate area of study. For that reason, few graduate programs have provided training in the study of human sexuality for fear that it would be a career liability. She describes the field as failing to advance due to the lack of training and the absence of a scholarly community engaged in research. This chapter presents our finding that in the absence of solid cross-cultural research on human sexuality, we have instead continued to rely on exotic erotics in publications and textbooks from dated and sometimes dubious sources that have not been validated by subsequent research.

PENISES AND THE MEANING OF NAKEDNESS IN WESTERN CULTURE

What does it really mean to be naked? The concept of "nakedness" varies from culture to culture. As previously mentioned, among the Awá-Guajá of Brazil, a man's exposure of his penis is not considered nudity unless he fails to tie up his foreskin with *tikwita*, a small piece of string made from palm fibers. In cultural anthropologist Adeline Masquelier's *Dirt, Undress, and Difference*, she describes the surface of the body as having been historically a "central terrain on which battles for salvations of souls and the fashioning of persons were waged through sartorial means."[4] She argues that in missionary and colonizing contexts, the nakedness of indigenous people signified their godlessness and need for intervention by Western cultures.

Although ideas of nakedness may appear universal, in the world's cultures today, which body parts are taboo to expose varies cross-culturally. The American humorist Lewis Grizzard put it well when he said, "In the south there's a difference between 'Naked' and 'Nekkid.' 'Naked' means you don't have any clothes on. 'Nekkid' means you don't have any clothes on . . . and you're up to somethin'!"[5] Janet Tamaro, in her book on breastfeeding, recounts a story of Muslim women breastfeeding in a maternity ward when a male physician entered. They rushed to cover themselves, but it was not their breasts that they covered but their heads, with the *hijab*.[6]

In much of the Western world today, female nipples are considered "nekkid." Women can wear clothing that exposes every other part of the breast, but exposing the nipples is taboo. In 2004, singer Janet Jackson was performing at a football halftime show when her nipple was accidentally exposed for a half-second. Many expressed complete outrage at this assault on morality and family values. Conservative commentator Phyllis Schlafly said, "The Super Bowl is supposed to be the preeminent family entertainment night of the year, and it is completely unacceptable for American families to be assaulted by obscenity in the middle of a football game."[7] Federal Communications Commission (FCC) chief Michael Powell made this statement: "Like millions of Americans, my family and I gathered around the television for a celebration. Instead, that celebration was tainted by a classless, crass and deplorable stunt. Our nation's children, parents and citizens deserve better."[8] US senator Zell Miller had a more colorful response but was equally outraged by the incident: "I don't know how many of you have ever run over a skunk with your car. I have many times and I can tell you, the stink says around for a long time. You can take the car through the wash and it's still there. So the scent of this Super Bowl halftime show will long linger in the nostrils of America."[9]

Miller also lamented about what a terrible position he was put in in trying to explain this "stink" to his eight-year-old grandson. The FCC received over a half a million complaints over the incident and CBS was initially fined $550,000 dollars, although the fine was later appealed and voided.[10] The problem with the attitude that we need to save our children from female nipples is, well, aren't they *for* children? In Western society, we have a long history of fashion trends that accentuate the female breasts, but the nipple of the breast is taboo. Oddly, no such taboo applies to exposure of male nipples, which look very much like female nipples. But our strange nipple-phobia pales in comparison with the taboos on viewing the penis in Western societies.

The full horror of seeing a penis was evident in the witch trials of fourteenth- through seventeenth-century Europe and America. According to David Friedman, author of *A Mind of Its Own: A Cultural History of the Penis*, one of the key crimes that women were charged with was knowledge of the Devil's penis.[11] Like many of the misdeeds women were accused of in the witch trials, this was a crime that was impossible to prove one way or the other. Women were often tortured into confession. In 1608, the Puritan preacher William Perkins described a popular method of determining whether a woman was a witch: throw her in water to see if she drowned.[12] If she did not drown, she was a witch; if she drowned, she was innocent. Failure to drown sometimes resulted in being burned at the stake. An accusation of witchcraft was in itself as good as a death sentence. Similarly, a woman had no rational way of arguing against the accusation that she had seen the Devil's penis, because, obviously, the premise itself was irrational. But what it points to is a very deep cultural fear that, inherently, there is something very, very bad about penises. The worst imaginable type of penis is the one attached to Satan himself.

The word "penis" itself has long been taboo in American culture. In the introduction, we described the public outrage after the word "penis" was uttered repeatedly in a *Saturday Night Live* sketch in 1988. Arguably, the taboo weakened somewhat in 1993 when the story broke that Lorena Bobbitt had used a 12-inch kitchen knife to sever the penis of her husband, John Wayne Bobbitt, and thrown it out the window of her car.[13] There was widespread media coverage of the story, and there was no other way to describe the incident without using the word "penis." Lorena Bobbitt was arrested and tried for the assault but was found not guilty by reason of insanity.[14] John Wayne Bobbitt's penis was reattached and he had a short-lived career as a porn star in the films *Frankenpenis* and *John Wayne Bobbitt: Uncut.*[15]

However, discomfort with the word "penis" remains, as is evidenced by the abundance of euphemisms for the member. Euphemisms are indirect or humorous references that serve to mask subjects that are considered impolite, taboo, vulgar, or socially sensitive. One study asked a dozen college students to write down as many euphemisms for "penis" as they could come up with in 30 minutes. The students listed nearly 200 terms, 144 by male students and 50 by female students.[16] The Urban Dictionary, a web-based listing of American slang, contained 377 listings for "penis" as of September 2012.[17] The online "Dicktionary" has nearly 2,000 listings.[18]

Just about the worst thing a person can say to another in the English language is "f*ck you." But why should that expression be a curse instead of a blessing? Could we not use it to mean, "I wish for you great pleasure"? The current negative connotation may suggest cursing another with a wish that he or she be raped. Linguist George Lakoff wrote in his book *Metaphors We Live By* that all language is deeply symbolic and reveals our cultural values and attitudes. He describes how we use military metaphors in common speech, such as in debates where one "defends a position" or "shoots down an argument."[19] Metaphors for male genitalia abound in the English language. While they are often considered vulgar, they are also often used to express compliments. To say that a man is "well-hung" or "packing" is a good thing. Likewise, to call a man's "family jewels," "cojones," or "balls" large is to suggest that he is adventurous or courageous. However, anyone would be hard put to find a metaphor for female genitalia that is used as a compliment. Equivalent expressions of female genitalia, such as "she's got clitoris" or "she's got vagina," do not exist. Our metaphors reveal that Western societies still have double standards for male and female sexuality.

Such double standards are found in scientific descriptions of male and female reproductive anatomy and processes. Anthropologist Emily Martin has suggested that we have created a myth or scientific fairy tale that uses gender stereotypes to describe the role of the egg and the sperm in reproduction.[20] The male sperm are given characteristics of aggression, competition, and power. The female egg is passive and weak. She describes textbooks as relating a romance wherein the sperm saves the egg, a damsel in distress. We find a passive egg being swept along the fallopian tubes. The sperm "activates" the developmental program of the egg, delivering genes. Sperm have "strong, efficiently powered tails" that burrow through the egg. A sperm is seen as "rescuing" an egg, for if one does not reach the egg, the egg will die.

Martin also describes our cultural perception of menstruation as a female "failure," as suggested in medical texts, and of sperm production as male "success." Menstruation is "wasted" fertility. The uterine lining is described as dead tissue and "debris" that is "sloughed off," which makes it sound like something rotting and decaying. Spermatogenesis, on the other hand, is "amazing in its magnitude" because men can manufacture several million sperm each day, while women "shed" only one egg per month. Describing the egg as being "shed" makes it sound like something cast off and abandoned. It would be easy to rewrite this scenario in a way that characterized sperm production as wasteful. Although men can produce millions of sperm each day, most of them die and never reach their destination because they are too defective or weak or are "shed" at the wrong time to impregnate a woman. Given that the average family has about two children, the odds of any one sperm winding up being useful is about a trillion to one.

But beyond talk of reproduction, it is the sight of the penis that is the strongest taboo in Western society. During the writing of this book, the so-called Weinergate scandal broke.[21] The career of New York congressman Anthony Weiner was ruined after he sexted pictures of his erect penis beneath his underwear and a towel to several women. His last name is now as unfortunately ironic as that of John Wayne Bobbitt. Football player Brett Favre sparked a similar scandal when he was accused of texting pictures of his penis to sports reporter Jenn Sterger.[22] Some celebrities, such the musicians Chris Brown[23] and Kanye West,[24] have been accused of intentionally leaking photos of their penises to garner media attention and publicity. Somewhat suspiciously, a sex tape has recently been leaked of West and a look-alike of his wife, reality TV star Kim Kardashian, who first came to fame after the leaking of a sex tape of her and musician Ray J (William Ray Norwood Jr.).[25] Negative publicity is still publicity, and there are few topics that attract more media coverage than the exposure of a celebrity's penis. Such contemporary cultural references will quickly date this book, but undoubtedly new personalities and new penises in compromising situations will appear on the scene.

EXOTIC EROTICS

The Western simultaneous obsession and anxiety over sexuality and the human body is also demonstrated in the history of anthropological thought. Anthropology is a relatively new science. The profession of anthropology dates only to the Victorian era, in the late nineteenth century. Some of the earliest ideas about non-Western peoples derived from sketchy sources such as explorers, missionaries, and sailors who brought back travel tales of exotic practices that were more fantasy than reality. In anthropology, we call the first anthropologists who tried to synthesize this information the "armchair anthropologists," for many did not actually do fieldwork but only compiled the tales of others. Those tales grew into theories about the development of human cultures, but many were based on either inadequate or false information.

The prevailing paradigm about human development in the late nineteenth century is known as cultural evolutionism. It posited that all cultures are on a continuum of development and are advancing in similar ways along a similar path. The belief was that some cultures were in a sense frozen in time and represented an earlier stage in human development. These have been called "primitives," "stone age cultures," among others terms. The notion of "primitive" human sexuality was one of the erroneous ideas of that time.

One example is the Swiss anthropologist Johann Jakob Bachofen's book *Das Mutterrecht* (The Mother Right), which appeared in 1861. In it, Bachofen proposed that in the earliest stages of human culture, we were matriarchal.[26] His work found a new audience in the latter part of the twentieth century with the advent of neopaganism and goddess spirituality and also with some in academia, such as with Marija Gimbutas, who proposed a pre-Christian matriarchal society in Europe.[27] However, Bachofen was not an advocate for women. Rather, he viewed the idea of women in charge as a situation that would create chaotic conditions. He argued that human society flourished once patriarchy was established and provided order and the foundations for productive human society.

It is important to bear in mind that these early anthropologists were products of their times (as are we). While they considered non-Western peoples to be primitives, they, at least, considered them to be fully human. Prevailing popular and scientific thought, on the other hand, equated non-Western peoples with apes on the evolutionary scale,[28] or if they considered them human, then they were apostate and fallen from the grace of god.[29] In American anthropology, the break with the cultural evolutionist paradigm came with the work of Franz Boas, who is considered the founder of modern American anthropology. His central tenet was cultural relativism, which stressed that cultures should be judged on their own terms and are products of their own unique histories. Boas not only was influential himself but also trained the bulk of the major American anthropologists at the beginning of the twentieth century. Moreover, Boas was unusual for his time in that he trained a number of female students who made important contributions to the study of sex and gender, such as Margaret Mead, Ruth Benedict, and Zora Neale Hurston.

Nonetheless, cultural relativism did not necessarily take hold outside the field of anthropology (and also among some anthropologists). This is especially true of matters dealing with sexuality. The conflicted Western attitudes toward sexuality are apparent in distorted views of indigenous people. Even today, much of the information that is published repeatedly on sexuality in non-Western cultures is wildly sensationalized. Such erotic exotics from dubious sources use supposed cultural evidence to contrast so-called primitive sexual behavior with that of civilized, modern Western societies. Even some early anthropologists told such tales. The problem is that misinformation can be more interesting that the truth. The wilder the tale, the more the tale is told. Once such a tale is published in a textbook, it is difficult to correct, for the textbook becomes the authority and the misinformation is cloned in other sources, with authors rarely bothering to check the validity of the original source.

Many of the exotic erotics are standard fare in college textbooks used in gender studies, sociology, and psychology classes. Much of the information comes from only a few sources that keep being repeated. One heavily cited source comes from the work of Yale University sociologist Clellan Ford and psychologist Frank Beach. Beginning in 1937, Ford and Beach began cataloging the sexual behavior of non-Western cultures. The result was the publication of *Patterns of Sexual Behavior*, in 1951.[30] It is still referred to as a classic. They claim to have gathered data on nearly 200 cultures for their work. Obviously they could not have personally done fieldwork of any quality in 200 different groups, so where did the research come from?

According to Judith Reisman, best known for her critique of the work of sex researcher Alfred Kinsey, the information was gathered by unnamed, untrained, and unsupervised Yale college students, many of whom were undergraduates. She writes, "Who the Ivy League kids were—and exactly what they were doing and with whom while in these exotic climes—is not included in the 'field reports,' but what they brought back was counted as solid scientific research as was used by many as the basis of books, articles, and university lectures preaching about the need to free ourselves from Western sexual inhibitions."[31]

Reisman has an axe to grind in her view on the problems with sexual permissiveness. And although she has been criticized for a number of extreme views on sexuality, homosexuality, and pornography, she makes a valid point about this so-called research. Few young undergraduate students have the training and experience necessary to conduct fieldwork independently, particularly on a subject as socially charged as human sexuality. Even if they had the maturity to conduct such fieldwork, these students could not have understood the languages of these cultures well enough to do solid ethnographic research. Cultural anthropologists are expected to spend at least a year in the field, learning the language and experiencing the culture on a daily basis, before their research is accepted as credible. As a case in point, the Yale students came back with a report that Hopi men enjoy sex with chickens.[32] We will never know if the Hopi were teasing the Yale students or if something was seriously lost in translation. This is laughable, but the work from the Yale Cross-Cultural Survey was incorporated into the Human Relations Area Files. The latter is a database that is currently used by some anthropologists to gather statistical information on cultural patterns.

MORE BAD SCIENCE: PURPORTED CROSS-CULTURAL EXAMPLES OF DEVIANT PRACTICES

Another example of exotic erotics is found in Robert Endleman's book *Love and Sex in Twelve Cultures*.[33] The cover art for the book is an armless, legless, red blob of a woman being pierced in the groin by a spear. We could probably just leave it at that and say no more to discredit this work. The book's aim is to use a dozen cross-cultural examples to demonstrate that sexuality in all cultures boils down to Freudian Oedipal conflicts. The crux of Freudian psychology is that there are two types of people in the world: those with penises and those without penises. These are not so much literal categories of men and women, as David Friedman[34] puts it, but states of mind about having a penis and about having had your penis castrated. According to Freud, girls suffer from penis envy.[35] Upon seeing the penises of their brothers or male playmates, girls may come to the realization that boys have a superior genital organ and that females have been cheated. Freud describes female sexuality as based upon the desire to get a penis the only way possible, by having sex with men.

According to Freud, the problem for boys is that although they have a penis, they are constantly in fear of losing it. Therefore, males suffer from castration anxiety.[36] When boys see the genitalia of their sisters and female playmates, they assume that they have been castrated and that their father must have done it. The boys are psychologically torn about what to do. Moreover, boys are said to sexually desire their mothers. However, they are afraid that if they pursue her, they will be castrated as their sisters have been. The term "Oedipus complex" derives from the Greek myth of Oedipus, the king of Thebes. Oedipus unwittingly murdered his father and married his mother. Freud viewed this myth as representing a psychic and historical reality for humanity. In *Totem and Taboo*, Freud argued that all of civilization is founded upon our prehistoric ancestor murdering his father in order to gain access to women.[37] For Freud, psychologically healthy men will resolve the dilemma and identify with their cruel, castrating fathers. Healthy men according to Freud are those who do not become homosexual or engage in other deviant sexual practices. It is from here that Endleman takes his inspiration in *Love and Sex in Twelve Cultures*.

The cultures chosen by Endleman are all viewed as sexually pathological in some way. He describes the core problem for each as being unique cultural variations on unresolved Oedipus complexes, which are exacerbated by terrible parenting, particularly on the part of the mother. For example, the Northern Athabaskans of Alaska are said to avoid sex altogether, unless they are drunk. Then, under the influence of alcohol, sex is violent and brutal. Athabaskan women consider all men to be rapists. The Apache Indians are said to be similarly sexually violent (because they are drunk), and relationships between men and women are extremely hostile. The Amazonian Mehinaku are said to have no concept of romantic love, and the men have a fear and dread of female genitalia. Anyi men of the Ivory Coast are said to have an extreme fear of castration by their mothers, and Lusaka women in Zambia are "coldly suspicious, quick to take offense, irresponsible, and prone to drink."[38] What is the message that we are supposed to take away from this cross-cultural survey? These stories teach us that non-Western cultures are composed of violent drunks, are sexually perverse, comprised of men and women who hate each other, and breed mothers that consistently fail at parenting, which results in disturbed children.

A somewhat similar account is given for the people of Inis Beag, a pseudonym of a small island community in Ireland. According to cultural anthropologist John Messenger, these people are extremely sexually repressed.[39] Men deal with their repression through fighting and drinking. This stereotype of the violent, drunken Irishman is similar to that of the violent, drunken Indian proposed by Endleman. Orgasm is unknown to Inis Beag women, according to Messenger. In general these people are said to prefer not to have sex at all, and when they do, they always keep their underclothing on. They are said to rarely bathe, except a sponging of their faces, arms, legs, hands, and feet once a week on Saturday night. They also avoid bathing their genitals. Moreover, Messenger claims that many people in this culture are mentally ill owing to their schizophrenogenic mothers.

The sex lives of the people of Mangaia in the Cook Islands have been greatly misconstrued by pseudo research. In his 1971 book chapter, anthropologist Donald Marshall claimed that Mangaians were obsessed with sex and particularly with the sight of genitalia. Marshall claimed they had no notion of love and no way to say "I love you" in their language; Mangaians only say, "I want to copulate with you."[40] Couples are reported to routinely have sex all night, and young women entertain a series of males at night in front of their parents, a display their parents actively encourage. Young males compete with each other to give women as many orgasms as possible, and it is not uncommon for females to have orgasms that last from thirty minutes to an hour. These tall tales of the Mangaia appear over and over in textbooks, including Endleman's book. They have been recently sensationalized in Jonathan Margolis's *O: The Intimate History of the Orgasm*[41] (2004) and in a social work textbook by Charles Zastrow, *Introduction to Social Work and Social Welfare: Empowering People*[42] (2010), to name a few examples.

Ten years before Margolis's *O: The Intimate History of the Orgasm*, anthropologist Helen Harris attempted to put the myths of Mangaia hypersexuality to rest.[43] When she told the Mangaia what was being written about them, they were appalled. They found it insulting that anyone would say that all they cared about was sex and that men and women did not love each other. Regarding their multiple-orgasmic all-night sex routine, they said it was untrue, adding, "After all, Mangaians are only human."[44] They also found the claim illogical, saying that Mangaians mainly sleep at night because they have work to do in the morning.

Margolis repeats another myth that the men of "Ponape" (i.e., Pohnpei) in Micronesia perform cunnilingus on females by inserting a fish into the vagina and licking it out. This tale comes from a single report in 1880 by a German ornithologist, Otto Finsch, who briefly visited the island.[45] Finsch also reported that old impotent men were given the job of lengthening the labia and clitoris of young girls. This so-called evidence comes from one bird-watcher 130 years ago, who did not know the language and had no training in studying cultural behaviors. Yet, it is presented as fact. Margolis makes other blatant errors, such as claiming that bonobos are monogamous, in his history of the orgasm.

A very popular textbook today in gender studies is Michael Kimmel's *The Gendered Society*.[46] He gives the following cross-cultural statistics on sex and orgasms. The Zande of Africa normally have sex two to three times a night and once upon wakening. Thonga men have sex with as many as three or four of their wives each night. Chaga men have 10 orgasms each night. However, Marquesan men have 10 to 30 orgasms per night. Kimmel does not clarify whether or not the Chaga and Marquesan men's orgasms are due to having sex with women, and he does not provide any data on the women of these cultures. At the other end of the extreme are the Yapese people. They are said to have sex only once a month, but in this case, sex is an all-day event. A Yapese man is said to partially insert his penis into a woman, thus bringing her to multiple orgasms for hours.

Here it seems that Kimmel is trying to situate Western sexual behavior on a continuum that extends from the Marquesa to the Yapese. Americans fall in the middle of Kimmel's scale, having our orgasms less than 30 times a night but more than once a month. However, let's take a step back and do the math for the Marquesans. If we assume an average of 8 hours for sleep, Kimmel's assertion would result in an orgasm about every 15 minutes. Obviously it is not possible for a man to orgasm 30 times in a night. This feat would challenge even the most dedicated man who is willing to work from dusk to dawn. Kimmel presents this information as fact without a critical look at the source of the data. In a footnote, Kimmel provides the reference as Yale-trained Edgar Gregersen's 1982 *Sexual Practices*.[47] Gregersen does not provide references for most of the material in his book, prefacing his bibliography by saying that only the most important references could be included due to problems of space. The reader is simply left to trust Gregersen.

It is also worth mentioning that exoticizing the other is not limited to relatively modern Western characterizations of indigenous peoples. Eva Keuls, in *The Reign of the Phallus*, describes the wild sexual practices that Greek historians attributed to their "barbarian" neighbors, the Etruscans.[48] Etruscans were said to have wild drinking parties where men had sex with each other's wives. The Greeks claimed the Egyptians had reversed their gender roles. Women did the selling at the market and urinated standing up, while men stayed home to weave and urinated sitting down. The Greek version of the Marquesans or Mangaians can be found in the Nasamones or Persians. At Nasamones wedding parties, everyone sleeps with the bride, and Persian men have sex with their mothers' sisters and their mothers' sisters' daughters, who would not be considered "blood" relatives in a patrilineal society. Lydian women were said to earn their dowries by prostitution, while Babylonian women must prostitute themselves to a stranger outside the temple of Aphrodite once in their lifetimes. According to Keuls, Herodotus noted that unattractive Babylonian women had to wait for up to four years before they could service a man.

THE AFRICAN PENIS

Perhaps the most exoticized penis in Western culture and ideology is the African penis. This exoticization extends to folk beliefs regarding African American men as well. In 1960, the reclusive Harper Lee published her first book, *To Kill a Mockingbird*, which was awarded the Pulitzer Prize in literature.[49] It was a semiautobiographical novel that was based on an incident in Lee's hometown, Monroeville, Alabama, in the 1930s when she was 10.[50] An African American man had been falsely accused of raping a white woman. The novel not only chronicles the deep cultural prejudice against African Americans in the Deep South but also exemplifies the commonly held stereotype of the black male as sexual predator.

Such stereotypes are very old and still exist today. Cornelius Eady's book of poetry *Brutal Imagination* (2001) recounts the story of Susan Smith from the perspective of an imagined black male perpetrator.[51] Smith was a South Carolina mother of two toddlers who reported in 1994 that she had been "carjacked by a black man."[52] The story immediately captured the public's attention and was all over the media as Smith tearfully pleaded for the return of her children. A nationwide search was begun for this "black man," who was feared to be doing god knows what to her children. After nine days, Smith confessed to murdering her children by putting them into her car and rolling them into a lake. Eady imagines that Smith's tale conjured this "black man" into existence for nine days; but more importantly, he has been conjured many times before. A similar sentiment was expressed 100 years earlier by George T. Winston, president of North Carolina State College of Agriculture and Mechanic Arts, in a publication in the *Annals of the American Academy of Political and Social Science*: "When a knock is heard at the door [a White woman] shudders with nameless horror. The black brute is lurking in the dark, a monstrous beast, crazed with lust. His ferocity is almost demoniacal. A mad bull or tiger would scarcely be more brutal. A whole community is frenzied with horror, with the blind and furious rage for vengeance."[53]

There is perhaps no greater mythology about the penis than that associated with the African penis, and by extension, the African American penis. Early accounts by European adventurers, explorers, and colonial administrators suggest that the African male's penis is big and his brain is small. The suggestion involves a kind of illogic whereby a man's body competes to develop the genitalia versus intelligence.

Unfortunately, this type of pseudo-science is not just a thing of the past. It has been perpetuated in Canadian psychologist J. Phillipe Rushton's *Race, Evolution, and Behavior*.[54] Rushton divides humanity into three broad racial groups: Black, Caucasian, and Oriental. Taking a "Goldilocks" framework, he finds that Caucasians are "just right." The three groups fall into categories labeled as "high," "intermediate," or "low" on a variety of physical and behavioral characteristics. Blacks are "high" for penis size, frequency of intercourse, permissiveness, aggressiveness, impulsivity, and self-concept, while they are "low" for brain size, IQ, mental stability, marital stability, cultural achievements, and abiding by the law. Orientals have the opposite profile, ranking "high" in all areas where blacks rank "low" and ranking "low" where blacks rank "high." Whites rank "intermediate" in all categories except for IQ and cultural achievements, wherein they also rank "high."

Rushton's work has been criticized for using unreliable sources and for misrepresenting the research literature.[55] But the question remains as to whether there really is a significant difference in penis size among the so-called races. Two early studies by sex researchers, one by Kinsey and another by Masters and Johnson, found little difference between black and white penises. The Kinsey Report found that, on average, erect penises of black males were 6.3 inches and white males were 6.2 inches.[56] However, these results may be biased because they had only 59 African American males in their sample compared to over 2,500 white males.[57] The Masters and Johnson study also found a slight difference but with the opposite result: black males averaged 6.2 inches and white males 6.4 inches.[58]

A more recent and comprehensive study (2014) suggests that Kinsey and Masters and Johnson may have overestimated the average length of an erect penis but nonetheless finds very little difference in erect penis size across the so-called races.[59] Herbenick et al. measured the erect penises of over 1,500 US males. They found that the average length was 14.15 centimeters (5.57 inches), with Asian Americans (n = 161) at 14.14 centimeters (5.57 inches), whites (n = 1,685) at 14.18 centimeters (5.58 inches), and black/African Americans (n = 38) at 14.66 centimeters (5.77 inches). The study indicates negligible differences between "whites" and "Asians" and a 0.2-inch difference increase in erect length in African American penises. The bias toward the mean for average penis size is due to the size of the sample groups, with far more whites sampled. In addition, although only eight Hawaiian/Pacific Islanders were sampled, their average erect penis size was the longest, at 14.88 centimeters (5.85 inches).

The studies do not suggest significant differences in penis size among U.S. men. Multiple problems exist with describing humans as belonging to separate biological races. While it is beyond the scope of this work to discuss these problems fully, the following excerpt from the American Anthropological Association demonstrates the biological invalidity of the notion:[60]

In the United States both scholars and the general public have been conditioned to viewing human races as natural and separate divisions within the human species based on visible physical differences. With the vast expansion of scientific knowledge in this century, however, it has become clear that human populations are not unambiguous, clearly demarcated, biologically distinct groups. Evidence from the analysis of genetics (e.g., DNA) indicates that most physical variation, about 94%, lies *within* so-called racial groups. Conventional geographic "racial" groupings differ from one another only in about 6% of their genes. This means that there is greater variation within "racial" groups than between them. In neighboring populations there is much overlapping of genes and their phenotypic (physical) expressions. Throughout history whenever different groups have come into contact, they have interbred. The continued sharing of genetic materials has maintained all of humankind as a single species.

Nonetheless, the perception of the African American male as danger-ously hypersexual with an oversized penis (relative to whites) remains an entrenched folk belief. The fictional trial in Harper Lee's *To Kill a Mocking-bird* was based on the reality that African American males were considered a threat to white women. Although slavery was officially abolished in the United States after the Civil War, racial biases did not change. In the Deep South, and to a lesser extent in the North, the Ku Klux Klan operated as a vigilante justice system, persecuting mainly black males for supposed crimes or simply for the crime of existing as a black male. But without a doubt, key to the Ku Klux Klan's lynching of black males was the belief that they posed a threat to white womanhood. All that was needed to justify the lynching of a black man was a vague accusation that he had made eye contact with a white woman.

In reality, it was not African American males who posed a threat to white women but white males who posed a threat to African American women. White male slave-owners used their positions of power to coerce black female slaves into sexual relationships. DNA evidence suggests than the American founding father Thomas Jefferson fathered the last child of his slave Sally Hemings.[61] Although some have raised the possibility that this was a consen-sual relationship,[62] it unlikely that a woman in a slave relationship with a man could ever really have a free choice.

While the Civil War abolished slavery, it did not abolish the inherent power relations between African Americans and whites. Strom Thurmond provides a case in point. He served as a South Carolina US senator from 1956 until the day he died in 2003, at the age of 100. He made a run for president in 1948 on a segregationist platform, stating in one speech, "I wanna tell you, ladies and gentlemen, that there's not enough troops in the army to force the Southern people to break down segregation and admit the nigger race into our theaters, into our swimming pools, into our homes, and into our churches."[63] Apparently, Thurmond was not as particular about his bedroom as he was his swimming pool. He fathered a child with the family's 16-year-old African American maid in the 1970s.[64] Had this occurred in a later place and time, Thurmond at least could have been prosecuted for statutory rape.

Anthropologist Ann Stoler makes a similar case for the practice of con-cubinage in European colonies in Southeast Asia and Africa.[65] Men would arrive first in the colonies and set up households with an indigenous female, who would be required to cook, clean, and perform sexual services. When their Victorian wives arrived, they had to be protected from the hypersexual male natives, who could not be trusted to control their sexual desires in the presence of a white woman. A Victorian woman was far too alluring and the natives far too primitive to be able to control their sexual urges. Race and sex were bound up with one another, with different rules applying to white men, white women, indigenous men, and indigenous women. A white man could not, technically, rape a native woman. Although she was required to be his sexual servant, this was not considered rape. Beyond that, she had to cook his breakfast and clean his bathroom. But all it took for a native man to receive a public flogging was for someone to *think* that he had looked the wrong way at a white woman. White Victorian women represented extreme purity, while native men were sexually perverse. This, despite the fact that it was white men who were abusing native women, not the other way around.

The cultural imperative to protect white women can still be found in the "Missing White Woman Syndrome," a phrase apparently coined by PBS journalist Gwen Ifill. It refers to the 24/7 news coverage that ensues when a white woman goes missing, particularly if she is young and blonde; no such attention is given to missing women of color or to men. This contrast was first made in the summer of 2005, when white Birmingham, Alabama, teenager Natalee Holloway disappeared on a senior trip to Aruba.[66] Over the summer, there were 1,800 print and broadcast stories on Holloway. That same summer, a young Latina woman, Latoyia Figueroa, also disappeared, but it was not reported at all in the media for nine days. Even then, it apparently received coverage only because an angry blogger wrote into the *Nancy Grace* television show, which addresses American current affairs and criminal justice issues. There are many other examples of media coverage of white women, who are viewed as damsels in distress, but not of women of color. Another example is the constant media coverage of the capture in 2003 of the white Jessica Lynch, a soldier in Iraq; little mention was made of African American Shoshona Johnson, who was captured in the *same* ambush. This is not to suggest that there should not be extreme public concern in any case of abduction, but the point Ifill makes, namely, that ethnicity drives media coverage, is valid.

Two other sources of information that perpetuate racially based penis stereotypes are related websites that purport to provide a map of penis size by country: "World Penis Average Size Database"[67] and "Penis Size Worldwide."[68] The latter provides the base material for the former and claims to provide information from "trusted research centers and reports worldwide." However, it should first be noted that the map is based on circa-1900 outdated and debunked so-called racial categories such as "Mongoloid" and "Caucasoid." The United States is color-coded into three categories: mulatto (black-European), from Texas and the Deep South up through New England, American multiracial (Amerindian, European, Black) in California, and European for the rest of the United States, including Alaska. In this bizarre ethnic grouping, US Native Americans are recognized only in California, Native American Inuit peoples are designated as "Mongoloid," and African American peoples exist only on the West Coast in California, on the East Coast, and in the southern interior in the United States. The big picture is that African penises are large, Euro penises are medium size, and Asian penises are small.

Although detailed statistical information is provided to give the site its scientific cachet, the information is largely irrelevant data on participants in the survey, including such variables as age, shoe size, GDP per capita, and AIDS rate. The critical information necessary for evaluating scientific validity and reliability, namely, variables such as sample size and how individuals were recruited, is not included. Moreover, individuals and affiliations are cited, but no references are provided that demonstrate that the so-called data was accepted in any peer-reviewed publications. Instead, rather vulgar pictures are provided as evidence, with men from various ethnic and geographic affiliations holding and exhibiting their erect penises.

This is again a J. Philippe Rushton–esque reiteration of the Goldilocks narrative that African penises are too big (while their brains too small), Asian penises are too small (while their brains are too big), and Europeans are just right. It suggests the compromise of the European male ideal wherein these men have the good sense not to grow their penises so large as to compromise their intellectual potential (making the African mistake) or so small as to compromise their masculinity (making the Asian mistake). Although this thinking—that African-descended males are hypersexual and underintellectual, while Asian-descended males are hyperintellectual and undersexual— has gained some traction in popular thought, there is no credible scientific evidence that penis size negatively correlates with brain size or intelligence. This is simply foolishness and plays into dangerous, silly, and ill-informed stereotypes.

CONCLUSION

This chapter demonstrates both the lay and scientific exoticization of the penis that have informed some of our contemporary ideas about sexuality and the penis. We separated the realities from the fantasies in accounts of human sexual behavior around the world. Many accounts of the sexuality of non-Western peoples have apparently been invented out of whole cloth by nonanthropologists, poorly trained students, and in some cases reputable researchers, including anthropologists. Such cross-cultural accounts often involve fantastic tales of exotic practices by "primitive Man" and can still be found today in college textbooks and scholarly publications. Although such accounts are often based on sketchy sources, they nonetheless have been presented as facts and perhaps reveal more about the researcher than the culture he or she claims to have studied.

Nakedness is a culturally defined concept; accordingly, there is no hard and fast rule for what is considered an acceptable or unacceptable degree of exposure that applies from one culture to the next. Interestingly, in Western culture, despite our linguistic and ideological bias toward the penis and male genitals (over female genitalia), there are strong taboos about discussing and viewing the penis. This Western paradox fundamentally involves an obsessive and anxious relationship to the body and sexuality.

The term "penis" is dangerous and to be avoided in polite conversation. As a result, our culture has invented hundreds of euphemisms to assist in our discussion of and dealing with this socially sensitive topic. On the other hand, an exploration of the terms we use to refer to the genitalia in males versus females makes it clear there are double standards associated with male and female sexuality in the United States and Western cultures generally. This bias and male preference has been, perhaps unwittingly, extended to the description of reproduction, thus anthropomorphizing the biological processes involved in sex and fertilization. Male sperm are described as strong and powerful in their quest to save the listless unfertilized egg. In the same vein, menstruation has been viewed as a female failure and a waste of fertility. Unfortunately this fiction has long been perpetuated, and we argue that it is part of the patriarchy seen in a range of cultures.

Another fiction lies in many of our ideas about variations in sexuality, which derive from fallacies generated long ago. Our modern understanding of erotic cultures began with the work of early anthropologists in the late nineteenth century and their attempts to explain wild customs that were originally recorded by the explorers and missionaries who first encountered non-Western peoples. The resulting theories about cultural evolution argued that the so-called primitive non-Western peoples were frozen in time and had not achieved the ultimate level of civilization (as represented by Victorian England, for example). Later, the work of Freud seriously influenced the understanding of sexuality, and the Oedipus complex continues to live a long and eventful life as a major character in the interpretation of sexual behaviors and psychology. Tales of exotic-erotic behavior have been passed down over the years and these frequently find their way into textbooks and popular culture.

Tendencies to exoticize the other are found in most cultures. These tendencies are widespread and are certainly not limited to Western characterizations of indigenous peoples. In our own culture the penis of an African or African American man is the most dangerous and exotic of all. In her recent article "Who's Afraid of Black Sexuality?" historian Stacey Patton argues, "If sex was once difficult to discuss openly, black sex was especially fraught. It touched on too many taboos: stereotypes and caricatures of 'black Hottentots' . . . lascivious Jezebels; of hypersexual black men lusting after white women."[69] While the old taboos are falling away among academics, this shift has yet to fully impact popular culture and the average American. Many people still hold spurious beliefs that black men have significantly larger penises than do men from other so-called races. While there is no data to support this assumption, it is still perpetuated and has connections with deep-rooted racist stereotypes. As with the other elements of sexuality we have discussed in this book, there is a tension between our fascination with the subject and our anxiety about it.

6

The Domesticated Penis

The Phallus and the Future

Today, modern technologies for modifying the penis have moved far beyond superincision, circumcision, and subincision. Surgical penis enlargements and implants make possible significant increases in size or rigidity. Drugs such as Viagra are available to improve male performance or to treat a condition known as "erectile dysfunction." Sex-change operations create penises for biological females or turn penises into vaginas for biological males.

In addition, human technology can have indirect side effects on the penis. A recent serious concern is the effect of the growing number of "environmental estrogens" on male sexuality and fertility. Environmental estrogens are synthetic chemicals that are by-products of industrial processes, which can accumulate in the air, water, and soils. High concentrations of environmental estrogens in water have caused sex reversals in fish, feminizing males. In addition, environmental estrogens have been implicated in lowering testosterone levels and sperm counts in human males across the globe.

Cultural change proceeds more rapidly than does evolutionary change. In human history, it took millions of years for sex to evolve from a simple act of biological reproduction to a human expression of sociality and sexuality. Even within the last 10,000 years, we have archaeological and ethnographic evidence of cultural diversification and of a wide range of human cultural attitudes toward the penis and human sexuality in general. Within the last 50 years, we have developed technologies that can chemically and surgically alter human biology. As such, the domestication of the penis remains a story that is very much ongoing.

How Does Penis Size Matter?

Contemporary pop cultural American beliefs seem to take it for granted that, for male humans anyway, the bigger the penis, the better. As we have seen, both cross-culturally and in the history of Western society, larger penises have not necessarily been valued over smaller ones. Nonetheless, in much of American society and much of the Western world, the very clear cultural message communicated and broadcast everywhere is that a large penis is a sign of superior masculinity.

We receive this message from multiple sources. Pornography, which is disproportionately marketed to and consumed by males,[1] features men with large, and sometimes extraordinarily long and thick, penises. The late pornography star John Holmes claimed to have the biggest penis in the world, with reports varying from 13.5 to 15 inches long.[2] Daniel Mead, aka "Long Dong Silver," was reported to have an 18-inch penis, although his penis was later revealed to be a prosthetic.[3] While the legendary accounts of both were exaggerations, as all legends are, they also contained some truth. Here, the truth is that the myth belies male desire to possess the ultimate penis. It is notable that the market for women's pornography is growing,[4] especially the market for erotica. E. L. James's novel *Fifty Shades of Grey* (2011), dubbed "mommy porn," was the fastest selling paperback of all time.[5] However, wide gender differences still exist in the consumption of pornography.

Advertising for penis enlargement intrudes upon us whether we wish to see it or not. While we now have fairly effective programs for blocking spam e-mails, there was a time when we had to manually block variations of the word "penis," such as "pen!s," "pen1s," and "p3nis," to avoid receiving unwanted solicitations to enlarge our penises, whether we are male or female, a child or an adult. Jokes about penis size are not only a staple of bawdy late-night comic routines but also pervade daytime talk shows and prime-time sitcoms. In our culture it is almost impossible *not* to get the message that men should have really big penises. The other side of the coin is the message that men whose penises are of average size are in fact not average but somewhat lacking. Men with smaller-than-average penises are to be pitied as inferior males.

Based on at the broad evolutionary picture, we argue that size does matter in terms of the evolution of the human penis, but it is relevant only from the standpoint of primate comparative anatomy. This is to say, the general size, shape, and performance of the human penis are critically important in understanding human evolution, but minor differences in the size of individual males' penises are less important. An analogy for this can be found in our Western cultural proclivity for large breasts in females. In both cases, it is important that we understand that we are looking at an aesthetic of a cultural moment. We need not exaggerate this sentiment and embue it with long-term evolutionary significance, for which there is simply no evidence. What human female choice selected for was a different kind of penis.

Nonetheless, there are always real-time consequences for any belief that a culture may hold. What a person believes to be true is not merely in his or her head but is acted upon in daily life and incorporated into identity and behavior. Contemporary psychological studies in Western societies do reflect the perceived relationship between penis size and masculinity. However, these attitudes are more pronounced in men than in women. If a large penis endowed males with an evolutionary advantage, we would expect to find that women are at least as concerned with the penis size of their partners as men are with comparing penis sizes. However, one recent large survey of heterosexual men and women found that 85 percent of women were satisfied with their partner's penis size, whereas 45 percent of men wanted to have larger penises.[6]

Urologists have coined the psychological term "small penis syndrome" to describe contemporary Western male anxiety that their penises are insufficient, despite falling well within the normal range.[7] Such unrealistic beliefs are as much a culture-bound syndrome as the more exoticized koro and penis-snatching beliefs in South Asia and Africa. They are all cut from the same cloth: cultural beliefs that not only erode our sense of worthiness but also motivate us into extreme action to remedy our flaws.

Two more familiar, contemporary culture-bound syndromes in Western society are male extreme bodybuilding and female self-starvation (i.e., anorexia nervosa), whereby males try to be as big as possible and females try to be as small as possible. Some males resort to testicle-shrinking, rage-inducing anabolic steroids to artificially pump themselves up.[8] Some females resort to starving and exercising themselves nearly (or actually) to death in order to become as thin and small as possible.[9] While we can rationalize these disorders as afflictions of a minority of psychologically disordered individuals, we cannot rationalize away the fact that these extreme behaviors reflect entrenched cultural beliefs. More to the point for our purposes here, contemporary male Western cultural beliefs value a penis that is physically larger than the norm and exhibits a puberty-like level of responsiveness. Outside of surgical intervention, it is extremely difficult to change one's penis size. But the desire to do so is strong enough to support a healthy market for penis enhancement, which entails, essentially, bogus advertising. While nonsurgical attempts to alter penis size are sketchy at best, penis performance can be altered with mechanical or chemical interventions.

VIAGRA NATION

The term "erectile dysfunction" is now well established in the common Western vernacular. Statistics suggest that some 30 million American men describe themselves as suffering from some form of erectile dysfunction.[10] While many men experience erectile dysfunction as an associated symptom of diabetes, coronary artery disease, or other health issues,[11] increasingly declining sexual function is associated with increasing age.[12] One causative factor is the naturally occurring decrease in testosterone levels as men age.[13] As such, erectile dysfunction can also be considered a culture-bound syndrome because in modern Western society we have raised the bar to a new normal for men. Attitudes have changed so that it is no longer considered natural for men's sexual function to decline with age; rather the cultural expectation is for men to maintain the performance levels that they had in their youth. If they cannot, Viagra and other drugs provide a solution to this newly recognized medical problem in Western society.

In 1998, the FDA approved Viagra as a treatment for erectile dysfunction (ED). By the end of that year, Viagra's manufacturer, Pfizer, hired Bob Dole for a television advertising campaign to promote the drug.[14] He was an excellent choice. Since he was the 1996 Republican nominee for president, he was immediately recognizable to the American public. Dole also held the distinction of being the second oldest presidential party nominee, at age 73 years and 1 month, just 5 months younger than Ronald Reagan.[15] Although Dole lost his presidential bid, he was a well-known public figure who had demonstrated his ability as a senior citizen to stand toe-to-toe with a rival nearly 30 years his junior. Dole helped Pfizer and Viagra reframe erectile dysfunction as an everyday problem that any man could face and conquer. However, Dole was not just any man: He was man who was a heartbeat away from becoming the leader of the free world. His long-term marriage to Elizabeth Dole certainly helped, since she was already an accomplished political figure in her own right, serving in the administrations of Nixon, Reagan, and George H. W. Bush, as well as serving as the president of the American Red Cross. Pfizer had indeed enlisted the ideal power couple to market their product. Bob Dole discussed erectile dysfunction openly and frankly, with no hint of embarrassment or shame. Although Elizabeth receives only a vague reference in Bob Dole's commercials, which describe ED as being an issue for men and their partners, the credentials of this particular partner loomed large.

By 2003, in just five short years, Viagra sales had reached 1.7 billion dollars and Viagra had been prescribed to six million men.[16] That figure likely underestimates the actual number of users and sales of Viagra because it does not include the ensuing robust Internet sales. It has been estimated that Internet-based pharmacies sell 2.3 million tablets per month; however, approximately 40 percent of those pills are counterfeit.[17] Between 2005 and 2008, 35.8 million counterfeit Viagra tablets were seized in Europe.[18] In 2010, an unprecedented step was taken in the United Kingdom to thwart the Internet market with the licensing of the supermarket chain Tesco to sell Viagra in 300 of its pharmacies without a prescription.[19] Whether the Viagra was legally prescribed or sold on the Internet, legitimate or placebo, sales boomed.

Before Viagra and its cogeners, treatment for what became known as ED relied primarily on prostheses and mechanical devices to induce erection. One of the earliest descriptions of penile prostheses dates from the sixteenth century. The French surgeon Ambrose Pare described the construction of an artificial penis from a wood pipe for individuals whose penises had been amputated.[20] The first penile implant was developed by the Russian surgeon Bogoraz in 1936 using rib cartilage to splint the penis, but the effectiveness of the procedure was temporary owing to the natural resorption of the bone material.[21] Innovations to Bogoraz's method, such as acrylic rods and inflatable devices, were introduced.[22]

In the early twentieth century, vacuum pumps were developed as a remedy for male sexual dysfunction. The concept of a negative-pressure vacuum pump originated with the physician John King, who described the use of a glass exhauster to produce an artificial erection. King's device, however, failed to sustain an erection once the device was removed.[23] The first effective vacuum constriction device was patented in 1917 by Otto Lederer, but this device did not become commercially available until 1974, when Geddins D. Osbon introduced his "youth equivalent device" called NuPotent, subsequently marketed in 1982 as ErecAid.[24] Many similar devices were soon marketed, all of which work using a vacuum chamber, a pump to produce negative pressure, and constriction rings.[25]

Also, just prior to the invention of Viagra, drug treatments using prostaglandins were introduced. In 1997, the prostaglandin transurethral suppository, MUSE, was marketed that worked by relaxing the smooth muscles of the penis to facilitate an erection.[26] A similar product, Caverject, was also a prostaglandin-based intervention, but it involved directly injecting the medication into the penis.[27]

With the simpler solution of Pfizer's so-called little blue pill, sales of MUSE and Caverject waned almost immediately.[28] Between 1998 and 2001, sales for Caverject dropped 33 percent and sales for MUSE dropped 67 percent.[29] Studies among users of both products suggest that men who took Viagra have higher satisfaction rates than those who use MUSE or Caverject.[30] However, Pfizer's Viagra began to face serious competition in 2003 with the introduction of two new ED drugs, Cialis and Levitra. One recent study found that among patients using Cialis (tadalafil) who switched to Viagra and patients using Viagra who switched to Cialis, Cialis was preferred.[31] Regardless of the particular drug of choice, the introduction of Viagra in 1997 was a watershed event.

Erectile dysfunction can indeed be a medical disorder affecting men with a wide variety of biological and psychological health issues. Nonetheless, research demonstrates that the bulk of ED identifiers are those experiencing the natural and age-related decline in male sexual responsiveness and performance. Viagra and other ED drugs provide men with a chemically induced fountain of youth; for as long as the drug is active in their systems, it can simulate their adolescent sexual responsiveness. Male cultural behaviors that alter sexual function are not limited to sexual performance enhancement. With the advent of new technologies, men are able to alter sexuality in new ways.

Castration and Sex Reassignment

While sex-reassignment surgery is a relatively recent phenomenon, castration has a long history in the ancient world. It has been estimated that hundreds of thousands of men were castrated in the Byzantine empire, the Ottoman empire, Chinese dynasties, and in Greco-Roman antiquity.[32] Castrated men most frequently worked as servants to royalty or the elite. The term "eunuch" derives from the Greek word for "bed" and refers to the early role of eunuchs in guarding the bedchambers of aristocrats.[33] In China, the role of the eunuch may have originated as an alternative for the death penalty.[34] In the nineteenth-century Ottoman empire, the African slave trade included castrating men who served as household servants.[35]

Voluntary castration has also been practiced for religious and other purposes. In Italy, from the latter half of the sixteenth century through the end of the nineteenth century, and particularly with the rise of the Italian opera, prepubescent boys were castrated to retain a high soprano and contralto voice.[36] Castrated boys who did not demonstrate musical ability were relegated to the priesthood.[37] The Skoptsy Christian sect, which emerged in late-eighteenth-century Russia, mandated male castration to control sexual urges.[38] Somewhat similarly, in Byzantine society, natural eunuchs were revered because it was believed that God had freed them from the sinfulness of sex.[39]

It should also be noted here that the precise meaning of what is translated or described in the older literature as a "eunuch" or person who has been castrated is not always clear. Even today, the term "castration" is used ambiguously to refer to orchiectomy (removal of the testicles, with or without retention of the scrotal sac), penectomy (removal of the penis), or altered sexual function such as chemical castration for sex offenders.[40] While the term "eunuch" most often refers to someone who has undergone an orchiectomy, "eunuch" may also refer to someone who is impotent or celibate.

Voluntary castration occurs today in a variety of contexts. As a pathology, it is called "genital self-mutilation" (GSM) or sometimes "Klingsor Syndrome," after the magician in Wagner's opera who castrated himself in an attempt to gain acceptance into the order of the Knights of the Holy Grail.[41] Genital self-mutilation is relatively uncommon, with males far outnumbering females, however, the rates may be increasing. Between 1900 and 1977 only 51 cases were reported, whereas by 1996 110 had been reported.[42]

Perhaps the best documented example comes from the *hijras* of India, which have been described in anthropologist Serena Nanda's ethnography *Neither Man Nor Woman*.[43] The *hijras* are an institutionalized third gender in Indian society who are devotees of the Bahuchara Mata, an aspect of the Hindu mother goddess. The term *hijra* comes from the Arabic term *ijara*, which means "eunich" or "castrated male." There is no analogue for *hijras* in Western society, for the gender role includes those born with ambiguous sexual anatomy, homosexual men, impotent or infertile men, and, less commonly, infertile women. According to Nanda, a defining characteristic of a *hijra* is sexual impotence. Hijras have an important ritual function in Indian society, which they perform in homes after the birth of a male child and at weddings, to bestow blessings. As a rite of passage, those born biologically male undergo surgical emasculation (removal of genitalia), which is considered to be the source of their ritual power. Recently, the Supreme Court of India recognized transgendered persons as an official third-gender category.[44] As such, the law protects enuchs, transgender people, and *hijras* from discrimination.

Cross-culturally, apart from ritual contexts, most clinically documented cases of men who remove or mutilate their genitals have been found to be suffering from psychosis[45] or an organic brain disorder.[46] In animals, penis self-mutilation has been reported in laboratory mice (8.5 percent of the population in one group)[47] and in canine separation anxiety.[48] Human GSM has also been documented in association with the abuse of substances such as cannabis,[49] methamphetamine,[50] and angel's trumpet (*Dadura sanguinea*)[51] and with delirium tremens during alcohol withdrawal.[52] Several cases of penectomy as a form of suicide attempt have been documented.[53] Other rarer causes are misguided self-treatment for scrotal hematoma and[54] self-incontinence[55] and personality disorders.[56] In one unusual case, the precipitating cause for a man of borderline intelligence who cut off his penis with a chain saw was allegedly massive media exposure to the Lorena Bobbitt case.[57] As previously described, Lorena Bobbitt cut off her husband's penis.

Second to psychiatric illness, GSM is most often found with what has been called Skoptic syndrome, in reference to the Russian sect.[58] Here, GSM occurs owing to guilt over the compulsion to masturbate or to a desire to control sexual urges that are believed to be morally wrong.[59] It occurs not only among Christians but also in a variety of religious contexts. There is one report of a Hindu man who performed a self-penectomy to avoid an arranged marriage out of fear that his erectile dysfunction would be exposed.[60]

A grayer area lies in cases of GSM in individuals with "gender identity disorder." Although many argue that this should not be considered a disorder, it was first characterized in the *DSM-III* in 1980 as a condition involving persistent cross-gender identification or discomfort with one's sex or the gender role for one's sex.[61] A number of cases have been documented of transgendered persons removing or mutilating their testicles because they were unable to obtain sexual reassignment surgery due to cost, time delay, incarceration, or medical/psychiatric ineligibility.[62]

Gender identity is complicated, involving a complex of cultural, historical, and biological factors. While it is far beyond the scope of this book to treat gender identity adequately, a few points should be addressed that are relevant to this work. In popular speech, the terms "sex" and "gender" are often used interchangeably. But in the social sciences, "sex" refers to one's biology while "gender" refers to one's role in a given culture or society. For the majority of people, sex is determined by one of two chromosome patterns: XX, for females, or XY, for males. However, chromosomal variations may occur in karyotypes including Turner's Syndrome (X0), Klinefelter's Syndrome (XXY), triple-X (XXX), and XYY.[63] Endocrine disorders such as congenital adrenal hyperplasia may masculinize XX females,[64] while androgen insensitivity may feminize XY males.[65] Much more rarely, individuals are intersexed as XXYY.[66]

Gender *roles* are much more fluid and changeable, both cross-culturally and over time. Nonetheless, gender theorist Judith Butler and others have characterized Western society as having a rather rigid gender binary whereby male and female gender roles have historically fallen into mutually exclusive categories of accepted masculine and feminine behaviors.[67] Gender identity disorder is a recognized diagnosis by the American Psychiatric Association wherein individuals feel that their biological sexual anatomy does not match their gender identity.[68] Modern medical technology has allowed for such individuals to undergo sex-reassignment surgery.

Magnus Hirschfield performed the first sex-reassignment surgery in Berlin over 100 years ago, in 1912.[69] Since that time, medical procedures have been developed and standardized, and they have become more widely available to those seeking sex reassignment. Surgical procedures for male-to-female (mtf) sex reassignment may include removal of the bulk of the penis, removal of the scrotum and testicles, breast augmentation, and construction of a simulated vulva, clitoris, and vagina.[70] Female-to-male (ftm) operative procedures include mastectomy, vaginectomy, and the creation of a simulated scrotum and penis.[71] Both mtf and ftm sex reassignment also involve hormone therapy to foster characteristics such as mammary development, facial and other hair growth, and respective male/female muscular development and body fat deposition ratios.[72] Other procedures to alter masculine or feminine appearance include simulating male/female body hair patterns through electrolysis or body hair implants and facial plastic surgery or transdermal injections to masculinize or feminize features.[73] Larger scale skeletal differences are more difficult to change. While there is a degree of variability in any chromosomal male or female, height and hip structure are substantially irreversible.

Two interesting statistics have emerged from the research on sexual reassignment surgery and procedures. One is that, overwhelmingly, most who undergo sex change surgery express satisfaction with the results.[74] Where dissatisfaction occurs, it mostly involves functional and mechanical postoperative genito-urinary difficulties or disappointment at not obtaining the desired result in sexual performance and functioning. Regret over having undergone sexual reassignment is rare. The second curious statistic is that three-fourths of sexual reassignment surgeries are male-to-female type.[75] We do not think it is too sweeping a generalization to suggest that today, cross-culturally, males have greater prestige, political authority, and general power than females do. From a purely cost-benefit analysis, it would seem that chromosomal females would have more to gain in becoming male than males would in becoming female. Paradoxically, one reason may be that there is greater stigma in Western society for males taking on a more feminine gender role than for females taking on a more masculine gender role. Because there is less stigma, there may be fewer social consequences for what is considered masculine behavior; this may provide females with greater flexibility in gender roles than males have. One example is that a boy who is called a sissy experiences greater social rejection than a girl who is called a tomboy.[76] Sissy and tomboy are not equivalent terms. Sissy is clearly a derogatory term for a male child who is not considered to be sufficiently masculine; tomboy is more neutral, describing a female child who enjoys stereotypical activities of boys.

Although male-to-female and female-to-male sexual reassignment procedures are relatively widespread and considered medically legitimate, a third form of procedure is emerging: male-to-eunuch (mte). Historically and cross-culturally, as previously described, eunuchs were largely individuals who were demasculinized either as children or against their will as adults. Most of the information on modern eunuchs is anecdotal or scattered in case studies.[77] However, this procedure is not common enough to prompt a discussion of the development of standards of care for individuals with a male-to-eunuch identity disorder.[78] In addition, the Eunuch Archive is a website founded in 1997 that serves as a resource and community for anyone interested in castration.[79] One study identified the term "eunuch calm" as a desire for castration, which permits freedom from sexual urges and feelings of aggression.[80] The male eunuch may be emerging as a new gender in Western society.

UNNATURAL SELECTION

Broadly, artificial selection involves the intentional (typically) human breeding of plants and animals to produce desirable traits. Today, increasingly more deleterious characteristics are being created due to the introduction of contaminants into the environment, which is, arguably, a process of "unnatural selection." Some of the unintended side effects of advances in human technology are the by-products that are created. The air, soil, and water on our planet are becoming increasingly saturated with chemicals and synthetic substances that have the potential to adversely affect not only our health but also the biology of other species on our planet. One of the most dangerous categories of pollutants are persistent organic pollutants (POPs), which can stay in the environment indefinitely. Some of the effects of these chemicals are known, but the long-term effects of many are not. To give one example, in the mid-twentieth century, dichlorodiphenyltrichloroethane (DDT) was used widely as a crop insecticide. Beginning in 1955, the World Health Organization began a global malaria eradication program relying on the use of DDT.[81] Due to what is referred to as the "grasshopper's effect," through rain and evaporation, DDT has spread far from its initial area of use; it has been detected in polar bears, penguins, and even the breast milk of Inuit women.[82]

One of the disturbing effects of the chemicals polluting our environment is their potential to affect reproductive anatomy and functioning. A serious problem is the accumulation of environmental estrogens, which have been implicated in both decreased sperm quality and increased disorders of the male reproductive tract.[83] Environmental estrogens, called "exogenous estrogens" or "xenoestrogens," are chemicals that imitate biological estrogen and can disrupt endocrine function. They either have an estrogen-like effect or substitute for estrogen and block natural biological estrogen; in effect, they can either masculinize or feminize organisms. Xenoestrogens are found in a wide variety of synthetic compounds including pesticides,[84] plastic water bottles,[85] food cans,[86] and body-care cosmetics.[87] In one research site, a population of alligators living in a lake contaminated with xenoestrogens (DDT and dicofol) produced females with abnormalities in ovarian morphology and male alligators with small phalluses and abnormal testes.[88]

The simpler forms of life are the most vulnerable to environmental estrogens. One particularly well-documented effect is found in sea snails contaminated with a chemical called tri-n-butyltin (TBT). The compound TBT has been used widely in antifouling paints.[89] Antifouling paints are applied to the hulls of boats to prevent the growth of barnacles, algae, and other sea life. Numerous species of aquatic snails (gastropods) exposed to TBT have developed a condition called "imposex" wherein females develop male sex organs (a penis and vas deferens).[90] The phenomenon of imposex has been reported in the waters of North America,[91] Europe and the Mediterranean,[92] Asia,[93] South America,[94] Africa,[95] and Australia.[96] Imposex females do not become males but develop both male and female reproductive anatomy. The growth of a penis and vas deferens interferes with the normal development of female reproductive anatomy, and these females become sterile, which threatens the survival of the snail populations. In addition, there is some evidence that TBT may affect the metabolism of sex hormones in humans.[97]

In a number of fish species, exposure to environmental estrogens has caused the development of males who are intersexed (having both male and female gonadal tissue) or who display inhibited testicular growth. Exposure to wastewater from sewage treatment plants has led to an increase in the frequency of intersex in fish such as the white sucker in the United States (*Catostomus commersoni*),[98] the roach fish (*Rutilus rutilus*)[99] and gudgeons (*Gobio gobio*)[100] in the United Kingdom, barbells (*Barbus plebejus*) in Italy,[101] and carp (*Cyprinus carpio*) in Spain.[102] In two UK sites near wastewater, 100 percent of the male roach fish (*Rutilus rutilus*) were intersexed.[103] Other pollutants such as mill pulp, municipal waste, and agricultural runoff have caused abnormalities including intersexuality, reduced gonad growth, and reduced plasma sex steroids in lake whitefish (*Coregonus clupeaformis*), perch (*Perca fluviatilis*), white suckers (*Catostomus commersoni*) in Canada,[104] and catfish (*Clarias gariepinus*) in South Africa.[105] Similar reproductive abnormalities have been seen in fishes with experimental exposure to estrogens, including European chub (*Leuciscus cephalus*),[106] coho salmon (*Oncorhynchus kisutch*),[107] rainbow trout (*Oncorhynchus mykiss*),[108] and the fathead minnow (*Pimephales promelas*).[109]

While the exposure of fishes to endocrine-disrupting substances has resulted in masculine females, in amphibian populations feminization of males has been documented. Such disruptions affect mating patterns and can lead to population decline. Many studies have documented and expressed concerns about a general global decline in amphibian populations.[110] A number of factors have been implicated in this general population decline, including infectious disease, climate change, habitat loss, and pollution. One concern has been the possibility that the widely used herbicide atrazine is causing reproductive abnormalities in amphibian males. Atrazine is a POP and one of the world's most heavily used pesticides.[111] Today, atrazine is found in soils, seawater, freshwater, groundwater, and drinking water all over the world including in North America,[112] South America,[113] Europe,[114] Asia,[115] Africa,[116] and Australia.[117]

Both experimental and field studies have demonstrated that reproductive abnormalities cause reduced testicular volume, reduced testosterone levels, retarded gonadal development, or intersexed males in several species of amphibians and mammals The "intersexed" or "hermaphroditic" male refers to what might better be called "pseudohermaphroditism." Here, a chromosomal male develops both male and female gonadal tissue. In review articles, some controversy surrounds the weight of the evidence demonstrating that atrazine can cause reproductive abnormalities at low levels of exposure.[118] Nonetheless, species where male abnormalities have been documented with atrazine exposure include the African clawed frog (*Xenopus laevis*),[119] the American/northern leopard frog (*Rana pipiens*),[120] the cricket frog (*Acris crepitans*),[121] and the green frog (*Rana clamitans*).[122] It is unclear what affects atrazine may have on humans. In rats, several studies have documented the disruption of prolactin and luteinizing hormones that regulate ovarian cycles, with exposure to this chemical.[123] There is also some evidence that atrazine may contribute to insulin resistance in the United States.[124]

In humans, the effects of environmental estrogens and other pollutants are not completely understood. It is known that many male reproductive disorders originate in utero with the exposure of the mother to exogenous estrogens and antiandrogens.[125] Several studies have associated air pollution with changes in sperm quality.[126] But perhaps most disturbing is information from a 1992 study that found that over the last 50 years from the time of the study, semen quality has decreased in human males worldwide.[127] In addition to sperm quality, other changes in male reproductive health include a rising incidence of testicular cancer, increasing frequencies of undescended testicles, and congenital hypospadias, wherein the urethra opens on the underside rather than at the end of the penis.[128] Again, we do not know how the environmental pollutants will ultimately affect the fate of human reproduction, but there is sufficient evidence for all of us to be extremely concerned.

CONCLUSION

In this chapter we explored the various ways in which the long process of domesticating the penis continues today. Human biocultural evolution involves changes in human biology and that of other species, as well as countless cultural and social developments. Our cultural behaviors and biological makeup have changed together over time. Moreover, our species is uniquely capable of significantly altering the biological makeup of the world around us. Our choices and technologies have an impact on a complex web of life that inhabits the planet with us. Unfortunately, some of our technologies and choices have negatively affected life on earth, including our own humankind.

Technological innovations in Western society to alter the penis have been documented since the sixteenth century and continue today with modern medical advances that enable men to enlarge their penises or enhance performance through chemical and mechanical means. The newly described Western condition of erectile dysfunction may be best understood from the anthropological perspective of a culture-bound syndrome. Although it is natural for men's sexual drive and function to decline with age, in our culture, this has become stigmatized, and it is increasingly a medical issue that demands attention.

Although castration has deep historical roots in a range of human cultures, sex reassignment surgery is a relatively new development. Both castration and sex-reassignment surgery alter or manipulate a person's body, genitals, and sexual abilities and activities. Bodily manipulation is a topic we have touched on frequently in this text, and we argue for its interpretation as a form of domestication. In some situations self-mutilation has been viewed as a pathology, as in cases of people suffering from psychosis or substance abuse. Extreme forms of body modification, including compulsive attention to specific areas of the body, may be a sign of body dysmorphic disorder (BDD), a mental illness that causes a person to become excessively concerned with perceived defects in their physical appearance.[129] However, some so-called disorders may explain more about a dominant cultural ideology concerning what is appropriate or inappropriate than about behaviors that truly create distress for the person engaging in them. Common forms of body modification such as plastic surgery or genital implants may be considered appropriate interventions that make the body look as the media tells us it should. However, if we do not necessarily privilege Western normative concepts of the body, we might view these behaviors as anxiety-driven excessive preoccupations with one's appearance (a form of BDD). Are cultural icons such as Michael Jackson, Mickey Rourke, Joan Rivers, and Cher, who have engaged in extensive plastic surgery and dieting, setting standards for American attractiveness or disfiguring themselves in the name of perfection?

In our culture there is a simultaneous anxiety about and fascination with the topics of sex and the penis. This is expressed in our contradictory mode of splashing sexuality across all forms of media while we express polite discomfort with open discussions surrounding the topic. Moreover, the word "penis" and its subject provoke especially hazardous sentiments. This response is partially due to Christian influences on our ideas about sexuality and the devilish potential of the penis, which must be controlled to maintain order, morality, and decorum. Of course these ideas are changing now, and with the help of products like Viagra, men are modifying their penises to make their organs serve their masters, rather than the other way around.

Epilogue

In these pages, we have presented an anthropological history of the penis that incorporates evidence from evolutionary theory, primatology, archaeology, and cultural anthropology. It is obvious that the human penis, when compared with that of our primate cousins, is unique in terms of its size, shape, and ability to prolong sexual activity while remaining erect. However, most discussions of human sexuality and evolution have long ignored one of the most intriguing aspects of the evolution of the human penis, that is, the role of female choice. Female choice has shaped the penis, in the process of domesticating it, and thus contributed to both the biological and cultural evolution of our species. Moreover, the human penis appears to have evolved for social sex rather than for strictly reproductive purposes. This argument sheds new light on the idea that alpha males, being aggressive and dominant, are able to mate with more females and produce more offspring. The alpha-male myth is debunked by the weight of data, which illustrates that cooperation, empathy, and positive social interactions convey advantageous reproductive success to individuals and groups.

Throughout this book we have emphasized several themes, including the role of female mate selection with an emphasis on social sex; the connection between agricultural practices and the rise of penis cults; the connection between an ideology of male dominance and elaborate phallus imagery as an expression of male control, in addition to other meanings; and the future of our relationship with the penis. From a historical perspective, it appears that the social roles of males and females shifted in association with, and perhaps as a result of, the development of agriculture. Gradual systematic changes in food production, society, and culture are evidenced in archaeological, ethnohistoric, and ethnographic data. For the majority of humanity, over time, the hunting and gathering and egalitarian way of life was replaced by one of elaborate food production. Males became associated with ownership of land, and, in some contexts, of people. Patriarchy and male control of the dominant political and public social spheres appear to have become increasingly common after the adoption of full-scale agriculture. Our review of data from around the globe provides ample evidence to support the notion that deep-rooted and pervasive connection exists between penis cults and agricultural societies.

While our cross-cultural investigation cannot examine all the specifics associated with each culture, ethnic group, gender, time, and place, we do find a pattern of cultural expressions, themes, and symbols. Phallic imagery, material culture, and written records of the past relating to phallocentrism are abundant. These varied lines of evidence suggest connections between concepts of domestication, fertility, creation, the legitimacy of rulers, and public expressions of masculine power. Another theme that appears in many cultural contexts is expressed as the opposition between male and female. We see widespread evidence from places as far-flung as Cambodia, Mexico, and Rome that social institutions drew power and support from phallic imagery that privileged masculine expressions. Daily reminders of masculine power appeared in religious rituals, texts, charms, and quotidian domestic objects. The phallus was also memorialized in elements of the landscape and as part of monumental architecture. In some cases, as in the Classic Mayan iconography of the Yucatán, shared cultural symbols of the phallus may have been a response to social and environmental stresses. In places such as ancient Egypt and Japan, the phallic symbol had clear associations with fertility, resurrection, and social order. While as symbols the penis and the phallus convey varied meanings in different cultural contexts, themes of bodily transformation, male versus female, phallic power, and both the natural and domesticated worlds are common. We argue that cultures focused on these subjects in the process of building and sustaining social institutions.

We have explored the way that ethnographically recorded cultural customs associated with the penis may be understood through the concept of the extended phenotype. Our review suggests that an ideology of patriarchy frequently appears when cross-cultural phallicism, rituals, and religion are examined. The penis is often a significant component of rituals, rites of passage, and mythological stories. This is evident in the practices of penis sheathing and modification and in the bullroarer complex. These customs domesticate the penis by altering it in culturally appropriate ways. Some practices are motivated by masculine anxiety and perhaps are efforts to ensure patriarchy and male superiority or power, as evidenced by modes of penis manipulation and accounts of penis theft and loss. As we have seen in the archaeological, ethnographic, and ethnohistoric records, phallic imagery and explicit expressions of maleness are related to male power and social position. By memorializing critical events with phallic imagery and rituals, those with power, and even those without power, reiterate the socially dominant role of males.

Although we argue that female choice shaped the evolution of the penis, in many cultures the phallus has been symbolically associated with power, masculinity, ownership, and control. Given the likelihood that females actually directed the evolution of our species with mate selection, the ideological position of the penis is somewhat surprising. Perhaps in the future we will follow the lead of our primate cousins the bonobos. Perhaps we will begin to act on the understandings that making peace is more productive than making war and that expressions of dominance and power are often less effective than empathy, compassion, and cooperation.

Notes

Chapter 1

1. Darwin (1871).
2. Gerhardt et al. (2000).
3. Wiber (1997).
4. Baumeister (2010).
5. Gray (1992).
6. McLean et al. (2010).
7. Herzing (2011).
8. Resko et al. (1996).
9. Hunter and Davis (1998).
10. de Waal and Lanting (1997), 105.
11. Grossman (2010).
12. Alam (2009), 25; and Hackworth and Akers (2010), 43.
13. Weaver (2005).
14. Rosenbaum (2009).
15. Grayson and Meltzer (2003); Koch and Barnosky (2006); Martin and Klein (1989); and Stuart (1999). Currently, the debate is falling in favor of environmental change over the human overkill hypothesis, although the two hypotheses are not necessarily mutually exclusive.
16. Baker (2008); Gignoux, Henn, and Mountain (2011); and Rosenberg (1990).
17. Some debate exists as to the extent of violence, particularly "warfare," in hunting and gathering societies (e.g., Ember 1978; Fry 2007, 2012; Pinker 2011; van der Dennen 2007; Wrangham and Peterson 1996; Wrangham and Glowacki 2012; Wrangham and Peterson 1996). Nonetheless, there is general agreement that there is a qualitative difference between hunter-gatherer violence and organized warfare.
18. Bittocchi et al. (2012); Merrill et al. (2009); Piperno and Flannery (2001); Smith (1997).
19. Huang et al. (2012); Lee et al. (2007); and Wong et al. (2004).
20. Bollongino et al. (2012); Kijas et al. (2012); and Luo et al. (2007).

21. Mirren (2011).
22. Leach (2003). Note that Leach focuses on artificial built environments that humans have created and on the outcome of sedentary lifestyles associated with the domestication of plants and animals. She posits that a shift in diet and decreased mobility are both responsible for morphological changes, specifically, decreases in body, brain, facial, and dental sizes. According to her argument, the morphological changes are evident in both humans and domestic animals.

Chapter 2

1. Darwin (1859); and Darwin and Wallace (1858).
2. Darwin (1871).
3. Darwin (1871), 570.
4. Milam (2010), 9.
5. Hrdy (1981); and Miller (1998).
6. Birkhead, Lee, and Young (1988); and Arnqvist and Henriksson (1997).
7. Murai (2006); and Schultz (1942).
8. Thorén, Lindenfors, and Kappeler (2006).
9. Galdikas (1983); and Mitani (1985). Fisher's (1915) term "runaway selection" describes a process by which a female's preference for male ornamentation can lead to a positive feedback process whereby increasingly exaggerated ornaments are selected for, even at a cost to males, such as bright feathers that make males more visible to predators.
10. Vanpé et al. (2007).
11. Grafen (1990); and Zahavi (1975).
12. Nell (2002).
13. Budras, Sack, and Röck (2011).
14. Slijper (1966).
15. Brennan et al. (2007).
16. Beja-Pereira et al. (2003); Métneki et al. (1984); Ransome-Kuti et al. (1975); and Sahi et al. (1973).
17 Haldane (1949); Livingstone (1958); and Weatherall and Clegg (2001). Other polymorphisms implicated in malaria resistance are thalassemia, glucose-6-phosphate deficiency, hereditary ovalocytosis, and RBC Duffy negativity. See also Cormier (2011).
18. Bertin and Fairbairn (2005); Briceño and Eberhard (2009); Briceño, Eberhard, and Robinson (2007); and Eberhard (1993, 2001, 2010).
19. United States: Dixson et al. (2010); Mautz et al. (2013); New Zealand: Dixson et al. (2010); China: Dixson et al. (2007a); and Cameroon: Dixson et al. (2007b).
20. However, in a recent study of 75 Czech women, Brody, Klapilova, and Krejčová (2013) found that women who experienced vaginal orgasms without clitoral stimulation stated a preference for longer penises.

21. Lloyd (2005).
22. Masters and Johnson (1966).
23. Freud (1962).
24. Kilchevsky et al. (2012); and Puppo and Gruenwald (2012).
25. Kilchevsky et al. (2012).
26. Ostrzenski et al. (2014).
27. Korda et al. (2010).
28. Zaviačič et al. (2000).
29. Irigaray (1985), 28.
30. Cain et al. (2003).
31. Robertiello (1970).
32. Tuana (2004).
33. O'Connell (2001).
34. Levin (2002).
35. Thornhill and Gangestad (2008).
36. Wrangham (1993).
37. de Waal (1995a, 1995b); Fruth and Hohmann (2006); Hohmann and Fruth (2000); Kano (1992); Manson, Perry, and Parish (1997); and Zamma and Fujita (2004).
38. Anestis (2004).
39. Chevalier-Skolnikoff (1974); and Goldfoot et al. (1980). Female orgasm in Rhesus macaques (*Macaca mulatta*) has also been experimentally induced though clitoral and vaginal stimulation with a silicon penis simulator; see Burton (1971).
40. Manson, Perry, and Parish (1997).
41. Pazol (2003).
42. de Waal and Lanting (1997); and de Waal (1995a, 1995b, 1998).
43. Lloyd (2005).
44. See Golde (1970) for an early discussion of the issue.
45. According to Kano (1986), orangutan copulations last about 10 minutes, in contrast to chimpanzee and bonobo copulations, which last less than 20 seconds.
46. Diamond (2006 [1992]), 76.
47. Diamond (1997), 145.
48. Dixson (1998).
49. Johnson and Halata (1991); Lemître et al. (2012); and Whitsett et al. (1984).
50. Cooper (1972); and Swanson et al. (2003).
51. McCracken (2000).
52. Hotzey and Arnqvist (2009); and Yamane and Miyatake (2010).
53. Torrentera and Belk (2002).
54. Brown (1983).
55. Jonestone and Keller (2000).
56. Hotzy and Arnqvist (2009); and Rönn and Hotzy (2012).
57. McLean et al. (2010).

58. de Waal (1995a).
59. McLean et al. (2010).
60. Prüfer et al. (2012).
61. Chimpanzee Sequencing and Analysis Consortium (2005).
62. Diamond (2006 [1992]).
63. Dixson and Mundy (1994).
64. Ibid.
65. de Waal (1995b).
66. Hobday (2000).
67. Ibid.
68. Berman, Ionica, and Li (2004); Bowler and Bodmer (2009); Green (1981); Wallis (1981); Jones (1983); and Yeager (1992). Among spotted hyenas, presentation of an erect penis or clitoris is a sign of submission; see East, Hofer, and Wickler (1993).
69. Hohmann and Fruth (2003).
70. Goodall (1986).
71. Galdikas (1985); and Nadler (1982).
72. Baldwin (1970); and Ploog and MacClean (1963). Male squirrel monkeys also display to other males.
73. Carosi and Visalberghi (2002); and Weigel (1979). *Sapajus apella* was formerly referred to as *Cebus apella*.
74. Sheets-Johnstone (1992).
75. Carosi and Visalberghi (2002).
76. Dixson (1998), 252.
77. Larivière and Ferguson (2002).
78. Dixson (1998).
79. Gilbert and Zevit (2001).
80. Ibid.
81. Dawkins (1989).
82. Dixson (1998); and Martin (2007).
83. Miller (1998).
84. Cold and McGrath (1999).
85. Dixson (1998).
86. Ibid.
87. Baker and Bellis (1995); and Gallup and Burch (2004).
88. Gallup et al. (2003).
89. BBC News (2003).
90. Dixson (1998).
91. Dixson (2002).
92. Díaz-Muñoz (2011); Schaffner and French (2004); and Terborgh and Goldizen (1985).
93. Kummer (1968); and Polo and Comenares (2012).
94. Cormier (2003).

95. Cormier and Jones (2010).

96. Malinowski (1929).

97. Williams (1957).

98. Hawkes, O'Connell, and Blurton Jones (1997).

99. Kim, Coxworth, and Hawkes (2012).

100. Cormier (2003).

101. Baumeister (2010), dustjacket.

102. Baumeister (2010), 125.

103. Baumeister (2010), 147.

104. Baumeister (2010) 140.

105. Gero and Conkey (1991).

106. Smuts (1985).

107. Fleagle (1999).

108. Baldwin (1971); Izar et al. (2009); and Kinzey (1997).

109. Du Mond and Hutchinson (1967).

110. Maggioncalda, Nacey and Sapolsky (2002); and Utami et al. (2002).

111. Díaz-Muñoz (2011); Schaffner and French (2004); and Terborgh and Goldizen (1985).

112. de Waal and Lanting (1997); and Furuichi (2011).

113. Strier (2011).

114. Pawłowski (1999).

115. Martin (2007).

116. Dahl (1986); and Graham (1981).

117. Dahl (1986); and Furuichi (1987).

118. Girolami and Bielert (1987); and Shaikh et al. (1982).

119. Clarke, Harvey, and Lindburg (1993); Thierry et al. (1996); and Thomson et al. (1992).

120. Smuts (2006); and Wrangham (1993).

121. Alexander and Noonan (1979); Benshoof and Thornhill (1979); Fox (1967); Schoröder (1993); Symons (1979); and Wilson (1975).

122. Smuts (2006) and Wrangham (1993) have suggested that sexual swellings likely evolved in bonobos and chimpanzees after their ancestors split from human ancestors.

123. Dahl (1986).

124. Smuts (2006).

125. Lee and DeVore (1968).

126. Morris (1967).

127. Wiber (1997).

128. Slocum (1975).

129. Zihlman (1981).

130. Pinker (2000 [1994]), 380.

131. Alexander and Noonan (1979).

132. Benshoof and Thornhill (1979).

133. Burley (1979).

134. Thornhill and Palmer (2000).

135. Wrangham and Peterson (1996).

136. Trivers (1972).

137. Moore (2007).

138. e.g. de Waal (2008).

139. Jewkes et al. (2009).

140. Epstein and Jewkes (2009).

141. Crocker and Crocker (2004).

142. Wilson (2000), 314.

143. Martin (2007).

Chapter 3

1. Ingold (1999), has described what is called demand sharing, which involves the social obligation to give when asked.

2. Hayden (2003); Gilligan (2007a, 2007b); and Kvavadze et al. (2009).

3. Kvavadze et al. (2009).

4. Gilligan (2007b), 14.

5. Gilligan (2007a), 499.

6. Gilligan (2007a), 499.

7. In the middle latitudes during the Late Pleistocene (ca. 126,000 to 10,000 years ago), a fluctuating climate, with mean annual temperatures below –7°C in some continental zones, made clothing necessary; see Gilligan (2010), 24.

8. Gilligan (2010).

9. Banks et al. (2008); and Gilligan (2007a).

10. Soffer et al. (2000).

11. Kvavadze et al. (2009), 1359.

12. Larsen (2006).

13. E.g., Ryan (2011); Fuller et al. (2011); and Deguilloux et al. (2012).

14. Flannery (1986); and Bellwood (2005).

15. Gerritsen (2008).

16. Bentley et al. (2012); Bramanti et al. (2009); Fuller et al. (2011); Lacan et al. (2011); and Ryan (2011).

17. Note that Shennan and Edinborough (2007) present evidence suggesting a drastic rise in population with the adoption of farming followed by a surprising and dramatic decline in populations in northern Europe at the end of the early Neolithic. They argue that this demographic decline lasted for nearly a thousand years, but there are no current agreed upon explanations for it. Nevertheless, a general trend in population increase is found in association with the initial adoption of agriculture prehistorically. See also Bentley et al. (2012); Fuller et al. (2011); Guzmán and Weisdorf (2011); and Peterson (2010).

18. Benz (2001).
19. Reitz and Wing (2008).
20. Eltsov (2008), 178.
21. Ibid.
22. Bentley et al. (2012); and Lacan et al. (2011).
23. Bentley et al. (2012).
24. Fuller et al. (2011); and Jones et al. (2011).
25. For example, see Lawler (2007, 1164), who reviews evidence that northern Mesopotamia rivaled the south in a "race to build cities," which resulted in rivalries, the creation of enemies, and conflict. Additional support for an increase in violence that accompanies the development of complex society comes from elsewhere in the Near East (McMahon et al. 2011), Italy (Robb 1997), and Asia (Domett et al. 2011).
26. For examples of summary evidence, see Gibbons (2012) and Lawler (2012).
27. We are aware that this interpretation privileges formal institutions and public structures over informal and domestic structures. Public symbolic life is more easily evidenced in terms of archaeology and architecture but may not represent the ideology and real lived life from the perspective of those not in public power. The lower classes and less privileged genders may have exercised different forms of power and autonomy, which we cannot easily understand. And, for the purposes of this text, we are interested in these public institutions in order to understand dominant ideologies and practices.
28. Hodder and Meskell (2011).
29. Schmandt-Besserat (2007).
30. Budge (2003); Hart (1986); and Ikram (2010).
31. Friedman (2001); and Ikram (2010).
32. Howard (1898), 85.
33. Budge (1926), 22; and Frankfort (1948), 381.
34. Frankfort (1948), 381.
35. Budge (2003); and Hart (1986).
36. Redford (2002).
37. Tyldesley (1995).
38. Redford (2002), 220.
39. Bleeker (1969), 70.
40. Bleeker (1969), 76.
41. Bleeker (1969), 57.
42. Ibid.
43. Selden (1998), 334.
44. Ikram (2010); and Redford (2002).
45. Budge (2003); and Hart (1986).
46. Redford (2002), 242.

47. Friedman (2001).
48. Ikram (2010).
49. Ikram (2010), 157.
50. Casadio (2003).
51. Hart (1986); and Ikram (2010).
52. Note that the story has many different versions and complicated twists, which we do not relay here. The story centers on important Egyptian themes of death, resurrection, fertility, and life. For example, when Isis mated with the resurrected Osiris, she was in the form of a black kite, the protector of the dead. Black kites are symbolic of funerary contexts and mourning, and they are associated with the goddesses Isis and her sister, Nephthys. See Ikram (2010) for a concise summary of the Osiris myth.
53. Howard (1898).
54. Robb (1997), 59–60.
55. Hogan (2007).
56. Daniélou (1995); Friedman (2001); and Howard (1898).
57. Howard (1898).
58. Larson (2007); and Mikalson (2005).
59. Mikalson (2005), 60–62.
60. Larson (2007); and Mikalson (2005).
61. Larson (2007), 128.
62. Ibid.
63. Csapo (1997).
64. Friedman (2001). The exact date of this event, referred to as the "Grand Procession of Ptolemy Philadelphus" and a "Pageant of Propaganda," is debated but probably occurred between 285 and 262 BCE, according to Nadig (2002).
65. Larson (2007, 130) makes this assertion, citing Clay (2002) and Jameson (1993). A more nuanced exploration of the phallic symbolism associated with Dionysus is discussed by Csapo (1997) in his article "Riding the Phallus for Dionysus."
66. Csapo (1997), 260.
67. Csapo goes on to argue, "The phallic power of Dionysus is a supreme expression of his character as interstructure precisely because of the symbolic importance of the phallus to social structure in ancient Greek society, and the habit of expressing social domination in the language of sexual domination" (Csapo 1997), 264–265.
68. Ibid.
69. Csapo (1997); Friedman (2001); and Larson (2007).
70. Larson (2007), 132–133.
71. Merival (1996), 9.
72. Larson (2007), 151.
73. Ibid.
74. Brown (1981), 62 and 64.

75. The Egyptian phallic god Min was identified by the Greeks as Pan (Csapo 1997, 273). They share many characteristics.

76. Rykvert (2011).

77. Grant (1997); Hallett and Skinner (1997); Rykvert (2011); and Varone (2001).

78. Grant (1997); Hallett and Skinner (1997); Rykvert (2011); and Varone (2001).

79. Much of the architecture and material culture of Pompeii were preserved with the eruption of Mount Vesuvius in 79 CE that covered the city with volcanic ash, thus fixing it in a moment in time.

80. Howard (1898); and Rykvert (2011).

81. Koloski-Ostrow (1997).

82. Koloski-Ostrow (1997), 254–257.

83. Friedman (2001), 22.

84. The Harappan culture is named after one of the Indus Valley's most spectacular and well-preserved cities of Harappa, dating to 3300 BCE and perhaps as early as 3500 BCE (McIntosh 2007), 65.

85. McIntosh (2001 and 2007); and Wright (2009).

86. McIntosh (2001 and 2007); and Wright (2009).

87. McIntosh (2007), 67–72.

88. Ibid. The cubic stone weights have also been recovered from this time period and they continue into the Mature Harappan period (2600–1900/1800 BCE).

89. McIntosh (2007), 285–286.

90. Klostermaier (1994); McIntosh (2007); and Wright (2009).

91. Klostermaier (1994), 145 and 263.

92. McIntosh (2001 and 2007); and Wright (2009).

93. Daniélou (1995). There is evidence, drawn from the Harappan period to modern times, that both male and female deities were worshipped in the Indian subcontinent and the surrounding region. In the Hindu traditions, however, these symbols may be interpreted as male dominated and focused primarily on the celebration of male power and creative energy.

94. Simmer-Brown (2001), 47.

95. McIntosh (2007), 286.

96. From Daniélou (1995), 13–14, citing the *Linga Purana*, 1.3.7 and 1.17.5.

97. Howard (1898), 77.

98. Klostermaier (1994), 143.

99. Bryant (2001); Klostermaier (1994); and McIntosh (2007).

100. Griffith (1899); and Klostermaier (1994).

101. Griffith (1899); and Klostermaier (1994).

102. Higham (2004); and O'Reilly (2007).

103. O'Reilly (2007), 54.

104. O'Reilly (2007)

105. Cort and Jett (2010), 154.

106. O'Reilly (2007), 191–194. The mandala tradition of government includes federated kingdoms under a central ruler. This was common in Southeast Asian political formations.

107. Kasahara (2009), 299.

108. Ibid.

109. Kasahara (2009), 446.

110. Ibid.

111. Ibid.

112. Buckley (1895); and Kasahara (2009).

113. Kasahara (2009), 449.

114. Lee (1995), 82–83. This festival has also been referred to as the "Festival of the Steel Phallus" and the "Festival of the Golden Testicles" Kasahara (2009); and Lee (1995).

115. Lee (1995)

116. Adams (2010).

117. Adams (2010) and Lee (1995). The modern Kanamara Matsuri is said to be associated with raising money for HIV research.

118. Buckley (1895); and Kasahara (2009).

119. Buckley (1895), 24.

120. Buckley (1895), 17; and Kasahara (2009).

121. Kvaerne (1996); and Snellgrove (2002).

122. Coleman and Jinpa (2005), 449; and Kvaerne (1996), 9. Notably, the soul of the dead person was accompanied by a domestic animal, usually a yak, horse, or sheep, that was later sacrificed as part of the funerary rituals (1996), 9.

123. Kvaerne (1996), 9.

124. Norbu (1995), 97–102.

125. Norbu (1995), 100–102.

126. Norbu (1995), 203–204.

127. Norbu (1995), 282.

128. Norbu (1995), 282.

129. Kvaerne (1996), 10.

130. Ibid.

131. Kvaerne (1996), 10; and Coleman and Jinpa (2005).

132. Kvaerne (1996), 10.

133. Ibid.

134. Coleman and Jinpa (2005).

135. Acharya (2003); Francke (1999); Richardson (1972); Rinpoche (1973); and Ward (1921).

136. Francke (1999); and Ward (1921), 156.

137. Francke (1999), 188.

138. Snellgrove (2002), 160.

139. Richardson (1972), 25; and Rinpoche (1973), 62. These discussions involve analysis of modern Buddhist practices, not just those of the ancient Bön tradition.

140. Richardson (1972), 25.

141. Acharya (2003).

142. Acharya (2003); Richardson (1972), 25; and Rinpoche (1973), 62.

143. Acharya (2003).

144. Daniélou (1995).

145. Acharya (2003).

146. Ibid.

147. Richardson (1972); and Rinpoche (1973).

148. Simmer-Brown (2001), 14–33.

149. Simmer-Brown (2001), 33.

150. Ibid.

151. Ibid.

152. Simmer-Brown (2001), 34.

153. Valeri (1985), 10–11. *Kino lau* literally translates as "four hundred bodies"; see Valeri (1985), 10.

154. Valeri (1985), 15.

155. Beckwith (1940), 15–16; and Valeri (1985), 13–15.

156. Handy and Handy (1991), 612; Pukui and Elbert (1986), 167; and Valeri (1985), 12.

157. Valeri (1985), 12.

158. Beckwith (1940); Handy (1927); Handy and Handy (1991); and Valeri (1985).

159. Valeri (1985), 13.

160. Beckwith (1940), 63–64; Handy and Handy (1991), 78; and Valeri (1985), 15–16.

161. Handy and Handy (1991), 19.

162. Handy and Handy (1991), 76–77. This fundamental concept, and that of the origin and nature of Earth and Sky, are discussed in great detail in Handy (1927) from a cross-cultural perspective within Polynesia.

163. Handy and Handy (1991), 311.

164. Valeri (1985), 45–46.

165. Valeri (1985), 354.

166. Valeri (1985), 302, citing Brigham (1908), 193.

167. Nichols and Pool (2012), 224, and 513–514.

168. Coe (2011), 93; and Freidel et al. (1993), 289.

169. Note that Venus is associated with the beginning of the rainy season.

170. The Nahua people are an ethnic group antecedent to the Toltec, Aztec, and other groups known from important cultural and archaeological remains in Mesoamerica.

171. Taube (1993), 37–39.

172. Ibid.

173. Diehl (2004), 102.

174. Harrison-Buck (2012).

175. Amrhein (2001); Ardren (2012); and Ardren and Hixson (2006).

176. Ardren (2012), 55, Figure 5.1.

177. Coe (2011); and Taube (1993).

178. Ardren and Hixson (2006). The authors argue that efforts to understand the meaning of the sexual and gender-based imagery of the Maya through the lens of Western perspectives and morality have resulted in a definition of male sexuality as procreative, heterosexual, and utilitarian. This idea has masked what some researchers think are realistic interpretations of Mayan concepts of masculinity (ideas that may not conform to mainstream Western sexuality).

179. Amrhein (2001); Ardren (2012), 56; Ardren and Hixson (2006), 8.

180. Amrhein (2001); Ardren (2012); and Ardren and Hixson (2006), 15.

181. Ardren and Hixson (2006), 16–17.

182. Ibid.

183. Looper (2009), 171–173.

184. Ibid.

185. Looper (2009), 171–172.

186. The Pawahtuns commemorate the role of the deities (and their wives) in establishing cosmic and sociopolitical order by assisting in the rebirth of the Maize God, who is represented by the ruler (Looper 2009), 171.

187. Ardren (2012), 60.

188. In Mesoamerican art, there tends to be more emphasis on the male body than on the female body in public settings; see Ardren (2012) and Harrison-Buck (2012).

189. Amrhein (2001); Ardren (2012); and Ardren and Hixson (2006).

190. Amrhein (2001), xv.

191. Ardren (2012), 54.

192. Thomas (1996).

193. Ardren (2012), 61; Coe (2011), 169–172; and McKillop (2004), 101.

194. Ardren (2012), 60–61.

195. Daniélou (1995).

196. Daniélou (1995), 6.

197. Howard (1898), 5.

198. Ardren (2012).

199. Thomas (1996).

Chapter 4

1. Fletcher (2003).

2. Lang (1893).

3. Haddon (1898).

4. Harding (1973/1974).

5. Haddon (1898), 327.

6. Frazer (1912, 1913); and Gladwin (1937).

7. Heine-Geldern (1964); Köepping (1983); and Lowie (1938).

8. Adams (2007); and Gronning, Sohl, and Singer (2007).

9. Dundes (2005); Gentile (2007); and Slattery (2005).

10. Lawergren (1988).

11. Frobenius (1898), cited in Von Hornbostel (1933).

12. Van Baal (1963).

13. Blanc (1961); Marett (1914); Zerries (1942), cited in Van Baal (1963).

14. Marett (1914).

15. Lowie (1920).

16. Von Hornbostel (1933).

17. Lang (1893).

18. Loeb (1931).

19. Haddon (1898).

20. Dundes (1976).

21. Berndt (1941). Also known as the Anta'kirinja or the Andekarinja.

22. Van Baal (1963). Also known as the Aranda.

23. Worms (1950).

24. Crawley (1927); and Mathews (1898). Also known as the Dieri.

25. Howitt (1885); and Mathews (1898). Also known as the Kurnai.

26. Mathews (1898). Also known as the Gamilaraay.

27. Piddington (1932).

28. Mathews (1898); and Mol (1979).

29. Mathews (1898). Also known as the Mycoolon.

30. Mol (1979); and Stanner (1963).

31. Berndt (1940).

32. Wild (1977). Also known as the Walbiri.

33. Berndt (1947); Eliade (1967); and Mol (1979). Also known as the Wiradjuri, Wuradjeri, Wirraayjuurray, or Wiradthuri.

34. Brown (1913). Also known as Kariera.

35. Van Baal (1963).

36. Van Baal (1963).

37. Worms (1950).

38. Berndt (1940).

39. Crawley (1927).

40. Mol (1979).

41. Wild (1977).

42. Elkin (1930). Also known as the Ungarinyin.

43. Radcliffe-Brown (1929). Also known as the Kumbaingeri.

44. McLean (1982).

45. McPherson (2012).

46. Langness (1974).

47. Lehner (1935).

48. Juillerat (2000).
49. Tuzin (1984).
50. Lattas (1989).
51. Chinnery and Beaver (1915).
52. Haddon (1900).
53. Albert (1989).
54. Van Baal (1963).
55. Kempf (1992).
56. Van Baal (1963). The group is not identified more specifically than as the people of the Trans-Fly region in Papua New Guinea.
57. McPherson (2012).
58. Kempf (1992).
59. Haddon (1900); and Van Baal (1963).
60. Lehner (1935).
61. Tuzin (1984).
62. Lattas (1989).
63. Chinnery and Beaver (1915).
64. Albert (1989).
65. Aufenanger (1977).
66. Tuzin (1984).
67. Aufenanger (1977).
68. Tuzin (1984).
69. Haddon (1900).
70. Van Baal (1963).
71. Whiting and Reed (1938).
72. Haddon (1900).
73. Kempf (1992).
74. Mead (1935). Also known as the Tchambuli.
75. Haddon (1900); and Van Baal (1963).
76. McPherson (2012).
77. Lattas (1989).
78. Van Baal (1963).
79. Chinnery and Beaver (1915).
80. Haddon (1900).
81. Lattas (1989).
82. Counts (1980).
83. Van Baal (1963).
84. Turnbull (1957).
85. Oliver (2001).
86. Lewis-Williams (1981).
87. Ratzel (1897).

88. Biobaku (1967); and de Cardi (1899).
89. Braithwaite Batty (1890); and Ellis (1894).
90. Ellis (1894); Marcuzzi (2010); and Morton-Williams (1964).
91. Dennett (1916).
92. Oso (1976).
93. Marcuzzi (2010).
94. Wilson-Haffenden (1927, 1930). Also known as the Kwotto/s.
95. Blench (1987).
96. Harris (1938). Also known as the Dakarari or Dakakari.
97. Smith (1953).
98. Wilson-Haffenden (1927, 1930). Also known as the Kwotto/s.
99. Aluede (2006).
100. Kubik (1975/1976). The umbrella term "Nyaneka-Nkhumbi" is used here in place of Kubik's term "Humbi," for the specific group to which he is referring is unclear.
101. Dieterlen (1989).
102. Biebuyck (1973, 1974).
103. Linton (1933).
104. Weeks (1914).
105. Nurse (1972).
106. Söderberg (1953).
107. Brown (1967); and Griffin (1967).
108. Loeb (1931).
109. Both (2006); Bourke (1892); Loftin (1936); Parsons (1939); and Tyler (1964).
110. Brown (1971); and Mason (1920).
111. Fowler and Matley (1979); Laird (1980); and Parkman (1993).
112. Parsons (1939).
113. Parkman (1993).
114. Flannery (1936).
115. Gifford (1939).
116. Perry (1983).
117. Bourke (1892).
118. Hill (1938); Lamphere (1969); and Murray (1989).
119. Benedict (1924).
120. Herzog (1928).
121. Bowen and Moser (1970); Harrington, Bernett, and Barnett (1988); and Hine (2000).
122. Speck (1944).
123. Kroeber (1929).
124. Hassrick and Carpenter (1944).
125. Murdoch (1892); and Whitridge (2004).
126. Lowie (1940).
127. Gregor (1987).

128. Lowie (1941).
129. Lowie (1940).
130. Murphy (1986).
131. Hill (1979).
132. Wright and Hill (1986).
133. Overing (1986).
134. Chernela, personal communication, cited in Shapiro (2009).
135. Haddon (1900).
136. Kartomi (1999).
137. Bakels (2004).
138. Dawkins (1982).
139. Cormier (2003).
140. Hood (1971); and Pendlebury (1991).
141. Rehak (1996).
142. Ucko (1969).
143. Ucko (1969).
144. Maybury-Lewis (1967).
145. Seeger (1975). Personal communication from Terence Turner.
146. Turner (1991).
147. Werner (1984).
148. Kracke (1981, 1988).
149. Lévi-Strauss (1969).
150. Heider (1969).
151. Benedict (1931).
152. Lüttenberg (2005).
153. Parsons (1989).
154. de la Cruz, Hacker, and Kandeel (2009).
155. Springer (2010).
156. Grancsay (1950).
157. Springer (2010).
158. Miller and Yavneh (2011).
159. Vicary (1989).
160. Reed (2004); and Vicary (1989).
161. Frick (2011).
162. Crawford (2003); and Persels (1997).
163. Hammond (1999).
164. Ackerknecht (1947).
165. Gollaher (2000).
166. Elliot-Smith (1908, 1910, 1929).
167. Shokeir and Hussein (1999).
168. Hodges (2001).

169. Speert (1953).
170. Freud (1939); Geller (1993).
171. Aggleton (2007); and Waszak (1978).
172. Hodges (2001).
173. Dunsmuir and Gordon (1999).
174. Gollaher (1994); and Sayre (1872).
175. Darby (2003); Dunsmuir and Gordon (1999); and Geller (1993).
176. Bell (2005).
177. Oliver (2002).
178. McPherson (1994, 2004, 2012).
179. Counts (1990).
180. Panoff (1968). Mengan speakers.
181. Kempf (2002).
182. McPherson (1994, 2004, 2012).
183. Kempf (2002)
184. Dari et al. (1994).
185. Rowanchilde (1996).
186. Kirkpatrick (1987).
187. Harrington (1968); and Whistler (1984).
188. Levy (1969, 1973).
189. Firth (1936a, 1936b).
190. Collecott (1921); and Douaire-Marsaudon (1996).
191. Brandewie (1973); and Rubel, Liu, and Brandewie (1971).
192. Gascon (2011).
193. Schneider and Schneider (1991).
194. Hoskins (2002).
195. Harrington (1968).
196. Bagge (1904). It is referred to as a circumcision, but the procedure described is a superincision.
197. Ashley-Montagu (1937).
198. Ibid.
199. Ibid.
200. Breault (1991). The candirú fish belong to the genus *Vandellia* and include *V. cirrhosa, V. plazai, V. beccarii, V. hasemani, V. weineri,* and *V. sanguinea.*
201. Ashley-Montagu (1937).
202. Ibid.
203. Whiting and Reed (1938).
204. Harrington (1968); and Hogbin (1970).
205. Cheng (1996).
206. American Psychiatric Association (1994).
207. Chowdhury (1996).

208. Durst and Rosca-Rebaudengo (1988); Joseph (1986); and Lapierre (1972).

209. Anderson (1990).

210. Chowdhury and Bagchi (1993); Chowdhury and Banerjee (1996); and Yap (1965).

211. Al-Sinawi, Al-Adawi, and Al-Guenedi (2008).

212. Earleywine (2001).

213. Chowdhury and Bera (1994).

214. Kalaitzi and Kalantzis (2006).

215. Bloor (2004).

216. Alvarez et al. (2012); Berrios and Morley (1984); Hawley and Owen (1988); Kennedy and McDonough (2002); and Sandford (1997).

217. Al-Hmoud (1999); Bersudsky et al. (1998); Hes and Nassi (1977); and Modai et al. (1986).

218. Tseng et al. (1988).

219. Ibid.

220. Aina and Morakinyo (2011); and Mather (2005).

221. Ilechukwu (1992).

222. Dzokoto and Adams (2005).

223. Smith (2002).

224. de la Cruz, Hacker, and Kandeel (2009).

225. Shepard (2002). The Matskigenka are also known as the Machiguenga and the Matsigenga.

226. de la Cruz, Hacker, and Kandeel (2009); and Keuls (1985).

227. English Heritage (2012).

228. Hutton (1991), 241.

229. Hutton (1991), 242.

230. Hutton (1991), 10.

231. Hutton (1991), 42–44.

232. Hutton (1991), 158.

233. Hutton (1991), 44–45.

234. Hutton (1991), 90.

235. Geertz (1972).

Chapter 5

1. Marcus and Fisher (1999 [1986]), i.

2. Davis and Whitten (1987).

3. Vance (2007).

4. Masquelier (2005), 2.

5. Grizzard (1994).

6. Tamaro (2005).

7. Schlafly (2004).

8. Powell (2004).
9. Miller (2004).
10. Horovitz (2005); and Lee (2011).
11. Friedman (2001).
12. Hill (2000).
13. Pershing (1996).
14. Frye (1996).
15. Elliott (2008); and Newitz and Wray (1996).
16. Cameron (1992).
17. Urban Dictionary (2012).
18. Dicktionary (2012).
19. Lakoff and Johnson (1980).
20. Martin (1991).
21. Marturano (2011).
22. Leonard and King (2011); and Merrill et al. (2012).
23. Cunningham (2012).
24. Weiss (2010).
25. Mattern (2012).
26. Bachofen (1861).
27. Gimbutas (1974, 1989, 1991).
28. Nott et al. (1854).
29. Harris (1968), 54–55.
30. Ford and Beach (1951).
31. Reisman (2010).
32. Ford and Beach (1951).
33. Endleman (1989).
34. Friedman (2001).
35. Freud (1962 [1905]).
36. Freud (1962 [1905]).
37. Freud (1918).
38. Endleman (1989), 64.
39. Messenger (1971).
40. Marshall (1971), 117.
41. Margolis (2004).
42. Zastrow (2010).
43. Harris (1997).
44. Harris (1997), 108.
45. Finsch (1880); see also Howes (2011).
46. Kimmel (2000).
47. Gregersen (1982).

48. Keuls (1985).
49. Lee (1960).
50. Shields (2006).
51. Eady (2001).
52. Patton and Snyder-Yuly (2007).
53. Winston (1901), 109.
54. Rushton (1995).
55. Weizmann et al. (1990).
56. Kinsey, Pomeroy, and Martin (1948).
57. It is worth mentioning that Rushton cites the Kinsey study as validating his findings that a significant difference in penis size exists among racial groups; in fact, Kinsey's study demonstrates very little difference.
58. Masters and Johnson (1966).
59. Herbenick et al. (2014).
60. American Anthropological Association (1998).
61. Foster et al. (1998).
62. Ellis (2000); Jones et al. (2011); and Kaplan (2009).
63. Asim (2007), 127; and Strom Thurmond cited in Nichols (2010).
64. Washington-Williams and Stadiem (2005).
65. Stoler (1989).
66. Leiber (2010).
67. World Penis Average Size Database (2012).
68. Penis Size Worldwide (2012).
69. Patton (2012).

Chapter 6

1. Hald (2006); Johansson and Hammarén (2007); Petersen and Hyde (2010, 2011); Romito and Beltramini (2011); and Træen, Spitznogle, and Beverfjord (2002).
2. Baxter (2009); Paley (1999); and Sager (1989).
3. Hanson (2008).
4. Corley and Hook (2012); and Sabo (2007).
5. Bentley (2012).
6. Lever, Frederick, and Peplau (2006).
7. Wylie and Eardley (2007).
8. Daigle (1990); Lloyd, Powell, and Murdoch (1996); and Pope and Kanayama (2004).
9. Bulik et al. (2012); Papadopoulos et al. (2009); and Wentz et al. (2009).
10. Feldman et al. (1994).
11. Araujo et al. (2010); Malaviage and Levy (2009); and Zias et al. (2009).
12. Cleveringa et al. (2009); Marumo, Nakashima, and Murai (2008); and Stranne et al. (2012).
13. Corona et al. (2009).

14. Lexchin (2006).
15. Dole is also the oldest first-time potential presidential nominee, at age 73. He also holds the dubious distinction of being the only person to lose as his party's nominee as both presidential and vice presidential candidate.
16. Conrad (2005).
17. Jackson et al. (2010).
18. Ibid.
19. Wise (2010).
20. Hellstrom et al. (2010).
21. Ibid.
22. Ibid.
23. Yuan et al. (2010).
24. Levine and Dimitriou (2001).
25. Levine and Dimitriou (2001); and Yuan et al. (2010).
26. Mulhall et al. (2001).
27. Brock, Tu, and Linet (2001).
28. Barnett, Robleda-Gomez, and Pachana (2012).
29. Wysowski and Swann (2003).
30. Sadeghi-Nejad et al. (2003).
31. Brock et al. (2007).
32. Stevenson (1995); Tsai (1996); and Wassersug, Zelenietz, and Squire (2004).
33. Ringrose (2007).
34. Tsai (1996).
35. Toledano (1984).
36. Peschel and Peschel (1987).
37. Rosselli (1988).
38. Tulpe and Torchinov (2000). Also spelled Skoptzy, Skoptsi, and so on.
39. Ringrose (2007).
40. Also referred to as an orchidectomy.
41. Bhattacharyya, Sanyal, and Roy (2011).
42. Eke (2000).
43. Nanda (1990).
44. McCarthy (2014).
45. Aboseif, Gomez, and McAninch (1993); Cheuk, Lee, and Ungvari (2009); Franke and Rush (2007); Greilsheimer and Groves (1979); Kabore et al. (2008); Kushner (1967); Lima et al. (2005); Ozturk et al. (2009); Qureshi (2009); Saldanha (1993); Siddiquee and Deshpande (2007); Schweitzer (1990); Stunell et al. (2006); Volkmer and Maier (2002); and Yusuf et al. (2009)
46. Patel et al. (2007).
47. Hong and Ediger (1978).
48. Ghaffari et al. (2007).

49. Ahsaini et al. (2011); and Khan, Usmani, and Hanif (2012).

50. Israel and Lee (2002).

51. Marneros, Gutmann, and Uhlmann (2006).

52. Charan and Reddy (2011).

53. Ajape et al. (2010); Money (1988); Rao, Bharathi, and Chate (2002); Razzaghi et al. (2009); Schweitzer (1990); and Tharoor (2007).

54. Murota-Kawano, Tosaka, and Ando (2001).

55. Mishra and Kar (2001).

56. Mago (2011).

57. Catalano et al. (1996).

58. Money (1988).

59. Dar et al. (2010); Hemphill (1951); Sharma et al. (2010); and Shimizu and Mizuta (1995).

60. Sudarshan, Rao, and Santosh (2006).

61. Zucker (2005); American Psychiatric Association (1980, 2000).

62. Brown (2010); Dunn et al. (2009); Haleem, Griffin, and Banerjee (2007); Millán-González (2010); Murphy, Murphy, and Grainger (2001); and St. Peter, Trinidad, and Irwig (2012).

63. Nielson and Wolhert (1991); Tüttelmann and Gromoll (2010); and Urbach and Benvenisty (2009).

64. Dessinioti and Katsambas (2009).

65. Greene, Symes, and Brook (1978).

66. Blackless et al. (2000).

67. Butler (1990); Carrera, DePalma, and Lameiras (2012); and Goldner (2011).

68. Cohen-Kettenis and Pfäfflin (2010).

69. Pfäefflin (1997).

70. Jarolím et al. (2009).

71. Monstrey, Ceulemans, and Hoebeke (2011).

72. Hembree et al. (2009).

73. Belmontesi, Grover, and Verpaele (2006); and Schroeter et al. (2003).

74. De Cuypere et al. (2006); Lawrence (2003); Lobato et al. (2006); and Nelson, Whallett, and McGregor (2009).

75. Pfäfflin and Junge (1998).

76. Skougard (2011).

77. Lenzer (2008); and Master and Santucci (2003).

78. Vale et al. (2010).

79. Dale (2006).

80. Wassersug, Zelenietz, and Squire (2004).

81. Matteson (1998).

82. Adeola (2004).

83. Sharpe and Shakkebaek (1993); and Fernandez and Olea (2012).

84. Mnif et al. (2011); and Olea-Serrano et al. (1999).

85. Wagner and Oehlmann (2009).

86. Brotons et al. (1995).

87. Harvey and Darbre (2004).

88. Guillette et al. (1994)

89. Garaventa, Failmali, and Terlizzi (2006).

90. Smith (1971).

91. Bryan et al. (1989); Short et al. (1989); and Tallmon and Hoferkamp (2009).

92. Bryan et al. (1986); and Horiguchi et al. (2012).

93. Chan et al. (2008); Ellis and Pattisina (1990); Mohamat-Yusuff et al. (2010); and Wu et al. (2010).

94. Castro and Fillmann (2012); and Penchaszadeh et al. (2009).

95. Marshall and Rajkumar (2003); and Lahbib et al. (2010).

96. Andersen (2004); Rees, Brady, and Fabris (2001); and Reitsema and Spickett (2003).

97. Heidrich, Steckelbroeck, and Klingmuller (2001).

98. Woodling et al. (2006).

99. Jobling et al. (1998).

100. Van Aerle et al. (2001).

101. Viganò et al. (2001).

102. Carballo et al. (2005); and Solé et al. (2003).

103. Jobling et al. (1998).

104. Anderssen et al. (1988); Mikaelian et al. (2002); and McMaster et al. (1994).

105. Barnhoorn et al. (2004).

106. Flammarion et al. (2000).

107. Piferrer and Donaldson (1989).

108. Jobling et al. (1996).

109. Kidd et al. (2007).

110. Alford (2011); Alford et al. (2001); Blaustein et al. (2011); Kiesecker, Blaustein, and Belden (2001); Hof et al. (2011); Houlahan et al. (2000); Sodhi et al. (2008); and Wake and Vrendenburg (2008).

111. Jablonowski, Schäffer, and Burauel (2011).

112. Benotti et al. (2009); Hua, Bennett, and Letcher (2006); Pereira, Rostad, and Leiker (1992).

113. Bedmar et al. (2004); Inoue et al. (2004); and Lanchote et al. (2000).

114. Bushway et al. (1991); Guzella, Pozzoni, and Guiliano (2006); and Law et al. (1994).

115. Alam, Dikshit, and Bandyopadhyay (2000); Fu et al. (2003); and Gfrerer et al. (2002).

116. du Preez and van Vuren (1992); London et al. (2004); and Pick, van Dyk, and Botha (1992).

117. Bowmer (1991); Jones et al. (2003); and Shaw and Müller (2005).

118. Rohr and McCoy (2010); and Solomon et al. (2008).

119. Hayes et al. (2002); and Tavera-Mendosa et al. (2002)

120. Hayes et al. (2002, 2003)
121. Reeder et al. (2005).
122. McDaniel et al. (2008).
123. Cooper et al. (1999).
124. Lim et al. (2009, 2010).
125. Skakkebæk, Rajpert-De Meyts, and Main (2001).
126. De Rosa et al. (2003); and Hammoud et al. (2010).
127. Carlsen et al. (1992).
128. Shakkebaek, Rajpert-De Meyts, and Main (2001).
129. Phillips (2009).

References

Aboseif, S., R. Gomez, and J. W. McAnich. 1993. Genital self-mutilation. *The Journal of Urology* 150(4): 1143–1146.

Acharya, Gopilal. 2003. Of phallus: An arcane symbol. *Kuensel Online, Bhutan's Daily News*. February 3, 2003. Retrieved on October 27, 2012, from http://www.kuenselonline.com.

Ackerknecht, Erwin H. 1947. Primitive Surgery. *American Anthropologist* 49(1): 25–45.

Adams, Jon. 2007. Making a Science of Literary Criticism. *Endeavor* 31(1): 30–33.

Adams, Jonathan. 2010. Japan: Nothing says springtime like penis and vagina festivals. *Global Post*. Retrieved on October 25, 2012, from http://www.globalpost.com.

Adeola, Francis O. 2004. Boon or bane? The environmental and health impacts of persistent organic oollutants. *Human Ecology Review* 11(1): 27–35.

Aggleton, Peter. 2007. "Just a snip"? A social history of male circumcision. *Reproductive Health Matters* 15(29): 15–21.

Ahsaini, Mustapha, Fadl Tazi, Abdelhak Khalouk, Karim Lahlaidi, Abderahim Bouazzaoui, Roos E. Stuurman-Wieringa, Mohammed Jamal Elfassi, and My Hassan Farih. 2011. Bilateral testicular self-castration due to cannabis abuse: A case report. *Journal of Medical Case Reports* 5: 404.

Aina, O. F., and O. Morakinyo. 2011. Culture-Bound Syndromes and the Neglect of Cultural Factors in Psychopathologies among Africans. *African Journal of Psychiatry* 14: 278–285.

Ajape, A. A., B. A. Issa, O. I. N. Buhari, P. O. Adeoye, A. L. Babata, and O. O. Abiola. 2010. Genital Self-Mutilation. *Annals of African Medicine* 9(1): 31–34.

Alam, J. B., A. K. Dikshit, and M. Bandyopadhyay. 2000. Efficacy of adsorbents for 2,4-D and atrazine removal from water environment. *Global Nest: The International Journal* 2(2): 139–148.

Alam, Manzoor. 2009. *War on Terrorism or American Strategy for Global Dominance: Islamic Perspective on the Afghan-Iraq War*. New York: Vantage.

Albert, Steven M. 1989. Cultural implication: Representing the domain of devils among the Lak. *Man* 24(2): 273–289.

Alexander, R., and K. M. Noonan. 1979. Concealment of ovulation, parental care, and human social evolution. In *Evolutionary Biology and Social Behavior*, ed. N. A. Chagnon and W. G. Irons, 436–453. North Scituate, MA: Duxbury.

Alford, Ross A. 2011. Ecology: Bleak future for amphibians. *Nature* 480: 461–462.

Alford, Ross A., Philip M. Dixon, and Joseph H. K. Pechmann. 2001. Ecology: Global amphibian population declines. *Nature* 412: 499–500.

Al-Hmoud, N. 1999. Koro-like syndrome in a Jordanian male. *Eastern Mediterranean Health Journal* 5(3): 611–613.

Al-Sinawi, Hamed, Samir Al-Adawi, and Amr Al-Guenedi. 2008. Ramadan fasting triggering Koro-like symptoms during acute alcohol withdrawal: A case report from Oman. *Transcultural Psychiatry* 45(4): 695–704.

Aluede, Charles O. 2006. The anthropomorphic attributes of musical instruments: History and use in Esan, Nigeria. *Anthropologist* 8(3): 157–160.

Alvarez, P., V. M. Puente, J. J. Blasco, P. Salgado, A. Merino, and A. Bulbena. 2012. Concurrent Koro and Cotard syndromes in a Spanish male patient with a psychotic depression and cerebrovascular disease. *Psychopathology* 45(2): 126–129.

American Anthropological Association. 1998. Statement on Race. Retrieved on January 30, 2015, from http://www.aaanet.org/stmts/racepp.htm.

American Psychiatric Association. 1994. *Diagnostic and Statistical Manual of Mental Disorder: DSM-IV*. Washington, DC: American Psychiatric Press.

———. 1980. *Diagnostic and Statistical Manual of Mental Disorder: DSM-III*. Washington, DC: American Psychiatric Press.

Amrhein, Marie. 2001. An iconographic and historic analysis of terminal classic Maya phallic imagery. PhD diss., Virginia Commonwealth University. UMI Microform 3042808. Ann Arbor, MI: ProQuest Information and Learning Company.

Andersen, L. E. 2004. Imposex: A biological effect of TBT contamination in Port Curtis, Queensland. *Australian Journal of Ecotoxicology* 10: 105–113.

Anderson, D. N. 1990. Koro: The genital retraction symptom after stroke. *The British Journal of Psychiatry* 157: 142–144.

Anderssen, Tommy, Lars Förlin, Jan Härdig, and Åke Larsson. 1988. Physiological disturbances in fish living in coastal water polluted with bleached kraft pulp mill effluents. *Canadian Journal of Fisheries and Aquatic Sciences* 45(9): 1525–1536.

Anestis, Stephanie Firos. 2004. Female genito-genital rubbing in a group of captive chimpanzees. *International Journal of Primatology* 25(2): 477–488.

Araujo, Andre B., Susan A. Hall, Peter Gantz, Gretchen R. Chiu, Raymond C. Rosen, Varant Kupelian, Thomas G. Travison, and John B. McKinlay. Does erectile dysfunction contribute to carviovascular disease risk prediction beyond the Framingham risk score? *Journal of the American College of Cardiology* 55(4): 350–356.

Ardren, Traci 2012. The phalli stones of the Classic Maya northern lowlands: Masculine anxiety and regional identity. In *Power and Identity in Archaeological Theory and Practice: Case Studies from Ancient Mesoamerica*, ed. Eleanor Harrison-

Buck, 53–62. University of Utah Press: Salt Lake City.

Ardren, Traci, and David Hixson. 2006. The unusual sculptures of Telantunich, Yucatán: Phalli and the concept of masculinity among the ancient Maya. *Cambridge Archaeological Journal* 16(1): 7–25.

Arnqvist, Göran, and Stefan Henriksson. Sexual cannibalism in the fishing spider and a model for the evolution of sexual cannibalism based on genetic constraints. *Evolutionary Ecology* 11(3): 255–273.

Ashley-Montagu, M. F. 1937. The origin of subincision in Australia. *Oceania* 8(2): 193–207.

Asim, Jabari. 2007. *The N Word: Who Can Say It, Who Shouldn't, and Why.* New York: Houghton Mifflin.

Aufenanger, Henry. 1977. Beliefs, customs, and rituals in the lower Yuat River Area, North-West New Guinea. *Asian Folklore Studies* 36(1): 117–132.

Bachofen, Johann Jakob. 1861. *Das Mutterecht.* Basel: Benno Schwabe.

Bagge, S. 1904. The circumcision ceremony among the Naivisha Masai. *Journal of the Anthropological Institute of Great Britain and Ireland* 34: 167–169.

Bakels, Jet. 2004. Farming the forest edge: Perceptions of wildlife among the Kerinci of Sumatra. In *Wildlife in Asia: Cultural Perspectives*, ed. John Knight, 147–164. London and New York: Routledge Curzon.

Baker, Lauren E. 2008. Local food networks and maize agrodiversity conservation: Two case studies from Mexico. *Local Environment* 13(3): 235–251.

Baker, R. Robin, and Mark A. Bellis. 1995. *Human Sperm Competition: Copulation, Masturbation, and Infidelity.* London: Chapman and Hall.

Baldwin, John D. 1971. The social organization of a semifree-ranging troop of squirrel monkeys (*Saimiri sciureus*). *Folia Primatologia* 14: 23–50.

———. 1970. Reproductive synchronization in squirrel monkeys (*Saimiri sciureus*). *Primates* 11(4): 317–326.

Banks, William E., Francisco d'Errico, A. Townsend Peterson, Masa Kageyama, Adriana Sima, and Maria-Fernanda Sánchez-Goñi. 2008. Neanderthal extinction by competitive exclusion. *PLoS ONE* 3(12): e3972. doi:10.1371/journal.pone.0003972.

Bannister, Robert C. 1979. *Social Darwinism: Science and Myth in Anglo-American Social Thought.* Philadelphia: Temple University Press.

Barnett, Zoë L., Sofia Robleda-Gomez, and Nancy A. Pachana. 2012. Viagra: The little blue pill with big repercussions. *Aging and Mental Health* 16(1): 84–88.

Barnhoorn, I. E. J., M. S. Bornman, G. M. Pieterse, and J. H. J. van Vuren. 2004. Histological evidence of intersex in feral sharptooth catfish (*Clarias gariepinus*) from an estrogen-polluted water source in Gauteng, South Africa. *Environmental Toxicology* 19(6): 603–608.

Baumeister, Roy. 2010. *Is There Anything Good About Men? How Cultures Flourish by Exploiting Men.* Oxford and New York: Oxford University Press.

Baxter, John. 2009. *Carnal Knowledge: Baxter's Concise Encyclopedia of Modern Sex.* New York: Harper Perennial.

BBC News. 2003. Penis is a competitive beast. Retrieved on January 30, 2015 from http://news.bbc.co.uk/2/hi/health/3128753.stm.

Beckwith, Martha W. 1940. *Hawaiian Mythology.* New Haven: Yale University Press.

Bedmar, Francisco, Jose Luis Costa, Elvira Suero, and Daniel Gimenez. 2004. Transport of atrazine and metribuzin in three soils of the humid pampas of Argentina. *Weed Technology* 18(1): 1–8.

Beja-Pereira, Albano, Gordon Luikart, Phillip R. England, Daniel G. Bradley, Oliver C. Jann, Giorgio Bertorelle, Andrew T. Chamberlain, Telmo P. Nunes, Stoitcho Metodiev, Nuno Ferrand, and Georg Erhardt. 2003. Gene-culture coevolution between cattle milk protein genes and human lactase genes. *Nature* 35(4): 311–313.

Bell, Kirsten. 2005. Genital cutting and Western discourses on sexuality. *Medical Anthropology Quarterly* 19(2): 125–148.

Bellwood, Peter. 2005. *First Farmers: The Origins of Agricultural Societies.* Oxford: Blackwell.

Belmontesi, Magda, Rjiv Grover, and Alexis Verpaele. 2006. Transdermal injection of Restylane SubQ for aesthetic contouring of the cheeks, chin, and mandible. *Aesthetic Surgery Journal* 26(1): S28–234.

Benedict, Ruth. 1931. Dress. In *Encyclopedia of the Social Sciences.* Vol. 5. New York: MacMillan.

———. 1924. A brief sketch of Serrano culture. *American Anthropologist* 26(3): 366–392.

Benotti, Mark J., Rebecca A. Trenholm, Brett J. Vanderford, Janie C. Holady, Benjamin D. Stanford, and Shane A. Snyder. 2009. Pharmaceuticals and endocrine disrupting compounds in U.S. drinking water. *Environmental Science Technology* 43(3): 597–603.

Benshoof, Lee, and Randy Thornhill. 1979. The evolution of monogamy and concealed ovulation in humans. In *Journal of Social and Biological Systems* 2(2): 95–106.

Benson, Larry V., Edward R. Cook, and Timothy R. Pauketat. 2009. Cahokia's boom and bust in the context of climate change. *American Antiquity* 74(3): 467–483.

Bentley, Paul. 2012. "Mummy porn": Fifty Shades of Grey outstrips Harry Potter to become fastest selling paperback of all time. *Daily Mail.* Retrieved on December 7, 2012, from http://www.dailymail.co.uk.

Bentley, R. Alexander, Penny Bickle, Linda Fibiger, Geoff M. Nowell, Christopher W. Dale, Robert E. M. Hedges, Julie Hamilton, Joachim Wahl, Michael Francken, Gisela Grupe, Eva Lenneis, Maria Teschler-Nicola, Rose-Marie Arbogast, Daniela Hofmann, and Alasdair Whittle. 2012. Community differentiation and kinship among Europe's first farmers. *Proceedings of the National Academy of Sciences* 109: 9326–9330.

Benz, Bruce F. 2001. Archaeological evidence of teosinte domestication from Guilá Naquitz, Oaxaca. *Proceedings of the National Academy of Sciences* 98(4): 2104–2106.

Berman, Carol M., Consuel S. Ionica, and Jinhua Li. 2004. Dominance style among *Macaca thibetana* on Mt. Huangshan, China. *International Journal of Primatology* 25(6): 1283–1312.

Berndt, R. M. 1947. Wuradjeri magic and "clever men." *Oceania* 17(4): 327–365.

———. 1941. Tribal migrations and myths centering on Ooldea, South Australia. *Oceania* 12(1): 1–20.

———. 1940. A curlew and owl legend from the Narunga tribe, South Australia. *Oceania* 10(4): 456–462.

Berrios, G. E., and S. J. Morley. Koro-like symptom in a non-Chinese subject. *The British Journal of Psychiatry* 145: 331–334.

Bersudsky, E., Y. Witztum, H. Mayodovnik, and M. Kotler. 1998. Koro-like syndrome in a Bedouin man. *Psychopathology* 31(4): 174–177.

Bertin, A., and D. J. Fairbairn. 2005. One tool, many uses: Precopulatory sexual selection on genital morphology in *Aquarius remigis*. *Journal of Evolutionary Biology* 18(4): 949–961.

Bettelheim, B. 1954. *Symbolic wounds: Puberty rites and the envious male*. New York: Free Press of Glencoe.

Bhattacharyya, Ranjan, Debasish Sanyal, and Krishna Roy. 2011. A case of Klingsor syndrome: When there is no longer psychosis. *Israeli Journal of Psychiatry Related Sciences* 48(1): 30–33.

Biebuyck, Daniel P. 1974. Mumbira: Musical instrument of a Nyanga initiation. *African Arts* 7(4): 42–45.

———. 1973. Nyanga circumcision masks and costumes. *African Arts* 6(2): 20–25.

Biobaku, Saburi. 1967. The effects of urbanization on education in Africa: The Nigerian experience. *International Review of Education* 13(4): 451–460.

Birkhead, T. R., K. E. Lee, and P. Young. 1988. Sexual cannibalism in praying mantis *Hierodula membranacea*. *Behaviour* 106(1–2): 112–118.

Birkhead, Tim. 2004. Survival of the biggest. *Science News: The Independent*. Retrieved on June 17, 2011, from http://www.independent.co.uk.

Bittocchi, Elena, Elia Belluci, Alessandro Giardini, Domenico Rau, Monica Rodriguez, Eleonora Biagetti, Rodolfo Santilocchi, Pierluigi Spagnoletti Zueli, Tania Gioia, Giuseppina Logozzo, Giovanna Attene, Laura Nanni, and Roberto Papa. 2012. Molecular analysis of the parallel domestication of the common bean (*Phaseolus vulgaris*) in Mesoamerica and the Andes. *New Phytologist*. Retrieved on December 14, 2012, from http://www.univpm.it.

Blackless, Melanie, Anthony Charuvastra, Amanda Derryck, Anne Fausto-Sterling, Karl Lauzanne, and Ellen Lee. 2000. How sexually dimorphic are we? Review and synthesis. *American Journal of Human Biology* 12(2): 151–166.

Blanc, Alberto C. 1961. *The Social Life of Early Man*. New York: Wenner-Gren Foundation for Anthropological Research.

Blaustein, Andrew R., Barbara A. Han, Rick A. Relyea, Peter T. J. Johnson, Julia C.

Buck, Stephanie S. Gervasi, and Lee B. Cats. 2011. The complexity of amphibian population declines: Understanding the role of cofactors in driving amphibian losses. *Annals of the New York Academy of Sciences* 1223: 108–119.

Bleeker, C. J. 1969. The religion of ancient Egypt. *Historia Religionum* 1: 40–114. Retrieved on November 3, 2012, from http://books.google.com.

Blench, Roger. 1987. Idoma musical instruments. *African Music* 6(4): 42–52.

Bloor, R. N. 2004. Whizz-Dick: Side effect, urban myth or amphetamine-related koro-like syndrome. *International Journal of Clinical Practice* 58(7): 717–719.

Bollongino, Ruth, Joachim Burger, Adam Powell, Marjan Mashkour, Jen-Denis Bigne, and Mark G. Thomas. 2012. Modern taurine cattle descended from small number of Near-Eastern founders. *Molecular Biology and Evolution* 29(9): 2101–2104.

Both, Arnd Adje. 2006. On the context of imitative and associative processes in Prehispanic music. In *Studien zur Musikärchaeologie V, Orient-Archäologie 20*, ed. E. Eichman, A. A. Both, and R. Eichmann, 319–332. Rahden/Westf.

Bourke, John G. 1892. *Medicine Men of the Apache, Ninth Annual Report of the Bureau of Ethnography*. Washington, DC: Government Printing Office.

Bowen, Thomas, and Edward Moser. 1970. Material and functional aspects of Seri instrumental music. *Kiva* 35(4): 178–200.

Bowler, Mark, and Richard Bodmer. 2009. Social behavior in fission-fusion groups of red uakari monkeys (*Cacajao calvus ucaylii*). *American Journal of Primatology* 71: 1–12.

Bowmer, K. H. 1991. Atrazine persistence and toxicity in two irrigated soils of Australia. *Australian Journal of Soil Research* 29(2): 339–350.

Braithwaite Batty, R. 1890. Notes on the Yoruba country. *The Journal of the Anthropological Institute of Great Britain and Ireland* 19: 160–164.

Bramanti, B., M. G. Thomas, W. Haak, M. Unterlaender, P. Jores, K. Tambets, I. Antanaitis-Jacobs, M. N. Haidle, R. Jankauskas, C.-J. Kind, F. Lueth, T. Terberger, J. Hiller, S. Matsumura, P. Forster, and J. Burger. 2009. Genetic discontinuity between local hunter-gatherers and Central Europe's first farmers. *Science* 326(5949): 137–140.

Brandewie, Ernest. 1973. Family size and kinship pressures in the Philippines. *Philippine Quarterly of Culture and Society* 1(1): 6–18.

Breault, J. L. 1991. Candirú: Amazonian parasitic fish. *Journal of Wilderness Medicine* 2: 304–312.

Brennan, P. L., R. O. Prum, K. G. McCracken, M. D. Sorenson, R. E. Wilson, and T. R. Birkhead. 2007. Coevolution of male and female genital morphology in waterfowl. *PLoS ONE* 2(5): e418. doi:10.1371/journal.pone.0000418.

Briceño, R. D., and W. G. Eberhard. 2009. Experiemental demonstration of possible cryptic female choice on male tsetse fly genitalia. *Journal of Insect Physiology* 55(11): 989–996.

Briceño, R. D., W. G. Eberhard, and A. S. Robinson. 2007. Copulation behavior of

Glossina pallidipes (Diptera: Muscidae) outside and inside the female, with a discussion of genitalic evolution. *Bulletin of Entomological Research* 97(5): 471–488.

Brigham, William Tufts. 1908. The ancient Hawaiian house. *Memories of the Bernice Pauahi Bishop Museum* 2(3): 185–378.

Brock, Gerald, John Chan, Serge Carrier, Melanie Chan, Luis Salgado, Alexander H. Klein, Clement Lang, Richard Horner, Stephen Gutkin, and Ruth Dickson. 2007. The treatment of erectile dysfunction study: Focus on treatment satisfaction of patients and partners. *British Journal of Urology International* 99(2): 376–382.

Brock, Gerald, Lei Mai Tu, and Otto I. Linet. 2001. Return of spontaneous erection during long-term intracavernosal alprostadil (Caverject) treatment. *Urology* 57(3): 536–541.

Brody, Stuart, Katerina Klapilova, and Lucie Krejčová. More frequent vaginal orgasm is associated with experiencing greater excitement from deep vaginal stimulation. *The Journal of Sexual Medicine* 10(7): 1730–1736.

Brotons, J. A., M. F. Olea-Serrano, M. Villalobos, V. Pedraza, and N. Olea. 1995. Xenoestrogens released from lacquer coatings in food cans. *Environmental Health Perspectives* 103(6): 608–612.

Brown, A. R. 1913. Three tribes of Western Australia. *The Journal of the Royal Institute of Great Britain and Ireland* 43: 143–194.

Brown, Donald N. 1971. Ethnomusicology and the Prehistoric Southwest. *Ethnomusicology* 15(3): 363–378.

———. 1967. The distribution of sound instruments in the prehistoric southwestern United States. *Ethnomusicology* 11(1): 71–90.

Brown, Edwin L. 1981. The Lucidas of Theocritus' Idylly7. *Harvard Studies in Classical Philology* 85: 59–100.

Brown, George R. 2010. Autocastration and autopenectomy as surgical self-treatment in incarcerated persons with gender identity disorder. *International Journal of Transgenderism* 12(1): 31–39.

Brown, Rosemary. 1983. Spermatophore transfer and subsequent sperm development in a homaloraghaid kinorhynch. *Zoologica Scripta* 12(4): 257–266.

Bryan, G. W., P. E. Gibbs, R. J. Huggett, L. A. Curtis, D. S. Bailey, and D. M. Dauer. 1989. Effects of tributyltin pollution on the mud snail, *Ilyanassa obsoleta*, from the York River and Sarah Creek, Chesapeake Bay. *Marine Pollution Bulletin* 20(9): 458–462.

Bryan, G. W., P. E. Gibbs, L. G. Hummerstone, and G. R. Burt. 1986. The decline of the castropod *Nucella lapillus* around South-West England: Evidence for the effect of tributyltin from antifouling paints. *Journal for the Marine Biological Association of the United Kingdom* 66: 611–640.

Bryant, Edwin. 2001. *The Quest for the Origins of Vedic Culture. The Indo-Aryan Migration Debate.* Oxford: Oxford University Press.

Buckley, Edmund. 1895. *Phallicism in Japan*. Chicago: University of Chicago Press.

Budge, E. A. Wallis. 2003. *From Fetish to God in Ancient Egypt*. Whitefish, MT: Kessinger.

————. 1926. *Cleopatra's Needles and Other Egyptian Obelisks*. London: Religious Tract Society.

Budras, Klaus-Dieter, W. O. Sack, and Sabine Röck. 2011. *Anatomy of the Horse*. 6th ed. Hannover, Germany: Schlütersche GmbH and Co, KG.

Bulik, Cynthia M., Kimberly A. Brownley, Jennifer R. Shapiro, and Nancy D. Berkman. 2012. Anorexia nervosa. In *Handbook of Evidence-Based Practice in Clinical Psychology*, ed. Peter Sturmey and Hichel Hersen, 575–597. Hoboken, NJ: John Wiley and Sons.

Burley, Nancy. 1979. The evolution of concealed ovulation. *The American Naturalist* 114(6): 835–858.

Burton, Frances D. 1971. Sexual climax in female *Macaca mulatta*. *Proceedings of the 3rd International Congress of Primatology*, Vol. 3: 181–191.

Bushway, Rodney J., Lewis B. Perkins, Ladislav Fukal, Robert O. Harrison, and Bruce S. Ferguson. 1991. Comparison of enzyme-linked immunosorbent assay and high-performance liquid chromatography for the analysis of atrazine in water from Czechoslovakia. *Archives of Environmental Contamination and Toxicology* 21(3): 365–370.

Butler, Judith. 1990. *Gender Trouble: Feminism and the Subversion of Identity*. New York: Routledge.

Cain, Virginia S., Catherine B. Johannes, Nancy E. Avis, Beth Mohr, Miriam Schocken, Joan Skurnick, and Marcia Ory. 2003. Sexual functioning and practices in a multi-ethnic study of midlife women: Baseline results from swan. *Journal of Sex Research* 40(3): 266–276.

Cameron, Deborah. 1992. Naming of parts: Gender, culture, and terms for the penis among American college students. *American Speech* 67(4): 367–382.

Carballo, Matilde, Sonia Aguayo, Ana de la Torre, and M. Jesús Muñoz. 2005. Plasma vitellogenin levels and gonadal morphology of wild carp (*Cyprinus carpio* L.) in a receiving rivers downstream of sewage treatment plants. *Science of the Total Environment* 341: 71–79.

Carlsen, Elisabeth. Aleksander Giwercman, Niels Keiding, and Niels E. Skakkebaek. 1992. Evidence for decreasing quality of semen during last 50 years. *British Medical Journal* 305: 609–613.

Carneiro, Robert L., and Robert G. Perrin. 2002. Herbert Spencer's *Principles of Sociology*: A centennial retrospective and appraisal. *Annals of Science* 59(3): 221–261.

Carosi, Monica, and Elisabetta Visalberghi. 2002. Analysis of tufted capuchin (*Cebus apella*) courtship and sexual behavior repertoire: Changes throughout the female cycle and female interindividual differences. *American Journal of Physical Anthropology* 118(1): 11–24.

Carrera, María Victoria, Renée DePalma, and Maria Lameiras. 2012. *Sexualities* 15(8): 995–1016.

Casadio, Giovanni. 2003. The failing male god: Emasculation, death and other accidents in the ancient Mediterranean world. *Numen* 50(3): 231–268.

Castro, Ítalo Braga, and Gilberto Fillmann. 2012. High tributyltin and imposex levels in the commercial muricid *Thai chocolata* from two Peruvian harbor areas. *Environmental Toxicology and Chemistry in Latin America* 31(5): 955–960.

Catalano, Glenn, Michael Morejon, Vicki A. Alberts, and Maria C. Catalano. 1996. Report of a case of male genital self-mutilation and the review of the literature, with special emphasis on the effects of media. *Journal of Sex and Marital Therapy* 22(1): 35–46.

Chan, Ka Ming, Kenneth Mei Yee Leung, Kwai Chung Cheung, Ming Hung Wong, and Jian-Wen Qiu. 2008. Seasonal changes in imposex and tissue burden of butyltin compounds in *Thais clavigera* populations along the coastal area of Mirs Bay, China. *Marine Pollution Bulletin* 57: 645–651.

Chand, Suma P. 1998. Koro associated with phobia for AIDS. *The International Journal of Psychiatry in Medicine* 28(3): 353–356.

Charan, Sri Hari, and C. M. Pavan Kumar Reddy. 2011. Genital self mutilation in alcohol withdrawal state complicated with delirium. *Indian Journal of Psychological Medicine* 33(2): 188–190.

Cheng, Sheung-Tak. 1996. A critical review of Chinese koro. *Culture, Medicine and Psychiatry* 20(1): 67–82.

Cheuk, J. T. Y., E. Lee, and G. S. Ungvari. 2009. A patient with chronic schizophrenia presenting with multiple deliberate self-harm and genital self-mutilation. *Hong Kong Journal of Psychiatry* 19: 87–89.

Chevalier-Skolnikoff, Suzanne. 1974. Male-female, female-female, and male-male sexual behavior in the stumptail monkey, with special attention to the female orgasm. *Archives of Sexual Behavior* 32(2): 95–116.

Childe, V. Gordon. 1936. *Man Makes Himself.* London: Watts.

Chimpanzee Sequencing and Analysis Consortium. 2005. Initial sequence of the chimpanzee genome and comparison with the human genome. *Nature* 437: 69–87.

Chinnery, E. W. P., and W. N. Beaver. 1915. Notes on the initiation ceremonies of Koko, Papua. *The Journal of the Royal Anthropological Institute of Great Britain and Ireland* 45: 69–78.

Chowdhury, Arabinda N. 1996. *Culture, Medicine, and Psychiatry* 20: 41–65.

Chowdhury, Arabinda N., and Gautam Banerjee. 1996. Recurrent Koro in repeated IV buprenorphine withdrawal. *Addiction* 91(1): 145–147.

Chowdhury, Arabinda N., and Dhrubo Jyoti Bagchi. 1993. Koro in heroin withdrawal. *Journal of Psychoactive Drugs* 25(3): 257–258.

Chowdhury, Arabinda N., and Nirmal K. Bera. 1994. Koro following cannabis smoking: Two case reports. *Addiction* 89(8): 1017–1020.

Clarke, A. S., N. C. Harvey, and D. G. Lingburg. 1993. Extended postpregnancy estrous cycles in female lion-tailed macaques. *American Journal of Primatology* 31: 275–285.

Clay, Diskin. 2002. The scandal of Dionysos on Paros: The Mnesiepes inscription E3. *Prometheus* 27: 97–111.

Cleveringa, Frits G., Margriet G. G. Meulenberg, Kees J. Gorter, Maureen van den Donk, and Guy E. H. M. Rutten. 2009. The association between erectile dysfunction and cardiovascular risk in men with type 2 diabetes in primary care: It is a matter of age. *Journal of Diabetes and its Complications* 23(3): 153–159.

Coe, Michael D. 2011. *The Maya.* 8th ed. New York: Thames & Hudson.

Cohen-Kettenis, Peggy T., and Friedemann Pfäfflin. 2010. The DSM diagnostic criteria for gender identity disorder in adolescents and adults. *Archives of Sexual Behavior* 39(2): 499–513.

Cold, Christopher J., and Kenneth A. McGrath. 1999. Anatomy and histology of the penile and clitoral prepuce in primates: An evolutionary perspective of the specialised sensory tissue of the external genitalia. In *Male and Female Circumcision: Medical, Legal, and Ethical Considerations in Pediatric Practice*, ed. George C. Denniston, Frederick Mansfield Hodges, and Marilyn Fayre Milos, 19–30. New York: Kluwer Academic/Plenum.

Coleman, Graham, and Thupten Jinpa, eds. 2005. *The Tibetan Book of the Dead, First Complete Translation.* London: Penguin Books.

Collecott, E. E. V. 1921. The supernatural in Tonga. *American Anthropologist* 23(4): 415–444.

Conrad, Peter. 2005. The shifting engines of medicalization. *Journal of Health and Social Behavior* 46(1): 3–14.

Cooper, Kenneth K. 1972. Cutaneous mechanoreceptors of the glans penis of the cat. *Physiology and Behavior* 8(5): 793–776.

Cooper, Ralph L., Tammy E. Stoker, Lee Tyrey, Jerome M. Goldman, and W. Keith McElroy. 2000. Atrazine disrupts the hypothalamic control of pituitary-ovarian function. *Toxicology Sciences* 53(2): 297–307.

Corley, M. Deborah, and Joshua N. Hook. 2012. Women, female sex and love addicts, and use of the Internet. *Sexual Addiction and Compulsivity: The Journal of Treatment and Prevention* 19(1–2): 53–76.

Cormier, Loretta A. 2011. *The Ten Thousand Year Fever: Rethinking Human and Wild Primate Malaria.* Walnut Creek, CA: Left Coast.

———. 2003. *Kinship with Monkeys: The Guajá Foragers of Eastern Amazonia.* New York: Columbia University Press.

Cormier, Loretta A., and Sharyn Jones. 2010. *Introductory Cultural Anthropology: An Interactive Approach.* El Cajon, CA: National Social Science Press.

Corona, G. E. Mannucci, V. Ricca, F. Lotti, V. Boddi, E. Bandini, G. Balercia, G. Forti, and M. Maggi. The age-related decline of testosterone is associated with different specific symptoms and signs in patients with sexual dysfunction. *International Journal of Andrology* 32(6): 720–728.

Cort, Louise Allison, and Paul Jett, eds. 2010. *Gods of Angkor: Bronzes from the National Museum of Cambodia.* Seattle: University of Washington Press.

Counts, Dorothy Ayers. 1990. Beaten wife, suicidal woman: Domestic violence in Kaliai, West New Britain. *Pacific Studies* 13: 151–169.

———. 1980. Fighting back is not the way: Suicide and the women of Kaliai. *American Ethnologist* 7(2): 332–351.

Couaire-Marsaudon, Françoise. 1996. Neither black nor white: The father's sister in Tonga. *The Journal of Polynesian Society* 105(2): 139–164.

Crawford, Katherine B. 2003. Love, sodomy, and scandal: Controlling the sexual reputation of Henry III. *Journal of the History of Sexuality* 12(4): 513–542.

Crawley, A. E. 1927. *The Mystic Rose: A Study of Primitive Marriage and of Primitive Thoughts in Its Bearing on Marriage.* New York: Boni and Liveright.

Crocker, William H., and Jean G. Crocker. 2004. *The Canela: Kinship, Ritual, and Sex in an Amazonian Tribe.* Belmont, CA: Wadsworth Publishing.

Crook, Paul. 1996. Social Darwinism: The concept. *History of European Ideas* 22(4): 261–274.

Csapo, Eric. 1997. Riding the phallus for Dionysus: Iconology, ritual, and gender-role de/construction. *Phoenix* 51(3–4): 253–295.

Cunningham, Shaundra. 2012. Thou shalt have no other gods before me: Myths, idols, and generational healing. In *The Black Church and Hip Hop Culture: Towards Bridging the Generational Divide*, ed. Emmett G. Price III, 67–80. Plymouth, UK: Scarecrow.

Dahl, Jeremy F. 1986. Cyclic perineal swelling during the intermenstrual intervals of captive female pygmy chimpanzees (*Pan paniscus*). *Journal of Human Evolution* 15(5): 369–385.

Daigle, Robert D. 1990. Anabolic steroids. *Journal of Psychoactive Drugs* 22(1): 77–80.

Dale, Joshua Paul. 2006. Intact or cut? Castration and the phallus in the new gender politics. *The Japanese Journal of American Studies* 17: 223–244.

Daniélou, Alain. 1995. *The Phallus: Sacred Symbol of Male Creative Power.* Rochester, VT: Inner Traditions International.

Dar, Tanveer Iqbal, Muneer Wani, Dara Singh, and Aijaz Mustafa. 2010. Self-amputation of testis: A case of compulsive masturbation. *Turkish Journal of Urology* 36(1): 95–96.

Darby, Robert J. L. 2003. The masturbation taboo and the rise of routine male circumcision: A review of the historiography. *Journal of Social History* 36(3): 737–757.

Dari, Willis, Basiti Ligairi, and Solange Petit-Skinner. 1994. *Adolescents in Fiji.* San Francisco: MacDuff.

Darwin, Charles. 1871. *The Descent of Man, and Selection in Relation to Sex.* London: Murray.

———. 1859. *On the Origin of Species by Means of Natural Selection, or, The Preservation of Favoured Races in the Struggle for Life.* London: John Murray.

Darwin, Charles, and Alfred Wallace. 1858. On the tendency of species to form varieties; and on the perpetuarion of varieties and species by means of natural selection. *Journal of the Proceedings of the Linnean Society of London. Zoology* 3(9): 45–62.

Davis, Daniel L., and R. G. Whitten. 1987. The cross-cultural study of human sexuality. *Annual Review of Anthropology* 16: 69–98.

Dawkins, Richard. 1982. *The Extended Phenotype.* San Francisco: Freeman.

———. 1989. *The Selfish Gene.* Oxford: Oxford University Press.

de Cardi, C. N. 1899. Ju-ju laws and customs in the Niger Delta. *Journal of the Anthropological Institute of Great Britain and Ireland* 29: 51–64.

De Cuypere, G., E. Elaut, G. Heylens, G. Van Maele, G. Selvaggi, G. T'sjoen, R. Rubens, P. Hoebeke, and S. Monstrey. 2006. Long-term follow-up: Psychosocial outcome of Belgian transsexuals after sex reassignment surgery. *Sexologies* 15(2): 126–133.

Deguilloux, Marie-France, Rachael Leahy, Marie-Hélène Pemonge, and Stephanie Rottier. 2012. European Neolithization and ancient DNA: An assessment. *Evolutionary Anthropology* 21(1): 24–37.

de la Cruz, Bernard J., Jeannette Hacker, and Fouad R. Kandeel. 2009. A history of the penis: Images, worship, and practices. In *Male Sexual Dysfunction: Pathophysiology and Treatment*, ed. Fouad R. Kandeel, 3–11. New York: Informa Healthcare.

Dennett, R. E. 1916. The Ogboni and other secret societies in Nigeria. *Journal of the Royal African Society* 16(61): 16–29.

De Rosa, Michele, Stefano Zarilli, Luigi Paesano, Umberto Carbone, Bartolomena Boggia, Mario Petretta, Antonella Maisto, Francesca Cimmino, Giancarmelo Puca, Annamaria Colao, and Gaetono Lombardi. 2003. Traffic pollutants affect fertility in men. *Human Reproduction* 18(5): 1055–1061.

Dessinioti, Cleo, and Andreas Katsambas. 2009. Congenital adrenal hyperplasia. *Dermato-Endocrinology* 1(2): 87–91.

de Waal, Frans B. M. 2008. Putting the altruism back into altruism: The evolution of empathy. *Annual Review of Pyschology* 59: 279–300.

———. 1995a. Bonobo sex and society. *Scientific American* 272: 82–88.

———. 1995b. Sex as an alternative to aggression in the bonobo. In *Sexual Nature Sexual Culture*, ed. Paul R. Abramson and Steven D. Pinkerton, 37–56. Chicago: University of Chicago Press.

de Waal, Frans B. M., and Frans Lanting. 1997. *Bonobo: The Forgotten Ape.* Berkeley: University of California Press.

Diamond, Jared. 2006 (1992). *The Third Chimpanzee: The Evolution and Future of the Human Animal.* New York: Harper Perennial.

———. 1997. *Why Is Sex Fun? The Evolution of Human Sexuality.* New York: Basic Books.

Díaz-Muñoz, Samuel L. 2011. Paternity and relatedness in a polyandrous nonhuman primate: Testing adaptive hypotheses of male reproductive cooperation. *Animal Behaviour* 82: 563–571.

Dicktionary (online list of penis euphemisms). 2012. http://gregology.net.

Diehl, Richard A. 2004. *The Olmecs: America's First Civilization.* New York: Thames & Hudson.

Dieterlen, Germaine. 1989. Masks and mythology among the Dogon. *African Arts* 22(3): 34–43.

Dixson, Alan. 2002. Sexual selection by cryptic female choice and the evolution of primate sexuality. *Evolutionary Anthropology: Issues, News, and Reviews* 11(S1): 195–199.

———. 1998. *Primate Sexuality: Comparative Studies of the Prosimians, Monkeys, Apes, and Human Beings.* Oxford: Oxford University Press.

Dixson, A. F., and N. I. Mundy. 1994. Sexual behavior, sexual swelling, and penile evolution in chimpanzees (*Pan troglodytes*). *Archives of Sexual Behavior* 23(3): 267–280.

Dixson, Barnaby J., Alan F. Dixson, Phil J. Bishop, and Amy Parish. 2010. Human physique and sexual attractiveness: A New-Zealand-US comparative study. *Archives of Sexual Behavior* 39(3): 798–806.

Dixson, Barnaby J., Alan F. Dixson, Baoguo Li, and M.J. Anderson. 2007a. Studies of human physique and sexual attractiveness: Sexual preferences of men and women in China. *American Journal of Human Biology* 19(1): 88–95.

Dixson, Barnaby J., Alan F. Discon, Bethan Morgan, and Matthew J. Anderson. 2007b. Human physique and sexual attractiveness: Sexual preferences of men and women in Bakossiland, Cameroon. *Archives of Sexual Behavior* 36(3): 369–75.

Domett, K. M., D. J. W. O'Reilly, and H. R. Buckley. 2011. Bioarchaeological evidence for conflict in Iron Age north-west Cambodia. *Antiquity* 85: 441–458.

Douaire-Marsaudon, Françoise. 1996. Neither black nor white: The father's sister in Tonga. *The Journal of the Polynesian* Society: 139–64.

Du Mond, Frank V., and Thomas C. Hutchinson. 1967. Squirrel monkey reproduction: The "fatted" male phenomenon and seasonal spermatogenesis. *Science* 158(3804): 1067–1070.

Dundes, Alan. 2005. Folklorists in the twenty-first century. *The Journal of American Folklore* 118(470): 385–408.

———. 1976. A psychoanalytic study of the bullroarer. *Man* 11(2): 220–238.

Dunn, Thomas M., Vincent Collins, Robert M. House, and Philippe Weintraub. 2009. Male genital self-mutilation with maggot infestation in an intoxicated individual. *Mental Health and Substance Use* 2(3): 235–238.

Dunsmuir, W. D., and E. M. Gordon. 1999. The history of circumcision. *British Journal of Urology* 83(S1): S1–S12.

Du Preez, Hein H., and J. H. H. van Vuren. 1992. Bioconcentration of atrazine in the banded tilapia, *Tilapia sparrmanii*. *Comparative Biochemistry and Physiology Part C.: Comparative Pharmacology* 101(3): 651–655.

Durst, R., and P. Rosca-Rebaudengo. 1988. Koro secondary to a tumour of the corpus callosum. *British Journal of Psychiatry* 153: 251–254.

Dzokoto, Vivian Afi, and Glenn Adams. 2005. Understanding genital-shrinking epidemics in West Africa: Koro, juju, or a mass psychogenic illness? *Culture, Medicine, and Psychiatry* 29: 53–78.

Eady, Cornelius. 2001. *Brutal Imagination*. New York: Penguin Putnam.

Earleywine, Mitchell. 2001. Cannibis-induced Koro in Americans. *Addiction* 96(11): 1663–1666.

East, Marion L., Heribert Hofer, and Wolfgang Wickler. 1993. The erect "penis" is a flag of submission in a female-dominated society: Greetings in Serengeti spotted hyenas. *Behavioral Ecology and Sociobiology* 33(6): 355–370.

Eberhard, William G. 2010. Evolution of genitalia: Theories, evidence, and new directions. *Genetica* 138(1): 5–18.

———. 2001. Species-specific genitalic copulatory courtship in sepsid flies (Diptera, sepsidae, microsepsis) and theories of genitalic evolution. *Evolution* 55(1): 93–102.

———. 1993. Evaluating models of sexual selection: Genitalia as a test case. *The American Naturalist* 142(3): 564–571.

Eke, N. 2000. Genital self-mutilation: There is no method in this madness. *British Journal of Urology International* 85(3): 295–298.

Eliade, Mircea. 1967. Australian religions. Part III: Initiation rites and secret cults. *History of Religions* 7(1): 61–90.

Elkin, A. P. 1930. The rainbow-serpent myth in north-west Australia. *Oceania* 1(3): 349–352.

Elliott, Kamilla. 2008. Gothic-film-parody. *Adaptation* 1(1): 24–43.

Elliot-Smith, Grafton. 1929. *The Migrations of Early Culture: A Study of the Significance of the Practice of Mummification as Evidence of the Migrations of Peoples and the Spread of Certain Customs and Beliefs*. Manchester: University Press.

———. 1910. Circumcision in ancient Egypt. *The British Medical Journal* 1(2561): 294.

———. 1908. The most ancient of splints. *The British Medical Journal* 1(2465): 732–734.

Ellis, Alfred B. 1894. *The Yoruba-Speaking Peoples of the Slave Coast of West Africa: Their Religion, Manners, Customs, Laws, Language, Etc.* London: Chapman and Hall.

Ellis, Derek V., and L. Agan Pattisina. 1990. Widespread neogastropod imposex: A biological indicator of global TBT contamination? *Marine Pollution Bulletin* 21(5): 248–253.

Ellis, Joseph J. 2000. Jefferson: Post-DNA. *The William and Mary Quarterly* 57(1): 125–138.

Eltsov, Piotr Andreevich. 2008. *From Harappa to Hastinapura: A Study of the Earliest South Asian City and Civilization*. Leiden, The Netherlands: Brill.

Ember, Carol R. 1978. Myths about hunter-gatherers. *Ethnology* 17(4): 439–448.

Endleman, Robert. 1989. *Love and Sex in Twelve Cultures*. New York: Psyche.

English Heritage. 2012. The National Heritage List for England. "Hill Figure Called The Giant." Retrieved on December 3, 2012, from: http://list.english-heritage.org.uk.

Epstein, Helen, and Rachel Jewkes. 2009. The myth of the virgin rape myth. *The Lancet* 374(9699): 1419.

Feldman, H.A., I. Goldstein, D. G. Hatzichristou, R. J. Crane, and J. B. McKinlay. 1994. Impotence and its medical and psychological correlates: Results of the Massachusetts aging study. *Journal of Urology* 151(1): 54–61.

Fernandez, Mariana F., and Nicolas Olea. 2012. Developmental exposure to endocrine disruptors and male urogenital tract malformations. In *Endocrine Disruptors and Puberty*, ed. E. Diamanti-Kandarakis and A. C. Gore, 225–239. New York: Humana.

Finsch, Otto. 1880. Ornithological letters from the Pacific. No II. *Ibis* 22(2): 218–220.

Firth, Raymond. 1936a. Tattooing in Tikopia. *Man* 36: 173–177.

———. 1936b. *We, the Tikopia: A Sociological Study of Kinship in Primitive Polynesia*. London: Allen and Unwin.

Fisher, R. A. 1915. The evolution of sexual preference. *Eugenics Review* 7: 184–192.

Flammarion, P., F. Brion, M. Babut, J. Garric, B. Migeon, P. Noury, E. Thybaud, X. Palazzi, and C. R. Tyler. 2000. Induction of fish vitellogenin and alterations in testicular structure: Preliminary results of estrogenic effects in chub (*Leuciscus cephalus*). *Exotoxicology* 9: 127–135.

Flannery, Kent V. 1986. *Guilá Naquitz: Archaic Foraging and Early Agriculture in Oaxaca, Mexico*. New York: Academic Press.

Flannery, Regina. 1936. Some aspects of James Bay recreative culture. *Primitive Man* 9(4): 49–56.

Fleagle, John G. 1999. *Primate Adaptation and Evolution*. San Diego, CA: Academic Press.

Fletcher, Neville H. 2003. Australian Aboriginal musical instruments: The didjeridu, the bullroarer, and the gumleaf. *Acoustics Australia* 31(2): 51–54.

Ford, Clellan S., and Frank A. Beach. 1951. *Patterns of Sexual Behavior*. New York: Harper and Brothers.

Foster, Eugene A., M. A. Jobling, P. G. Taylor, P. Donnelly, P. de Knijff, Rene Mieremet, T. Zerjal, and C. Tyler-Smith. 1998. Jefferson fathered slave's last child. *Nature* 396: 27–28.

Fowler, Don D., and John F. Matley. 1979. *Material Culture of the Numa: The John Wesley Powell Collection, 1867–1880*. Washington, DC: Smithsonian Institution Press.

Fox, Robin. 1967. In the beginning: Aspects of hominid behavioural evolution. *Man* 2(3): 415–433.

Francke, August Hermann. 1999 (1907). *History of Western Tibet: One of the Unknown Empires*. Kathmandu: Pilgrims.

Franke, Craig B., and James A. Rush. 2007. Autocastration and autoamputation of the penis in a patient with delusions of sexual guilt. *Jefferson Journal of Psychiatry* 21(1). Retrieved on August 26, 2012, from http://jdc.jefferson.edu.

Frankfort, Henri. 1948. *Kinship and the Gods: A Study of Ancient Near Eastern Religion as the Integration of Society and Nature.* Chicago: University of Chicago Press.

Frazer, James George. 1913. *The Golden Bough: A Study in Magic and Religion, Volume 11, Balder the Beautiful* (Part 2). London: Macmillan.

———. 1912. *The Golden Bough: A Study in Magic and Religion, Volume 7, Spirits of the Corn and of the Wild* (Part 1). London: Macmillan.

Freidel, Davide, Linda Schele, and Joy Parker. 1993. *Maya Cosmos: Three Thousand Years on the Shaman's Path.* New York: William Morrow.

Freud, Sigmund. 1962 (1905). *Three Contributions to the Theory of Sex.* New York: E. P. Dutton.

———. 1939. *Moses and Monotheism.* New York: Vintage Books.

———. 1918. *Totem and Taboo.* New York: Moffat Yard.

Frick, Carole Collier. 2011. Boys to men: Codpieces and masculinity in sixteenth-century Europe. In *Gender and Early Modern Constructions of Childhood*, ed. Naomi J. Miller and Naomi Yavneh, 157–180. Burlington, VT: Ashgate Publishing.

Friedman, David M. 2001. *A Mind of Its Own: A Cultural History of the Penis.* New York: Penguin Books.

Frobenius, Leo. 1988. *Der Ursprung der afridanischen Kulturen.* Vol. 1. Berlin: Gebrüder Borntraeger.

Fruth, Barbara, and Gottfried Hohmann. 2006. Social grease for females? Same-sex genital contacts in wild bonobos. In *Homosexual Behavior in Animals: An Evolutionary Perspective*, ed. P. L. Vasey and V. Sommer: 294–315. Cambridge University Press.

Fry, Douglas P. 2012. Life Without War. *Science* 336: 879–884.

———. 2007. *Beyond War: The Human Potential for Peace.* Oxford: Oxford University Press.

Frye, Marilyn. 1996. The necessity of differences: Constructing a positive category of women. *Signs* 21(4): 991–1010.

Fu, Jiamo, Bixian Mai, Guoying Seng, Gan Zhang, Xinming Wang, Ping'an Peng, Xianming Xiao, Rong Ran, Fanzhong Cheng, Xianshi Peng, Zhishi Wnng, and U Wa Tang. 2003. Persistent organic pollutants in environment of the Pearl River Delta, China: An overview. *Chemosphere* 52: 1411–1422.

Fuentes, Augustin. 1998. Re-evaluating primate monogamy. *American Anthropologist* 100(4): 890–907.

Fuller, Dorian Q., George Willcox, and Robin G. Allaby. 2011. Cultivation and domestication had multiple origins: Arguments against the core area hypothesis for the origins of agriculture in the Near East. *World Archaeology* 43(4): 628–652.

Furuichi, Takeshi. 2011. Female contributions to the peaceful nature of bonobo society. *Evolutionary Ecology* 20: 131–142.

————. 1987. Sexual swelling, receptivity, and group of wild chimpanzee females at Wamba, Zaire. *Primates* 28(3): 309–318.

Galdikas, B. M. F. 1985. Subadult male orangutan sociality and reproductive behavior at Tanjung Puting. *American Journal of Primatology* 8: 87–99.

————. 1983. The orangutan long call and snag crashing at Tanjung Puting Reserve. *Primates* 24(3): 371–384.

Gallup, Gordon G., Jr., and Rebecca L. Burch. 2004. Semen displacement as a sperm competition strategy in humans. *Evolutionary Psychology* 2: 12–23.

Gallup, Gordon G., Jr., Rebecca L. Burch, M. L. Zappieri, R. Parvez, M. Stockwell, and J. Davis. 2003. The human penis as a semen displacement device. *Evolution and Human Behavior* 24: 277–289.

Garaventa, F., M. Faimali, and A. Terlizzi. 2006. Imposex in pre-pollution times: Is TBT to blame? *Marine Pollution Bulletin* 52: 696–718.

Gascon, Mervin G. 2011. Traditional and modern practices enhance health knowledge of the Babogo tribe. *Asian Journal of Health* 1(1): 143–159.

Geertz, Clifford. 1972. Deep play: Notes on the Balinese cockfight. *Daedulus* 101(1): 1–37.

Geller, Jay. 1993. A paleontological view of Freud's study of religion: Unearthing the "leitfossil" circumcision. *Modern Judaism* 13(1): 49–70.

Gentile, John S. 2007. The scholar as mystic: The poetic mysticism of Joseph Campbell. *Storytelling, Self, and Society: An Interdisciplinary Journal of Storytelling Studies* 3(3): 195–204.

Gerhardt, H. Carl, Steven D. Tanner, Candice M. Corrigan, and Hilary C. Walton. 2000. Female preference functions based on call duration in the gray tree frog (*Hyla versicolor*), *Behavioral Ecology* 11(6): 663–669.

Gero, Joan, and Margaret Conkey, eds. 1991. *Engendering Archaeology: Women in Prehistory*. Oxford, UK: Blackwell.

Gerritsen, Rupert. 2008. *Australia and the Origins of Agriculture*. British Archaeological Reports International Series. Oxford: Archaeopress.

Gfrerer, Marion, Thomas Wenzl, Xie Quan, Bernhard Platzer, and Ernst Lankmayr. 2002. Occurrence of triazines in surface and drinking water of Liaoning Province in eastern China. *Journal of Biochemical and Biophysical Methods* 53: 217–288.

Ghaffari, M. Selk, N. Khoami, M. Majani, and S. J. Adavood. 2007. Penile self-mutilation as an unusual sign of a separation-related problem in a cross-breed dog. *Journal of Small Animal Practice* 48(11): 651–653.

Gibbons, Ann. 2012. The ultimate sacrifice. *Science* 336: 834–837.

Gifford, E. W. 1939. The Coast Yuki. *Anthropos* 34(1): 292–375.

Gignoux, Christopher R., Brenna M. Henn, and Johanna L. Mountain. 2011. Rapid global demographic expansions after the origins of agriculture. *Proceedings of the National Academy of Sciences* 108(13): 5154–5162.

Gilbert, Scott F., and Ziony Zevit. 2001. Congenital baculum deficiency: The generative bone of Genesis 2: 21–23. *American Journal of Medical Genetics* 101(3): 284–285.

Gilligan, Ian. 2007a. Neanderthal extinction and modern human behaviour: The role of climate change and clothing. *World Archaeology* 39(4): 499–514.

———. 2007b. Clothing and farming origins: The Indo-Pacific evidence. *Bulletin of the Indo-Pacific Prehistory Association* 27: 12–21.

———. 2010. The prehistoric development of clothing: Archaeological implications for a thermal model. *Journal of Archaeological Method and Theory* 17: 15–80.

Gimbutas, Marija. 1991. *The Civilization of the Goddess.* San Francisco: Harper and Row.

———. 1989. *The Language of the Goddess: Unearthing the Hidden Symbols of Western Civilization.* San Francisco: Harper and Row.

———. 1974. *The Goddesses and Gods of Old Europe: 7000–3500 BC, Myths, Legends and Cult Images.* London: Thames and Hudson.

Girolami, L., and C. Bielert. 1987. Female perineal swelling and its effect on male sexual arousal: An apparent sexual releaser in the chacma baboon (*Papio ursinus*). *International Journal of Primatology* 8: 651–661.

Gladwin, Harold S. 1937. Independent invention versus diffusion. *American Antiquity* 3(2): 156–160.

Golde, Peggy, ed. 1970. *Women in the Field: Anthropological Experiences.* Chicago: Aldine.

Goldfoot, D.A., H. Westerborg-van Loon, W. Groeneveld, and A.K. Slob. 1980. Behavioral and physiological evidence of sexual climax in the female stump-tailed macaque (*Macaca arctoides*). *Science* 208(4451): 1477–1479.

Goldner, Virginia. 2011. Deconstructing the gender binary. *Psychoanalytic Dialogues* 21:159–171.

Goodall, Jane. 1986. *The Chimpanzees of Gombe: Patterns of Behavior.* Cambridge, MA: Belknap.

Gollaher, David L. 2000. *Circumcision: A History of the World's Most Controversial Surgery.* New York: Basic Books.

———. 1994. From ritual to science: The medical transformation of circumcision in America. *Journal of Social History* 28(1): 5–36.

Grafen, Alan. 1990. Biological signals as handicaps. *Journal of Theoretical Biology* 144: 517–546.

Graham, Charles. E. 1981. Menstrual cycle of the great apes. In *Reproductive Biology of the Great Apes*, ed. Charles E. Graham, 1–43. New York: Academic Press.

Grancsay, Stephen V. 1950. The interrelationships of costume and armor. *The Metropolitan Museum of Art Bulletin* 8(6): 177–188.

Grant, Michael. 1997. *Eros in Pompeii: The Erotic Art Collection of the Museum of Naples.* New York: Stewart Tabori & Chang.

Gray, John. 1992. *Men Are from Mars, Women Are from Venus.* New York: HarperCollins.

Grayson, Donald K., and David J. Meltzer. 2003. A requiem for North American overkill. *Journal of Archaeological Science* 30(5): 585–593.

Green, K. M. 1981. Preliminary observations on the ecology and behavior of the capped langur, *Presbytis pileatus*, in the Madhapur forest of Bangladesh. *International Journal of Primatology* 2(2): 131–151.

Greene, S. A., E. Symes, and C. G. Brook. 1978. 5-alpha-reductase deficiency causing male pseudohermaphroditism. *Archives of Disease in Childhood* 53(9): 751–753.

Gregersen, Edgar. 1982. *Sexual Practices: The Story of Human Sexuality*. New York: Franklin Watts.

Gregor, Thomas. 1987. *Anxious Pleasures: The Sexual Lives of an Amazonian People*. Chicago: University of Chicago Press.

Greilsheimer, Howard, and James E. Groves. 1979. Male genital self-mutilation. *Archives of General Psychiatry* 36(4): 441–446.

Griffin, P. Bio. 1967. A high status burial from Grasshopper Ruin. *Kiva* 33(2): 37–53.

Griffith, Ralph T. H. 1899. *The Texts of the White Yajurveda, Translated with a Popular Commentary*. Benares: E. J. Lazarus and Co. Retrieved on October 24, 2012, from https://play.google.com.

Grizzard, Lewis. 1994. *The Best of Lewis Grizzard*. Southern Track Records.

Gronning, Torben, Patricia Sohl, and Thomas Singer. 2007. ARAS: Archetypal symbolism and images. *Visual Resources: An International Journal of Documentation* 23(3): 245–267.

Grossman, Catherine Lynn. 2010. Muslim cleric joins Rev. Pat Roberson blaming quakes on sinners. *USA Today*. Retrieved on June 27, 2010, from http://content.usatoday.com.

Guillette, Louis J., Timothy S. Gross, Greg R. Masson, John M. Matter, H. Franklin Percival, and Allan R. Woodward. 1994. Developmental abnormalities of the gonad and abnormal sex hormone concentrations in juvenile alligators from contaminated and control lakes in Florida. *Environmental Health Perspectives* 102(8): 680–688.

Guzella, Licia, Fiorenzo Pozzoni, and Giuseppe Giuliano. 2006. Herbicide contamination of surficial groundwater in Northern Italy. *Environmental Pollution* 142(2): 344–353.

Guzmán, Ricardo Andrés, and Jacob Weisdorf. 2011. The Neolithic Revolution from a price-theoretic perspective. *Journal of Development Economics* 96(2): 209–219.

Hackworth, Jason, and Joshua Akers. 2010. Faith in the neoliberalisation of post-Katrina New Orleans. *Tijdschrift Voor Economishce en Social Geografie* 102(1): 39–54.

Haddon, Alfred C. 1900. Studies in the anthropogeography of British New Guinea. *The Geographic Journal* 16(4): 414–440.

———. 1898. *The Study of Man*. New York: G. P. Putnam.

Hald, Gert Martin. 2006. Gender differences in pornography consumption among young heterosexual Danish adults. *Archives of Sexual Behavior* 35: 577–585.

Haldane, J. B. S. 1949. The rate of mutation of human genes. *Proceedings of the VIII International Congress of Genetics Hereditas* 35: 267–273.

Haleem, S., S. J. Griffin, and G. K. Banerjee. 2007. Self-castration: A case report. *Grand Rounds* 7: 9–12.

Hallett, Judith P., and Marilyn B. Skinner. 1997. *Roman Sexualities*. Princeton, NJ: Princeton University Press.

Halliday, R. J. 1971. Social Darwinism: A definition. *Victorian Studies* 14(4): 389–405.

Hammond, T. 1999. A preliminary poll of men circumcised in infancy or childhood. *British Journal of Urology International* 83(S1): S85–S92.

Hammoud, Ahman, Douglass T. Carrell, Mark Gibson, Matt Sanderson, Kirtly Parker-Jones, and C. Matthew Peterson. 2010. Decreased sperm motility is associated with air pollution in Salt Lake City. *Fertility and Sterility* 93(6): 1875–1879.

Handy, E. S. Craighill. 1927. Polynesian religion. *Bernice P. Bishop Museum Bulletin 34*. Honolulu: Bishop Museum Press.

Handy, E. S. Craighill, and Elizabeth Green Handy. 1991 [1972]. Native planters in old Hawaii: Their life, lore, and environment. Rev. ed. *Bernice P. Bishop Museum Bulletin 233*. Honolulu: Bishop Museum Press.

Hanson, Dian, ed. 2008. *The Big Penis Book*. Los Angeles: Taschen America.

Harding, J. R. 1973/1974. The bull roarer in history and antiquity. *African Music* 5(3): 40–42.

Harrington, Charles. 1968. Sexual differentiation and socialization and some male genital mutilations. *American Anthropologist* 70(5): 951–956.

Harrington, Gwyneth, Miguel Bernett, and Victoria Barnett. 1988. Seri dreams. *Journal of the Southwest* 30(4): 502–521.

Harris, Helen. 1997. Rethinking Polynesian heterosexual relationships: A case study on Mangaia, Cook Islands. In *Romantic Passion: A Universal Experience?*, ed. Robert Jankowiak, 95–127. New York: Columbia University Press.

Harris, Marvin. 1968. *The Rise of Anthropological Theory: A History of Theories of Culture*. New York: HarperCollins.

Harris, P. G. 1938. Notes on the Dakarari peoples of Sokoto Province, Nigeria. *The Journal of the Royal Institute of Great Britain and Ireland* 68: 113–152.

Harrison-Buck, Eleanor, ed. 2012. *Power and Identity in Archaeological Theory and Practice: Case Studies from Ancient Mesoamerica*. Salt Lake City: University of Utah Press.

Hart, George. 1986. *A Dictionary of Egyptian Gods and Goddesses*. London: Routledge & Kegan Paul.

Harvey, Philip W., and Philippa Darbre. 2004. Endocrine disrupters and human health: Could oestrongenic chemicals in body care cosmetics adverse affect breast cancer incidence in women? *Journal of Applied Toxicology* 24(3): 167–176.

Hassrick, Royal, and Edmund Carpenter. 1944. Rappahannock games and amusements. *Primitive Man* 17: 29–39.

Hawkes, K., J. F. O'Connell, and N. G. Blurton Jones. 1997. Hadza women's time allocation, offspring provisioning, and the evolution of long postmenopausal lifespans. *Current Anthropology* 38(4): 551–577.

Hawkins, Mike. 1997. *Social Darwinism in European and American Thought: 1860–1945.* Cambridge: Cambridge University Press.

Hawley, Richard M., and John H. Owen. 1988. Koro: Its presentation in an elderly male. *International Journal of Geriatric Psychiatry* 3(1): 69–72.

Hayden, B. 2003. Were luxury goods the first domesticates? Ethnoarchaeological perspectives from Southeast Asia. *World Archaeology* 34: 458–469.

Hayes, Tyrone B., Atif Collins, Melissa Lee, Magdlena Mendoza, Nigel Noriega, A. Ali Stuart, and Aaron Vonk. 2002. Hermaphroditic, demasculinized frogs after exposure to the herbicide atrazine at low ecologically relevant doses. *Proceedings of the National Academy of Sciences, USA* 99(8): 5476–5480.

Hayes, Tyrone, Kelly Haston, Mable Tsui, Anhthu Hoang, Cathryn Haeffele, and Aaron Vonk. 2002. Herbicides: Feminization of male frogs in the wild. *Nature* 419: 895–896.

———. 2003. Atrazine-induced hermaphroditism at 0.1 ppb in American leopard frogs (*Rana pipiens*): Laboratory and field evidence. *Environmental Health Perspectives* 111(4): 568–575.

Heider, Karl G. 1969. Attributes and categories in the study of material culture: New Guinea Dani attire. *Man* 4(3): 379–391.

Heidrich, Dagmar D., Stephen Steckelbroeck, and Dietrich Klingmuller. 2001. Inhibition of human cytochrome P450 aromatase activity by butyltins. *Steroids* 66(10): 763–769.

Heine-Geldern, Robert. 1964. One hundred years of ethnological theory in the German-speaking countries: Some milestones. *Current Anthropology* 5(5): 407–418.

Hellstrom, Wayne J. G., Drogo K. Montague, Ignacio Moncada, Culley Carson, Suks Minhas, Geraldo Faria, and Sudhakar Krishnamurti. 2010. Implants, mechanical devices, and vascular surgery for erectile dysfunction. *Journal of Sexual Medicine* 7: 501–523.

Hembree, Wylie C., Peggy Cohen-Kettenis, Henriette A. Delemarre-van de Waal, Louis J. Gooren, Walter J. Metyer III, Norman P. Spack, Vin Tanpricha, and Victor M. Montori. 2009. Endocrine treatment of transsexual persons: An endocrine society clinical practice guideline. *Journal of Clinical Endocrinology and Metabolism* 94(9): 3132–3154.

Hemphill, R. E. 1951. A case of genital self-mutilation. *British Journal of Medical Psychology* 24(4): 291–295.

Herbenick, Debby, Michael Reece, Vanessa Schick, and Stephanie A. Sanders. 2014. Erect penile length and circumference dimensions of 1,661 sexually active men in the United States. *The Journal of Sexual Medicine* 11(1):93–101.

Herzing, Denise L. 2011. *Dolphin Diaries: My 25 Years with Spotted Dolphins in the Bahamas.* New York: St. Martin's.

Herzog, George. 1928. The Yuman musical style. *The Journal of American Folklore* 41(160): 183–231.

Hes, J. P., and G. Nassi. 1977. Koro in a Yemenite and a Georgian Jewish Immigrant. *Confinia Psychiatrica* 20: 180–184.

Higham, Charles. 2004. *The Civilization of Angkor.* Berkley: University of California Press.

Hill, Frances. 2000. *The Salem Witch Trials Reader.* Boston: Da Capo.

Hill, Gertrude. 1938. The use of turquoise among the Navajo. *Kiva* 4(3): 11–14.

Hill, Jonathan. 1979. Kamayurá flute music: A study of music as meta-communication. *Ethnomusicology* 23(3): 417–432.

Hine, Charles Henri. 2000. Five Seri spirit songs. *Journal of the Southwest* 42(3): 589–609.

Hobday, Alistair. 2000. Where is the human baculum? *Mankind Quarterly* 41(1): 43–58.

Hodder, Ian, and Lynn Meskell. 2011. A "curious and sometimes macabre artistry." *Current Anthropology* 52(2): 235–263.

Hodges, Frederick M. 2001. The ideal prepuce in ancient Greece and Rome: Male genital aesthetics and their relation to *Lipodermos*, circumcision, foreskin restoration, and the *Kynodesmē*. *Bulletin of the History of Medicine* 75: 375–405.

Hof, Christian, Miguel B. Araújo, Walter Jetz, and Carsten Rahbek. 2011. Additive threats from pathogens, climate and land-use change for global amphibian diversity. *Nature* 480: 516–519.

Hofstadter, Richard. 1944. *Social Darwinism in American Thought.* Philadelphia: University of Pennsylvania Press.

Hogan, C. Michael. 2007. Knossos Fieldnotes. *The Modern Antiquarian.* Retrieved on October 19, 2012, from http://www.themodernantiquarian.com.

Hogbin, H. Ian. 1970. *The Island of Menstruating Men: Religion in Wogeo, New Guinea.* Scranton: Chandler.

Hohmann, Gottfried, and Barbara Fruth. 2003. Intra- and inter-sexual aggression by bonobos in the context of mating. *Behaviour* 140(11/12): 1389–1413.

———. 2000. Use and function of genital contacts among female bonobos. *Animal Behaviour* 60(2): 107–120.

Hood, Sinclair. 1971. *The Minoans: The Story of Bronze Age Crete.* New York: Praeger.

Hong, Chou C., and Raymond D. Ediger. 1978. Self-mutilation of the penis in C57BL/6N mice. *Laboratory Animals* 12: 55–57.

Horiguchi, Toshihiro, Yasuhiko Ohta, Hiroshi Urushitani, Jeong-Hoon Lee, Jeong-Chae Park, Hyeon-Seo Cho, and Hiroaki Shiraishi. 2012. Vas deferens and penis development in the imposex-exhibiting female rock shell, *Thais clavigera*. *Marine Environmental Research* 76: 71–79.

Horovitz, Bruce. 2005. NFL strives to ensure superclean Super Bowl. *USA Today*, retrieved on December 1, 2012, from http://usatoday30.usatoday.com.

Hoskins, Janet. 2002. The menstrual hut and the witch's lair in two eastern Indonesian societies. *Ethnology* 41(4): 317–333.

Hotzy, Cosima, and Göran Arnqvist. 2009. Sperm competition favors harmful males in seed beetles. *Current Biology* 19(5): 404–407.

Houlahan, Jeff E., C. Scott Findlay, Benedikt R. Schmidt, Andrea H. Meyer, and Serfius L. Kuzmin. 2000. Quantitative evidence for global amphibian population declines. *Nature* 404: 742–755.

Howard, Clifford. 1898. *Sex Worship: An Exposition of the Phallic Origin of Religion.* 2nd ed. Washington, DC: published by the author.

Howes, Hilary S. 2011. "It is not so!" Otto Finsch, expectations and encounters in the Pacific, 1865–85. *Historical Records of Australian Science* 22: 32–52.

Howitt, A. W. 1885. The Jeraeil, or initiation ceremonies of the Kurnai tribe. *The Journal of the Anthropological Institute of Great Britain and Ireland* 14: 301–325.

Hrdy, S. Blaffer. 1981. *The Woman That Never Evolved.* Cambridge: Harvard University Press.

Hua, Wenyi, Erin R. Bennett, and Robert J. Letcher. 2006. Ozone treatment and the depletion of detectable pharmaceuticals and atrazine herbicide in drinking water sourced from the upper Detroit River, Ontario, Canada. *Water Research* 40(12): 2259–2266.

Huang, Xuehui, Nori Kurata, Xinghua Wei, Zi-Xuan Wang, Ahong Want, Quiang Zhao, Yan Zhao, Kunyan Liu, Hengyun Lu, Wenjun Li, Yunli Guo, Yiqi Lu, Concong Zhou, Danlin Fan, Qijun Weng, Chuanrang Zhu, Tao Huang, Lei Zhang, Yonchun Wang, Lei Feng, Hiroyasu Furuumi, Takahiko Kubo, Toshie Miyabayashi, Xiaoping Yuan, Qun Zu, Guojun Dong, Qilin Zhan, Canyang Li, Asao Fujiyama, Atsushi Toyoda, Tingting Lu, Qi Feng, Qian Qian, Jiayang Li, and Bin Han. 2012. A map of rice genome variation reveals the origin of cultivated rice. *Nature* 490(7421): 497–501.

Hunter, F. M., and L. S. Davis. 1998. Female Adélie penguins acquire next material from extrapair males after engaging in extrapair copulations. *The Auk* 115(2): 526–528.

Hutton, Ronald. 1991. *The Pagan Religions of the Ancient British Isles: Their Nature and Legacy.* Oxford, UK: Blackwell.

Ikram, Salima. 2010. *Ancient Egypt: An Introduction.* Cambridge: Cambridge University Press.

Ilechukwu, Sunny T. C. 1992. Magical penis loss in Nigeria: Report of a recent epidemic of a koro-like syndrome. *Transcultural Psychiatry* 29(2): 91–108.

Ingold, Tim. 1999. On the social relations of the hunter-gatherer band. In *The Cambridge Encyclopedia of Hunters and Gatherers*, ed., R. B. Lee and R. H. Daly, 399–410. Cambridge, UK: Cambridge University Press.

———. 1980. *Hunters, Pastoralists, and Ranchers: Reindeer Economies and Their Transformations.* Cambridge: Cambridge University Press.

Inoue, Miriam H., Rubem S. Oliveira Jr., Jussara B. Regitano, Cássio A. Tormena, Jamil Constantin, and Valdemar L. Tornisielo. 2004. Sorption Kinetics of

Atrazine and Diuron in Soils from Southern Brazil. *Journal of Environmental Science and Health Part B: Pesticides, Food Contaminants, and Agricultural Wastes* 39(4): 589–601.

Irigaray, Luce. 1985. *This Sex Which Is Not One.* Ithaca, NY: Cornell University Press.

Israel, Joshua A., and Kewchang Lee. 2002. Amphetamine usage and genital self-mutilation. 97(9): 1215–1218.

Izar, Patrícia, Anita Stone, Sarah Carnegie, and Érica S. Nakai. 2009. Sexual selection, female choice, and mating systems. In *South American Primates: Comparative Perspectives in the Study of Behavior, Ecology, and Conservation,* ed. Paul A. Garber, Alejandro Estrada, Julio Cesar Bicca-Marges, Eckhard W. Heymann, and Karen B. Strier, 157–189. New York: Springer.

Jablonowski, Nicolai David, Andreas Schäffer, and Peter Burauel. 2011. Still present after all these years: Persistence plus potential toxicity raise questions about the use of atrazine. *Environmental Science Pollution Research* 18: 328–331.

Jackson, G., S. Arver, I. Banks, and V. J. Stecher. 2010. Counterfeit phosphodiesterase type 5 inhibitors pose significant safety risks. *International Journal of Clinical Practice* 64(4): 497–504.

Jameson, Michael H. 1993. The asexuality of Dionysus. In *Masks of Dionysus,* ed. T. H. Carpenter and C. A. Faraone, 44–64. Ithaca, NY: Cornell University Press.

Jarolím, Ladislav, Jirí Sedy, Marek Schmidt, Andrej Nanka, René Foltán, and Ivan Kawaciuk. 2009. Gender reassignment surgery in male-to-female transsexualism: A retrospective 3-month follow-up with anatomical remarks. *Journal of Sexual Medicine* 6(6): 1635–1644.

Jewkes, Rachel, Yandisa Sikweyiya, Robert Morrell, and Kristen Dunkle. 2009. Understanding men's health and use of violence: Interface of rape and HIV in South Africa. Gender and Health Research Unit, Medical Research Council. Pretoria, South Africa. Retrieved on June 14, 2012, from http://www.mrc.ac.za.

Jobling, Susan, Monique Nolan, Charles R. Tyler, Geoff Brighty, and John P. Sumpter. 1998. Widespread sexual disruption in wild fish. *Environmental Science Technology* 32(17): 2498–2506.

Jobling, Susan, John P. Sumpter, David Sheahan, Julia A. Osborne, and Peter Matthiessen. 1996. Inhibition of testicular growth in rainbow trout (*Oncorhynchus mykiss*) exposed to estrogenic alkylphenolic chemicals. *Environmental Toxicology and Chemistry* 15(2): 194–202.

Johansson, Thomas, and Nils Hammarén. 2007. Hegemonic masculinity and pornography: Young people's attitudes towards and relations to pornography. *The Journal of Men's Studies* 15(1): 57–70.

Johnson, Richard D., and Zdenek Halata. 1991. Topography and ultrastructure of sensory nerve endings in the glans penis of the rat. *The Journal of Comparative Neurology* 312(2): 299–310.

Jones, Clara B. 1983. Social organization of captive black howler monkeys (*Alouatta caraya*): Social competition and the use of non-damaging behavior. *Primates* 24(1): 25–39.

Jones, Martin, Harriet Hunt, Emma Lightfoot, Diane Xinyu Liu, and Giedre Motuzaite-Matuzeviciute. 2011. Food globalization in prehistory. *World Archaeology* 43(4): 665–675.

Jones, Ross J., Jochen Muller, David Haynes, and Ulrich Schreiber. 2003. Effects of herbicides diuron and atrazine on corals of the Great Barrier Reef, Australia. *Marine Ecology Progress Series* 251: 153–167.

Jones, Suzanne W. 2001. Imagining Jefferson and Hemings in Paris. *Transatlantica: Revue D'études Américanes/American Studies Journal* 1: 2–10.

Jonestone, Rufus A., and Laurent Keller. 2000. How males can gain by harming their mates: Sexual conflict, seminal toxins, and the cost of mating. *The American Naturalist* 156(4): 368–377.

Joseph, Anthony B. 1986. Koro: Computed tomography and brain electrical activity mapping in two patients. *Journal of Clinical Psychiatry* 47(8): 430–432.

Juillerat, Bernard. 2000. Do the Banaro really exist? *Oceania* 71(1): 46–66.

Kabore, Fasnéwindé Aristide, Papa Ahmed Fall, Babacar Diao, Boubacar Fall, Anani Odzegbe, Yahya Ould Tfeil, and Baye Assane Diagne. 2008. Auto-amputation récidivante du pénis sur terrain schizophrène: À propos d'un cas. *Andrologie* 18(3): 224–226.

Kalaitzi, C. K., and A. Kalantzis. 2006. Cannibis-induced koro-like syndrome. *Urologia Internationalis* 76(3): 276–280.

Kano, Takayoshi. 1992. *The Last Ape: Pygmy Chimpanzee Behavior and Ecology*. Redwood City, CA: Stanford University Press.

Kaplan, Sara Clarke. 2009. Our founding (m)other: Erotic love and social death in Sally Hemings and the president's daughter. *Callaloo* 32(3): 773–791.

Kartomi, Margaret J. 1999. The music-culture of South-Coast West Sumatra: Backwater of Minangkabau "heartland" or home of the sacred mermaid and the earth goddess? *Asian Music* 30(1): 133–181.

Kasahara, Kazuo, ed. 2009. *A History of Japanese Religion*. Translated by P. McCarthy and G. Sekimori. Tokyo: Kosei Publishing Co.

Kempf, Wolfgang. 2002. The politics of incorporation: Masculinity, spatiality, and modernity among the Ngaing of Papua New Guinea. *Oceania* 73(1): 56–77.

———. 1992. "The Second Coming of the Lord": Early Christianization, episodic time, and the cultural construction of continuity in Sibog. *Oceania* 63(1): 72–86.

Kennedy, N., and M. McDonough. 2002. Koro: A case report in an Eastern European asylum seeker in Ireland. *Irish Journal of Psychological Medicine* 19: 130–131.

Keuls, Eva C. 1985. *The Reign of the Phallus: Sexual Politics in Ancient Athens*. Berkeley: University of California Press.

Khan, Mohammed Kaleem, Mohammed Amir Usmani, and Shaukat A. Hanif. 2012. A case of self amputation of penis by cannabis induced psychosis. *Journal of Forensic and Legal Medicine* 19(6): 355–357.

Kidd, Karen A., Paul J. Blanchfield, Kenneth H. Mills, Vince P. Palace, Robert E. Evans, James M. Lazorchak, and Robert W. Flick. 2007. Collapse of a fish population after exposure to a synthetic estrogen. *Proceedings of the National Academy of Science: USA* 104(21): 8897–8901.

Kiesecker, Joseph M., Andrew R. Blaustein, and Lisa K. Belden. 2001. Complex causes of amphibian declines. *Nature* 410: 681–684.

Kijas, James W., Johannes A. Lenstra, Ben Hayes, Simon Boitard, Laercio R. Porto Neto, Magali San Cristobal, Bertrand Servin, Russell McCulloch, Vicki Whan, Kimberly Gietzen, Samuel Paiva, William Barendse, Elena Ciani, Herman Raadsma, John McEwan, Brian Dalrymple, and other members of the International Sheep Genomics Consortium. 2012. Genome-wide analysis of the world's sheep breeds reveals high levels of historic mixture and strong recent selection. *PLoS Biology* 10(2): e1001258. Retrieved on December 14, 2012, from http://www.plosbiology.org.

Kilchevsky, Amichai, Yoram Vardi, Lior Lowenstein, and Ilan Gruenwald. 2012. Is the female G-spot truly a distinct anatomic entity? *The Journal of Sexual Medicine* 9(3):719–726.

Kim, Peter S., James E. Coxworth, and Kristen Hawkes. 2012. Increased longevity evolves from grandmothering. *Proceedings of the Royal Society, Biological Sciences.* Preprint edition: doi:10.1098/rspb.2012.1751.

Kimmel, Michael S. 2000. *The Gendered Society.* Oxford: Oxford University Press.

Kinsey, Alfred C., Wardell B. Pomeroy, and Clyde E. Martin. 1948. *Sexual Behavior in the Human Male.* Philadelphia: W. B. Saunders.

Kinzey, Warren G., ed. 1997. *New World Primates: Ecology, Evolution, and Behavior.* Piscataway, NJ: Transaction Publishers.

Kirkpatrick, John. 1987. Taure'are'a: A liminal category and passage to Marquesan adulthood. *Ethos* 15(4): 382–405.

Klostermaier, Klaus K. 1994. *A Survey of Hinduism.* 2nd ed. Albany, NY: State University of New York Press.

Koch, Paul L., and Anthony B. Barnosky. 2006. Late Quaternary extinctions: State of the debate. *Annual Review of Ecology, Evolution, and Systematics* 37: 215–250.

Köepping, Klaus-Peter. 1983. *Adolf Bastian and the Psychic Unity of Mankind: The Foundations of Anthropology in Nineteenth Century Germany.* St. Lucia, Australia: University of Queensland Press.

Koloski-Ostrow, Ann Olga. 1997. Violent stages in two Pompeian Houses: Imperial taste, aristocratic response, and messages of male control. In *Naked Truths: Women, Sexuality, and Gender in Classical Art and Archaeology,* ed. Olga Koloski-Ostrow and Claire L. Lyons, 243–266. London: Routledge.

Korda, Joanna B., Sue W. Goldstein, and Frank Sommer. 2010. Sexual medicine and history: The history of female ejaculation. *The Journal of Sexual Medicine* 7(5): 1965–1975.

Kracke, Waud H. 1988. Kagwahiv mourning II: Ghosts, grief, and reminiscences. *Ethos* 16(2): 209–222.

———. 1981. Kagwahiv mourning: Dreams of a bereaved father. *Ethos* 9(4): 258–275.

Kroeber, A. L. 1929. The Valley Nisenan. *University of California Publications in American Archaeology and Ethnography* 24(4): 253–290.

Kubik, Gerhard. 1975/1976. Musical bows in South-Western Angola, 1965. *African Music* 5(4): 98–104.

Kummer, Harold. 1968. *Social Organization of Hamadryas Baboons.* Basel and New York: Karger.

Kushner, A. W. 1967. Two cases of auto-castration due to religious delusions. *British Journal of Medical Psychology* 40(3): 293–298.

Kvaerne, Per. 1996. *The Bön Religion of Tibet: The Iconography of a Living Tradition.* Boston: Shambhala.

Kvavadze, Eliso, Ofer Bar-Yosef, Anna Belfer-Cohen, Elisabetta Boaretto, Nino Jakeli, Zinovi Matskevich, and Tengiz Meshveliani. 2009. 30,000-year-old wild flax fibers. *Science* 325: 1359.

Lacan, Marie, Christine Keyser, François-Xavier Ricaut, Nicolas Brucato, Francis Duranthon, Jean Guilaine, Eric Crubézy, and Bertrand Ludes. 2011. Ancient DNA reveals male diffusion through the Neolithic Mediterranean route. *Proceedings of the National Academy of Sciences* 108(2): 9788–9791.

Lahbib, Youssef, Sami Abidli, Jean-Francois Chiffoleau, Bernard Averty, and Najoua Trigui El Menif. 2010. Imposex and butyltin concentrations in snails from the lagoon of Bizerta (northern Tunesia). *Marine Biology Research* 6(6): 600–607.

Laird, Carobeth. 1980. Chemehuevi shamanism, sorcery, and charms. *Journal of California and Great Basin Anthropology* 2(1): 80–87.

Lakoff, George, and Mark Johnson. 1980. *Metaphors We Live By.* Chicago: University of Chicago Press.

Lamphere, Louise. 1969. Symbolic elements in Navajo ritual. *Journal of Anthropological Research* 25(3): 279–305.

Lanchote, Vera Lucia, Pierina Sueli Bonato, Antonio Luiz Cerdeira, Neife Aparecida Guinain Santos, Dermeval de Carvalho, and Marco Antonio Gomes. 2000. HPLC screening and GC-MS confirmation of triazine herbicides resideues in drinking water from sugar cane area in Brazil. *Water, Air, and Soil Pollution* 118: 329–338.

Lang, Andrew. 1983. *Custom and Myth.* London: Longmans, Green.

Langness, L. L. 1974. Ritual, power, and male dominance. *Ethos* 2(3): 189–212.

Lapierre, Y. D. 1972. Koro in a French Canadian. *Canadian Psychiatric Association Journal* 17(4): 333–334.

Larsen, Clark S. 2006. The agricultural revolution as environmental catastrophe:

Implications for health and lifestyle in the Holocene. *Quaternary International* 150: 12–20.

Larson, Jennifer. 2007. *Ancient Greek Cults: A Guide*. New York: Routledge.

Lattas, Andrew. 1989. Trickery and sacrifice: Tambarins and the appropriation of female reproductive powers in male initiation ceremonies in West New Britain. *Man* 24(3): 451–469.

Larivière, S., and S. H. Ferguson. 2002. On the evolution of the mammalian baculum: Vaginal friction, prolonged intromission or induced ovulation. *Mammal Review* 32(4): 283–294.

Law, R. J., M. J. Waldock, C. R. Allchin, R. E. Laslett, and K. J. Bailey. 1994. Contaminants in seawater around England and Wales: Results from monitoring surveys, 1990–1992. *Marine Pollution Bulletin* 28(11): 668–675.

Lawergren, Bo. 1988. The origin of musical instruments and sounds. *Anthropos* 83: 31–45.

Lawler, Andrew. 2007. Murder in Mesopotamia? *Science* 317: 1164–1165.

———. 2012. Civilization's Double-Edged Sword. *Science* 336: 832–833.

Lawrence, Ann A. 2003. Factors associated with satisfaction or regret following male-to-female sex reassignment surgery. *Archives of Sexual Behavior* 32(4): 299–315.

Leach, Helen M. 2003. Human Domestication Reconsidered. *Current Anthropology* 44(3): 349–368.

Lee, Gyoung-Ah, Gary W. Crawford, Li Liu, and Xingcan Chin. 2007. Plants and people from the early Neolithic to Shang periods in North China. *Proceedings of the National Academy of Sciences of the United States of America* 104(3): 1087–1092.

Lee, Harper. 1960. *To Kill a Mockingbird*. Philadelphia: J. B. Lippencott.

Lee, Khoon Choy. 1995. *Japan: Between Myth and Reality*. Singapore: World Scientific.

Lee, Richard B., and Irven DeVore, eds. 1968. *Man the Hunter*. New York: Aldine.

Lee, Timothy B. 2011. Court rules Janet Jackson nipplegate fine was unfair to CBS. *Ars Technica*. Retrieved on December 1, 2012, from http://arstechnica.com/tech-policy/2011/11/court-rules-nipplegate-fine-was-unfair-to-cbs/.

Lehner, Stephen. 1935. The balum cult of the Bukaua of Huon Gulf, New Guinea. *Oceania* 5(3): 338–345.

Leiber, Carol M. 2010. Me(di)a culpa: The "Missing White Woman Syndrome" and media self-critique. *Communication, Culture, & Critique* 3: 549–565.

Lemaître, Jean-François, Steven A. Ramm, Nicola Jennings, and Paula Stockley. 2012. Genital morphology linked to social status in the bank vole (*Myodes glareolus*). *Behavioral Ecology and Sociobiology* 66: 97–105.

Lenzer, Jeanne. 2008. Obituary: Felix Spector. *British Medical Journal* 336: 726.

Leonard, David J., and C. Richard King. 2011. Lack of black opps: Kobe Bryant and the difficult path of redemption. *Journal of Sports and Social Issues* 35(2): 209–223.

Lever, Janet, David A. Frederick, and Letitia Anne Peplau. 2006. Does size matter? Men's and women's views on penis size across the lifespan. *Psychology of Men & Masculinity* 7(3): 129–143.

Levin, Roy J. 2002. The physiology of sexual arousal in the human female: A recreational and procreational synthesis. *Archives of Sexual Behavior* 31(5): 405–411.

Levine, Laurence A., and Robert J. Dimitriou. 2001. Vacuum constriction and external erection devices in erectile dysfunction. *Urologic Clinics of North America* 28(2): 335–342.

Lévi-Strauss, Claude. 1969. *The Raw and the Cooked: An Introduction to a Science of Mythology*, Vol. 1. New York: Harper and Row.

Levy, Robert I. 1973. *Tahitians: Mind and Experience in the Society Islands*. Chicago: University of Chicago Press.

———. 1969. Child management structure in Tahitian families. *Journal of Polynesian Society* 78(1): 35–43.

Lewis-Williams, J. D. 1981. The thin red line: Southern San notions and rock paintings of supernatural potency. *The South African Archaeological Bulletin* 36(133): 5–13.

Lexchin, Joel. 2006. Bigger and better: How Pfizer redefined erectile dysfunction. *PLoS Medicine* 3(4); e132. Retrieved on December 7, 2012, from http://www.plosmedicine.org.

Lim, Soo, Sun Young Ahn, In Chan Song, Myung Hee Chung, Hak Chul Jang, Kyong Soo Park, Ki-Up Lee, Youngmi Kim Pak, and Hong Kyu Lee. 2009. Chronic exposure to the herbicide atrazine causes mitochondrial dysfunction and insulin resistance. *PLoS One* 4(4): e5186. Retrieved on September 16, 2012, from http://www.plosone.org.

Lim, Soo, Young Min Cho, Kyong Soo Park, and Hong Kyu Lee. 2010. Persistent organic pollutants, mitochondrial dysfunction, and metabolic syndrome. *Annals of the New York Academy of Sciences* 1201(1): 166–176.

Lima, David Souza, Kamila Prior, Richardo Uchida, Sérgio Brotto, Regiane Garrido, Sérgio Tamai, and Marsal Sanches. 2005. Mutilação genital e psicose. *Revista de Psiquiatria Clínica* 32(2): 88–90.

Linton, Ralph. 1933. The Tanala: A hill tribe of Madagascar. *Publications of the Field Museum of Natural History. Anthropological Series* 22: 1–334.

Livingstone, Frank B. 1958. Anthropological implications of sickle cell gene distribution in West Africa. *American Anthropologist* 60: 533–562.

Lloyd, Elizabeth Anne. 2009. *The Case of the Female Orgasm: Bias in the Science of Evolution*. Cambridge: Harvard University Press.

Lloyd, F. H., P. Powell, and A. P. Murdoch. 1996. Anabolic steroid abuse by body builders and male subfertility. *British Medical Journal* 313: 100–101.

Lobato, Maria Inês Inês, Walter José Koff, Carlo Manenti, Déborah da Fonseca Seger, Jaqueline Salvador, Maria da Graça Borges Fortes, Analída Rodolpho Petry, Esalba Silveira, and Alexandre Annes Henriques. 2006. Follow-up of sex reassignment surgery in transsexuals: A Brazilian cohort. *Archives of Sexual Behavior* 35: 711–735.

Loeb, E. M. 1931. The religious organizations of north central California and Tierra Del Fuego. *American Anthropologist* 33(4): 517–556.

Loftin, John D. Supplication and participation: The distance and relation of the sacred in Hopi prayer rites. *Anthropos* 81: 177–201.

London, L., M. A. Dalvie, A. Nowicki, and E. Cairncross. 2004. Approaches for regulating water in South Africa for the presence of pesticides. *Water SA* 31(1): 53–60.

Looper, Matthew G. 2009. *To Be Like Gods: Dance in Ancient Maya Civilization*. Austin: University of Texas Press.

Lowie, Robert H. 1941. A note on the Gê tribes of Brazil. *American Anthropologist* 43(2): 188–196.

———. 1940. American culture history. *American Anthropologist* 42(3): 409–428.

———. 1938. *The History of Ethnological Theory*. New York: Farrar and Rinehart.

———. 1920. *Primitive Society*. New York: Boni and Liveright.

Luo, M-C, Z-L Yang, F. M. You, T. Kawahara, J. G. Waines, and J. Dvorak. 2007. The structure of wild and domesticated emmer wheat populations, gene flow between them, and the site of emmer domestication. *TAG Theoretical and Applied Genetics* 114(6): 947–959.

Lüttenberg, Thomas. 2005. The codpiece: A Renaissance fashion between sign and artefact. *The Medieval History Journal* 8(1): 49–80.

Maggioncalda, Anne Nacey, and Robert M. Sapolsky. 2002. *Scientific American* 286(6): 60–65.

Mago, Vishal. 2011. Male genital self-mutilation. *Indian Journal of Psychiatry* 53(2): 168–169.

Malinowski, Bronislaw. 1929. *The Sexual Life of Savages in North-Western Melanesia: An Ethnographic Account of Courtship, Marriage and Family Life among the Natives of the Trobriand Islands*. London: Routledge.

Malviage, Lasantha S., and Jonathan C. Levy. 2009. Erectile dysfunction in diabetes mellitus. *The Journal of Sexual Medicine* 6(5): 1232–1247.

Manson, Joseph H., Susan Perry, and Amy R. Parish. 1997. Nonconceptual sexual behavior in bonobos and capuchins. *International Journal of Primatology* 18(5): 767–786.

Marcus, George E., and Michael M. J. Fischer. 1999. *Anthropology as Cultural Critique: An Experimental Moment in the Human Sciences*. 2nd ed. Chicago: University of Chicago Press.

Marcuzzi, Michael. 2010. The bullroarer cult in Cuba. *Latin American Music Review* 31(2): 151–181.

Marett, Robert Ranulph. 1914. *The Threshold of Religion*. New York: Macmillan.

Margolis, Jonathan. 2004. *O: The Intimate History of the Orgasm*. New York: Random House.

Marneros, Andreas, Philipp Gutmann, and Frank Uhlmann. 2006. Self-amputation of the penis and tongue after use of Angel's Trumpet. *European Archives of Psychiatry and Clinical Neuroscience* 256(7): 458–459.

Marshall, David J., and Anisha Rajkumar. 2003. Imposex in the indigenous *Nassarius kraussianus* (Mollusca: Neogasropoda) from South African harbours. *Marine Pollution Bulletin* 46(9): 1150–1155.

Marshall, Donald S. 1971. Sexual Behavior on Mangaia. In *Human Sexual Behavior,* ed. D. S. Marshall and R. C. Suggs, 103–162. The Institute for Sex Research. New York: Basic Books.

Martin, Emily. 1991. The egg and the sperm: How science has constructed a romance based on male-female roles. *Signs: Journal of Women in Culture and Society* 16(3): 485–501.

Martin, Paul S., and Richard G. Klein. 1989. *Quaternary Extinctions: A Prehistoric Revolution.* Tucson: University of Arizona Press.

Martin, Robert D. 2007. The evolution of human reproduction: A primatological perspective. *Yearbook of Physical Anthropology* 50: 59–84.

Marturano, Antonio. 2011. The ethics of online social networks: An introduction. *International Review of Information Ethics* 16: 3–5.

Marumo, Ken, Jun Nakashima, and Masar Murai. 2008. Age-related prevalence of erectile dysfunction in Japan: Assessment by the International Index of Erectile Function. *International Journal of Urology* 8(2): 53–59.

Mason, J. Alden. 1920. The Papago harvest festival. *American Anthropologist* 22(1): 13–25.

Masquelier, Adeline, ed. 2005. Dirt, undress, and difference: An introduction. In *Dirt, Undress, and Difference: Critical Perspectives on the Body's Surface,* ed. Adeline Masquelier, 1–33, Bloomington: Indiana University Press.

Master, Viraj, and Richard Santucci. 2003. An American hijra: A report of a case of genital self-mutilation to become India's "third sex." *Urology* 62(6): 1121.

Masters, William H., and Virginia E. Johnson. *Human Sexual Response.* Boston: Little, Brown.

Mather, Charles. 2005. Accusations of genital theft: A case from Northern Ghana. *Culture, Medicine, and Psychiatry* 29: 33–52.

Mathews, R. H. 1898. Bullroarers used by the Australian Aborigines. *The Journal of the Anthropological Institute of Great Britain and Ireland* 27: 52–60.

Mattern, Joanne. 2012. *Kim Kardashian: Reality TV Star.* North Mankato, MN: ABDO.

Matteson, Patricia. 1998. *Resolving the DDT Dilemma: Protecting Biodiversity and Human Health.* Washington, DC: World Wildlife Fund.

Mautz, Brian S., Bob B. M. Wong, Richard A. Peters, and Michael D. Jennions. 2013. Penis size interacts with body shape and height to influence male attractiveness. *Proceedings of the National Academy of Sciences* 110(17): 6925–6930.

Maybury-Lewis, David. 1967. *Akwe-Shavante Society.* Oxford: Clarendon.

McCarthy, Julie. 2014. In India, landmark ruling recognizes transgender citizens. *NPR International.* Retrieved on January 7, 2015 from http://www.npr.org/blogs/thetwo-way/2014/04/15/303408581/in-india-landmark-ruling-recognizes-transgender-citizens.

McCracken, Kevin G. 2000. The 20-cm spiny penis of the Argentine Lake Duck (Oxyuravittata). The Auk (117): 820–825.

McDaniel, Tana V., Pamela A. Martin, John Struger, Jim Sterry, Chris H. Marvin, Mark E. McMaster, Stacey Clarence, and Gerald Tetreault. 2008. Potential endocrine disruption of sexual development in free ranging male northern leopard frogs (*Rana pipiens*) and green frogs (*Rana clamitans*) from areas of intensive row crop agriculture. *Aquatic Toxicology* 88(4): 230–242.

McIntosh, Jane. 2001. *A Peaceful Realm: The Rise and Fall of the Indus Civilization.* Oxford: Westview Press.

———. 2007. *The Ancient Indus Valley: New Perspectives.* Santa Barbara, CA: ABC Clio.

McKillop, Heather. 2004. *The Ancient Maya: New Perspectives.* New York: W. W. Norton.

McLean, Cory Y., Philip L. Reno, Alex A. Pollen, Abraham I. Bassan, Terence De. Capellini, Catherine Guenther, Vahan B. Indjeian, Xihong Lim, Douglas B. Menke, Bruce T. Schaar, Aaron M. Wenger, Gill Bejerano, and David M. Kingsley. 2010. Human-specific loss of regulatory DNA and the evolution of human-specific traits. *Nature* 471: 216–219.

McLean, Mervyn. 1982. A chronological and geographic sequence of Maori flute scales. *Man* 17(1): 123–157.

McMahon, Augusta, Arkadiusz Sołtysiak, and Jill Weber. 2011. Late Chalcolithic mass graves at Tell Brak, Syria, and violent conflict during the growth of early city-states. *Journal of Field Archaeology* 36(3): 201–220.

McMaster, M. E., K. R. Munkittrick, P. L. Luxon, and G. J. Vanderkraak. 1994. Impact of low-level sampling stress on interpretation of physiological responses of white sucker exposed to effluent from a bleached kraft pulp mill. *Ecotoxicity and Environmental Safety* 27(3): 251–264.

McPherson, Naomi M. 2012. Black and blue: Shades of violence in West New Britain, PNG. In *Engendering Violence in Papua New Guinea*, ed. Margaret Jolly and Christine Stewart with Carolyn Brewer, 47–72. Canberra: Australian National University Press.

———. 2004. Gender and cosmos emplaced: Women's houses and men's houses in Bariai, West New Britain, Papua New Guinea. *Pacific Studies* 27(1): 68–96.

———. 1994. The legacy of Moro the Snake-Man in Bariai. *Pacific Studies* 17(4): 153–181.

Mead, Margaret. 1935. *Sex and Temperament in Three Primitive Societies.* New York: William and Morrow.

Mellars, Paul. 2009. Origins of the female image. *Nature* 459: 176–177.

Merival, Patricia. 1996. *Pan the Goat-God: His Myth in Modern Times.* Cambridge: Harvard University Press.

Merrill, Kenneth, Aidan Bryant, Emily Dolan, and Siying Chang. 2012. The male gaze and online sports punditry: Reactions to the Inez Sainz controversy on the sports blogosphere. *Journal of Sports and Social Issues.* Retrieved on December 1, 2012, from http://jss.sagepub.com.

Merrill, William L., Robert J. Hard, Jonathan B. Mabry, Gayle J. Fritz, Karen R. Adams, John R. Roney, and A. C. MacWilliams. 2009. The diffusion of maize to the southwestern United States and its impact. *Proceedings of the National Academy of the Sciences of the United States of America* 105(50): 21019–21026.

Messenger, John C. 1971. Sex and repression in an Irish folk community. In *Human Sexual Behavior: Variations in the Ethnographic Spectrum*, ed. D. S. Marshall and R. C. Suggs, 3–37. New York: Basic Books.

Métneki, Julia, A. Czeizel, Sibylle D. Flatz, and G. Flatz. 1984. A study of lactose absorption capacity in twins. *Human Genetics* 67: 296–300.

Métraux, Alfred. 1948. Tribes of Eastern Bolivia and the Madeira headwaters. In *Handbook of South American Indians, Volume 3: The Tropical Forest Tribes*, ed. Julian H. Steward, 381–454, Washington, DC: Government Printing Office.

Mikaelian, Igor, Yves De Latontaine, John C. Harshbarger, Lucy L. J. Lee, and Caniel Marineau. 2002. *Environmental Toxicology and Chemistry* 21(3): 532–541.

Mikalson, Jon D. 2005. *Ancient Greek Religion.* Oxford: Blackwell.

Milam, Erika L. 2010. *Looking for a Few Good Males: Female Choice in Evolutionary Biology.* Baltimore: Johns Hopkins University Press.

Millán-González, Ricardo. 2010. Mutilación genital en paciente transsexual: ¿Manifestación de un espectro patológico imprecisamente definido? *Revista Colombiana de Psiquiatría* 39(3): 624–634.

Miller, Geoffrey F. 1998. How mate choice shaped human culture: A review of sexual selection in human evolution. *Handbook of Evolutionary Psychology: Ideas, Issues, and Applications*, eds. Charles B. Crawford and Dennis Krebs, 87–129. Hillsdale, NJ: Lawrence Erlbaum.

Miller, Naomi J., and Naomi Yavneh, eds. 2011. *Gender and Early Modern Constructions of Childhood.* Burlington, VT: Ashgate Publishing.

Miller, Zell. 2004. Free Republic. Retrieved on June 7, 2011, from http://www.freerepublic.com.

Mirren, Helen. 2011. Helen Mirren accuses Hollywood of penis worship. *The Guardian.* Retrieved on June 16, 2011, from http://www.guardian.co.uk.

Mishra, Baikunthanath, and Nilamadhab Kar. 2001. Genital self amputation for urinary symptom relief or suicide? *Indian Journal of Psychiatry* 43(4): 342–344.

Mitani, John C. 1985. Sexual selection and adult male orangutan long calls. *Animal Behaviour* 33(1): 272–283.

Mnif, Wissem, Aziza Ibn Hadj Hassine, Aicha Bouaziz, Aghleb Bartegi, Olivier Thomas, and Benoit Roig. 2011. Effect of endocrine disruptor pesticides: A review. *International Journal of Environmental Research and Public Health* 8(6): 2265–2303.

Modai, I., H. Munitz, and D. Aizenberg. 1986. Koro in an Israeli male. *British Journal of Psychiatry* 149: 503–505.

Mohamat-Yusuff, Ferdaus, Syaizwan Zahmir Zulkifli, Ahman Ismil, Hiroya Harino, Mohd Kamil Yusoff, and Takaomi Arai. 2010. Imposex in *Thais gradata* as a biomarker for TBT contamination on the southern coast of peninsular Malaysia. *Water, Air, and Soil Pollution* 211: 443–457.

Mol, Hans. 1979. The origin and function of religion: A critique of, and alternative to, Durkheim's interpretation of the religion of the Australian aborigines. *Journal for the Scientific Study of Religion* 18(4): 379–389.

Money, John. 1988. The Skoptic syndrome: Castration and genital self-mutilation as an example of sexual body-image pathology. *Journal of Psychology and Human Sexuality* 1(1): 113–118.

Monstrey, Stan J., Peter Ceulemans, and Piet Hoebeke. 2011. Sex reassignment surgery in the female-to-male transsexual. *Seminars in Plastic Surgery* 25(3): 229–244.

Moore, Lisa Jean. 2007. *Sperm Counts: Overcome by Man's Most Precious Fluid*. New York: New York University Press.

Morris, Desmond. 1967. *The Naked Ape*. New York: Dell.

Morton-Williams. 1964. An outline of the cosmology and cult organization of the Yoruba. *Africa: Journal of the International African Institute* 34(3): 243–261.

Mulhall, John P., Andrew E. Jahoda, Absaar Ahmed, and Marilyn Parker. 2001. Analysis of the consistency of intraurethral prostaglandin E_1 (MUSE) during at-home use. *Urology* 58(2): 262–266.

Murai, Tadahiro. 2006. Mating behaviors of the proboscis monkey. *American Journal of Primatology* 68(8): 832–837.

Murdoch, John. 1982. *Ethnological Results of the Point Barrow Expedition, Ninth Annual Report of the Bureau of Ethnology*. Washington, DC: Government Printing Office.

Murota-Kawano, Akiko, Akira Tosaka, and Masao Ando. 2001. Autohemicastration in a man without schizophrenia. *International Journal of Urology* 8(5): 257–259.

Murphy, D., M. Murphy, and R. Grainger. 2001. Self-castration. *Irish Journal of Medical Science* 170(3): 195.

Murphy, Robert F. 1986. Social structure and sex antagonism. *Journal of Anthropological Research* 42(3): 407–416.

Murray, D. W. 1989. Transposing symbolic forms: Actor awareness of language structures in Navajo ritual. *Anthropological Linguistics* 31: 195–208.

Nadig, Peter C. 2002. Review of R. A. Hazzard, "Imagination of a Monarchy: Studies in Ptolemaic Propaganda" (Phoenix Supplementary Volume, 37). Toronto: University of Toronto Press, 2000. *Bryn Mawr Classical Review* 9(2). Retrieved on October 17, 2012, from http://bmcr.brynmawr.edu.

Nadler, R. D. 1982. Reproductive behavior and endocrinology of orangutans. In *Orangutan: Its Biology and Conservation*, ed. L. E. M. de Boer, 231–248. The Hague: W. Junk.

Nanda, Serena. 1990. *Neither Man Nor Woman*. Bellmont, CA: Wadsworth

Nell, Victor. 2002. Why young men drive dangerously: Implications for injury prevention. *Current Directions in Psychological Science* 11(2): 75–79.

Nelson, L., E. J. Whallett, and J. C. McGregor. 2009. Transgender patient satisfaction following reduction mammoplasty. *Journal of Plastic, Reconstructive, and Aesthetic Surgery* 62(3): 331–334.

Newitz, Annalee, and Matthrew Wray. 1996. What is "white trash"? Stereotypes and economic conditions of poor whites in the U.S. *Minnesota Review* 47: 57–72.

Nichols, Deborah L., and Christopher A. Pool. 2012. *The Oxford Handbook of Mesoamerican Archaeology*. Oxford: Oxford University Press.

Nichols, John. 2010. Strom Thurmond's kid loses GOP bid to an African-American candidate. *The Nation*. Retrieved on December 1, 2012, from http://www.thenation.com.

Nielson, Johannes, and Mogens Wohlert. 1991. Chromosomal abnormalities found among 34,910 newborn children: Results from a 13-year incidence study in Arhus, Denmark. *Human Genetics* 87(1): 81–83.

Norbu, Namkhai. 1995. *Drung, Deu and Bön: Narrations, Symbolic Languages and the Bön Tradition in Ancient Tibet*. Dharamsala, India: Library of Tibetan Works and Archives.

Nott, Josiah Clark, George R. Gliddon, Samuel George Morton, Louis Agassiz, William Usher, and Henry S. Patterson. 1854. *Types of Mankind: Or, Ethnological Researchers: Based upon the Ancient Monuments, Paintings, Sculptures, and Crania of Races, and Upon their Natural, Geographical, Philological and Biblical History*. Philadelphia: Lippincott, Grambo.

Nurse, G. T. 1972. Musical instrumentation among the San (Bushmen) of the Central Kalahari. *African Music* 5(2): 23–27.

O'Connell, Helen E. and Kalavamparan V. Sanjeevan. Anatomy of female genitalia. In *Women's Sexual Function and Dysfunction: Study, Diagnosis and Treatment*, eds. Irwin Goldstein, Cindy M. Meston, Susan Davis, and Abdulmaged Traish, 105–112. Boca Raton, FL: Taylor and Francis.

Olea-Serrano, Fátima, Pablo Lardelli-Claret, Ana Rivas, Alberto Barba-Navarro, and Nicolás Olea. 1999. Inadvertent exposure to xenoestrogens in children. *Toxicology and Industrial Health* 14(1–2): 152–159.

Oliver, Douglas. 2002. *Polynesia in Early Historic Times*. Honolulu: Bess Press.

Oliver, Emmanuelle. 2001. Categorizing the Ju/'hoan musical heritage. *African Study Monographs* (S27): S11–S27.

O'Reilly, Donald J. W. 2007. *Early Civilizations of Southeast Asia*. Lanham, MD: Altamira.

Oso, B. A. 1976. *Phallus aruantiacus* from Nigeria. *Mycologica* 68(5): 1076–1082.

Ostrzenski, A., P. Krajewski, P. Ganjei-Azar, A. J. Wasiutynski, M. N. Scheinberg, S.

Tarka, and Fudalej. Verification of the anatomy and newly discovered histology of the G-spot complex. *BJOG: An International Journal of Obstetrics & Gynaecology* 121(11): 1333–1340.

Overing, Joanna. 1986. Images of cannibalism, death, and domination in a "non violent" society. *Journal de la Société des Américanistes* 72: 133–156.

Ozturk, Ahmet, Mehmet Kilinc, Selcuk Guven, Niyazi Gormus, Metin Belviranli, Mehmet Kaynar, and Mehmet Arslan. 2009. Penis replantation after self-mutilation. *International Urology and Nephrology* 41: 109–111.

Paley, Maggie. 1999. *The Book of the Penis*. New York: Grove.

Panoff, Michel. 1968. The notion of the double self among the Maenge. *The Journal of Polynesian Society* 77(3): 275–295.

Papadopoulos, Fotios C. Anders Ekbom, Lena Brandt, and Lisa Ekselius. 2009. Excess mortality, causes of death, and prognostic factors in anorexia nervosa. *British Journal of Psychiatry* 194: 10–17.

Parkman, E. Breck. 1993. Creating thunder: The Western rain-making process. *Journal of California and Great Basin Anthropology* 15(1): 90–110.

Parsons, Alexandra. 1989. *Facts and Phalluses: A Collection of Bizarre and Intriguing Truths, Legends, and Measurements*. New York: St. Martin's.

Parsons, Elsie Clews. 1939. *Pueblo Indian Religion*. Vol 1. Chicago: University of Chicago Press.

Patel, Sutchin R., Simone Thavaseelan, Liann N. Handel, Arthur Wong, and Mark Sigman. 2007. Bilateral externalization of testis with self-castration in a patient with prion disease. *Urology* 70(3): 590–591.

Patton, Stacey. 2012. "Who's afraid of black sexuality?" *The Chronicle of Higher Education*, December 3, 2012.

Patton, Tracey Owens, and Julie Snyder-Yuly. 2007. Any four black men will do: Rape, race, and the ultimate scapegoat. *Journal of Black Studies* 37(6): 859–895.

Pawlowski, Boguslaw. 1999. Loss of oestrus and concealed ovulation in human evolution: The case against the sexual-selection hypothesis. *Current Anthropology* 40(3): 257–276.

Pazol, Karen. 2003. Mating in the Kakamega Forest blue monkeys (*Cercopithecus mitis*): Does female sexual behavior function to manipulate paternity assessment? *Behaviour* 140(4): 473–499.

Penchaszadeh, Pablo E., Carlos Sánchez Atelo, Soledad Zabala, and Gregorio Bigatti. 2009. Reproduction and imposex in the edible snail *Adelomelon ancilla* from northern Patagonia, Argentia. *Marine Biology* 156(9): 1929–1939.

Pendlebury, J. D. S. 1991. *The Archaeology of Crete*. Cheshire, CT: Biblo-Moser.

Penis Size Worldwide. 2012. Retrieved on October 15, 2012, from http://www.targetmap.com.

Pereira, W. E., C. E. Rostad, and T. J. Leiker. 1992. Synthetic organic agrochemicals in the lower Mississippi River and its major tributaries: Distribution, transport, fate. *Journal of Contaminant Hydrology* 9: 175–188.

Perry, Richard J. 1983. Proto-Athapaskan culture: The use of ethnographic reconstruction. *American Anthropologist* 10(4): 715–733.

Persels, Jeffery C. 1997. Bragueta humanistica, or humanism's codpiece. *The Sixteenth Century Journal* 28(1): 79–99.

Pershing, Linda. 1996. "His wife seized his prize and cut it to size": Folk and popular commentary on Lorena Bobbitt. *NWSA Journal* 8(3): 1–35.

Peschel, Enid Rhodes, and Richard E. Peschel. 1987. Medical insights into the castrati in opera. *American Scientist* 75(6): 578–583.

Peterson, Jane. 2010. Domesticating gender: Neolithic patterns from the southern Levant. *Journal of Anthropological Archaeology* 29(3): 249–264.

Petersen, Jennifer L., and Janet Shibley Hyde. 2010. A meta-analytic review of gender differences in sexuality, 1993–2007. *Psychological Bulletin* 136(1): 21–38.

———. 2011. Gender differences in sexual attitudes and behaviors: A review of meta-analytic results and large datasets. *Journal of Sex Research* 48(2–3): 149–165.

Pfäfflin, Friedemann. 1997. Sex reassignment, Harry Benjamin, and some European roots. *The International Journal of Transgenderism* 1(2). Retrieved online on December 7, 2012, from http://www.wpath/journal/www.iiav.nl.

Pfäfflin, F., and A. Junge. 1998. *Sex Reassignment: Thirty Years of International Follow-up Studies after Sex Reassignment Surgery; A Comprehensive Review, 1961–1991.* R. B. Jacobson and A. B. Meier, trans. Symposion Publishing. Retrieved from http://www.symposion.com.

Phillips, Katharine A. 2009. *Understanding Body Dysmorphic Disorder: An Essential Guide.* New York: Oxford University Press.

Pick, Frans E., Louis P. van Kyk, and Estelle Botha. 1992. Atrazine in ground and surface water in maize production areas of the Transvaal, South Africa. *Chemosphere* 24(3): 335–341.

Piddington, Ralph. 1932. Karadjeri initiation. *Oceania* 3(1): 46–87.

Piferrer, Francesc, and Edward M. Donaldson. 1989. Gonadal differentiation in coho salmon, *Oncorynchus kisutch*, after a single treatment with androgen or estrogen at different states during ontogenesis. *Aquaculture* 77: 251–262.

Pinker, Steven. 2011. *The Better Angels of Our Nature: How Violence Has Declined.* New York: Viking.

———. 2000 (1994). *The Language Instinct: How the Mind Creates Language.* New York: HarperCollins.

Piperno, D. R., and K. V. Flannery. 2001. The earliest archaeological maize (*Zea mays* L.) from highland Mexico: New accelerator mass spectrometry dates and their implications. *Proceedings of the National Academy of Sciences of the United States of America* 98(4): 2101–2103.

Ploog, Detlev, and Paul D. MacClean. 1963. Display of penile erection in squirrel monkey (*Saimiri sciureus*). *Animal Behaviour* 11(1): 33–39.

Polo, Pablo, and Fernando Colmenares. 2012. Behavioural processes in social context: Female abductions, male herding and female grooming in hamadyras baboons. *Behavioural Processes* 90(2): 238–245.

Pope, Harrison G., Jr., and Gen Kanayama. 2004. Bodybuilding's dark side: Clues to anabolic steroid use. *Current Psychiatry* 3(12): 1–8.

Powell, Michael. 2004. FCC to investigate Jackson's display at Super Bowl. *The Washington Post*. Retrieved on June 7, 2011, from http://www.washingtonpost.com.

Prüfer, Kay, Kasper Munch, Ines Hellman, Keiko Akagi, Jason R. Miller, Brian Walenz, Sergey Koren, Granger Sutton, Chinnappa Kodira, Roger Winer, James R. Knight, James C. Mullikin, Stephen J. Meader, Chris P. Ponting, Gerton Lunter, Saneyuki Higashino, Asger Holboth, Julien Dutheil, Emre Karakoç, Can Alkan, Saba Sajjadian, Claudia Rita Catacchio, Mario Ventura, Tomas Marques-Bonet, Evan E. Eichler, Claudine André, Rebeca Atencia, Lawrence Mugisha, Jörg Junhold, Nick Patterson, Michael Siebauer, Jeffrey M. Good, Anne Fischer, Susan E. Ptak, Michael Lachmann, David E. Symer, Thomas Mailund, Mikkel H. Schierup, Aida M. Andrés, Janet Kelso, and Svante Pääbo. 2012. The bonobo genome compared with the chimpanzee and human genomes. *Nature*. Retrieved on November 9, 2012, from http://www.nature.com.

Pukui, Mary Kawena, and Samuel H. Elbert. 1986 (1957). *Hawaiian Dictionary*. Rev. and enlarged ed. Honolulu: University of Hawaii Press.

Puppo, Vincenzo, and Ilan Gruenwald. 2010. Does the G-spot exist? A review of the current literature. *International Urogynecology Journal* 23(12) 1665–1669.

Qureshi, Naseem A. 2009. Male genital self-mutilation with special emphasis on the sociocultural meanings. *Neurosciences* 14(2): 178–181.

Radcliffe-Brown, A. R. 1929. Notes on totemism in Eastern Australia. *The Journal of the Royal Anthropological Institute of Great Britain and Ireland* 59: 399–415.

Ransome-Kuti, O., N. Kretchmer, J. D. Johnson, and J. T. Gribble. 1975. A genetic study of lactose digestion in Nigerian families. *Gastroenterology* 68(3): 431–436.

Rao, K. Nagaraja, G. Bharathi, and Sameeran Chate. 2002. Genital self-mutilation in depression: A case report. *Indian Journal of Psychiatry* 44(3): 297–300.

Ratzel, Friedrich. 1897. *The History of Mankind*. Vol. 2. New York: Macmillan.

Razzaghi, Mohammad, Alireza Rezaei, Mohammad Mohsen Mazloomfard, Babak Javanmand, Mojtaba Mohammadhossein, and Iraj Rezaei. 2009. Successful macrosurgical reimplantation of an amputated penis. *Urology Journal* 6(4): 306–308.

Redford, Donald B. 2002. *The Ancient Gods Speak: A Guide to Egyptian Religion*. Oxford: Oxford University Press.

Reed, C. S. 2004. The codpiece: Social fashion or medical need. *Internal Medicine Journal* 34: 684–686.

Reeder, Amy L., Marilyn O. Ruiz, Allan Pessier, Lauren E. Brown, Jeffrey M. Levengood, Christopher A. Phillips, Matthew B. Wheeler, Richard E. Warner, and Val R. Beasley. 2005. Intersexuality and the cricket frog decline: Historic and geographic trends. *Environmental Health Perspectives* 113(3): 261–265.

Rees, C. M., B. A. Brady, and G. J. Fabris. 2001. Incidence of imposex in *Thais orbita* from Port Phillip Bay (Victoria, Australia), following 10 years of regulation on use of TBT. *Marine Pollution Bulletin* 42(10): 873–878.

Rehak, Paul. 1996. Aegean breechcloths, kilts, and the Keftiu paintings. *American Journal of Archaeology* 100(1): 35–51.

Reichard, Ulrich. 1995. Extra-pair copulations in a monogamous gibbon (*Hylobates lar*). *Ethology* 100(2): 99–112.

Reichard, Ulrich H., and Claudia Barellii. 2008. Life history and reproductive strategies of Khao Yai *Hylobates lar*: Implications for social evolution in apes. *International Journal of Primatology* 29: 823–844.

Reisman, Judith. 2010. Anthropological tourists: Mead and the young sex mavens. *Salvo Magazine*. Retrieved on December 1, 2012, from http://www.salvomag.com.

Reitsema, T. J., and J. T. Spickett. 2003. Imposex in *Morula granulata* as a bioindicator of tributyltin (TBT) contamination in the Dampier Archipelago, Western Australia. *Marine Pollution Bulletin* 39: 280–284.

Reitz, Elizabeth J., and Elizabeth S. Wing. 2008. *Zooarchaeology*. 2nd ed. Cambridge: Cambridge University Press.

Resko, John A., Anne Perkins, Charles E. Roselli, James A. Fitzgerald, Jerome V. A. Choate, and Fredrick Stormshak. 1996. Endocrine correlates of partner preference behavior in rams. *Biology of Reproduction* 55: 120–126.

Richardson, Hugh E. 1972. Phallic symbols in Tibet. *Bulletin of Tibetology* 9(2): 25–27.

Rick, Torben C., Erlandson, Jon M., and Cristopher B. Wolff. 2008. Sex and symbolism: A Middle Holocene phallic artifact from Santa Rosa Island, California. *Pacific Coast Archaeological Society Quarterly* 40(1): 47–52.

Ringrose, Kathryn M. 2007. Eunuchs in historical perspective. *History Compass* 5(2): 495–506.

Rinpoche, Rechung. 1973. Note III: Phallic Symbols. *Bulletin of Tibetology* 10(1): 60–62.

Robb, John. 1997. Female beauty and male violence in early Italian society. In *Naked Truths: Women, Sexuality, and Gender in Classical Art and Archaeology*, ed. Olga Koloski-Ostrow and Claire L. Lyons, 43–65. London: Routledge.

Robertiello, Richard C. 1970. The "clitoral versus vaginal orgasm" controversy and some of its ramifications. *Journal of Sex Research* 6(4): 307–311.

Rogers, James Allen. 1972. Darwinism and Social Darwinism. *Journal of the History of Ideas* 33(2): 265–280.

Rohatynskyj, Marta. 1990. The larger context of Omie sex affiliation. *The Journal of the Royal Anthropological Institute of Great Britain and Ireland* 25(3): 434–453.

Rohr, Jason R., and Krista A. McCoy. 2010. A qualitative meta-analysis reveals consistent effects of atrazine on freshwater fish and amphibians. *Environmental Health Perspectives* 118(1): 20–32.

Romito, Patrizia, and Lucia Beltramini. 2011. Watching pornography: Gender differences, violence and victimization; An exploratory study in Italy. *Violence against Women* 17(10): 1313–1326.

Rönn, Johanna L., and Cosima Hotzy. 2012. Do longer genital spines in male seed beetles function as better anchors in mating? *Animal Behaviour* 83(1): 75–79.

Rosenbaum, Janet Elise. 2009. Patient teenagers? A comparison of the sexual behavior of virginity pledgers and matched nonpledgers. *Pediatrics* 1(1): e110–e120. Retrieved on December 14, 2012, from http://www.pediatricsdigest.mobi.

Rosenberg, Michael. 1990. The mother of invention: Evolutionary theory, territoriality, and the origins of agriculture. *American Anthropologist* 92(2): 399–415.

Rosselli, John. 1988. The castrati as a professional group and a social phenomenon. *Acta Musicologica* 60(2): 143–179.

Rowenchilde, Raven. 1996. Male genital modification: A sexual selection interpretation. *Human Nature* 7(2): 189–215.

Rubel, Arthur J., William T. Liu, and Ernest Brandewie. 1971. Genital mutilation and adult role behavior among lowland Christian Filipinos of Cebu. *American Anthropologist* 73(3): 806–810.

Rushton, J. Phillipe. 1995. *Race, Evolution, and Behavior: A Life History Perspective.* New Brunswick: Transaction Publishers.

Ryan, Philippa. 2011. Plants as material culture in the Near Eastern Neolithic: Perspectives from the silica skeleton artifactual remains at Çatalhöyük. *Journal of Anthropological Archaeology* 30(3): 292–305.

Rykvert, Joseph. 2011. *The Idea of a Town: The Anthropology of Urban Form in Rome, Italy, and the Ancient World.* London: Faber and Faber.

Sabo, Anne G. 2007. A new vision of porn: How women are revising porn to match a time of greater gender equality. In *Generation P? Youth, Gender and Pornography,* ed. Susanne V. Knudsen, Lotta Löfgren-Mårtenson, and Sven-Axel Månsson, 221–237. Copenhagen: Danish University of Education Press.

Sadeghi-Nejad, H., H. Lim, K. Long, and P. Gilhooly. 2003. Assessment of efficacy of Viagra® (Sildenafil citrate) using the erectile dysfunction inventory of treatment satisfaction (EDITS). *Urologia Internationalis* 71(1): 100–102.

Sager, Mike. 1989. The devil and John Holmes. *Los Angeles Times.* Retrieved on December 7, 2012, from http://byliner.com.

Sahi, T., M. Isokoski, J. Jussila, K. Launiala, and K. Pyörälä. 1973. Recessive inheritance of adult-type lactose malabsorption. *The Lancet* 302(7833): 823–826.

Saitoti, Tepilit Ole. 1986. *The Worlds of A Maasai Warrior: An Autobiography.* Berkeley: University of California Press.

Saldanha, D. 1993. Genital self mutilation. *Indian Journal of Psychiatry* 35(4): 226–227.

Sandford, John. 1997. Koro in a Caucasian male with panic disorder. *International Journal of Psychiatry in Clinical Practice* 1(4): 295.

Sapolsky, Robert M. 2006. A natural history of peace. *Foreign Affairs* 85(1): 104–120.

Sapolsky, Robert M., and Lisa J. Share. 2004. A pacific culture among wild baboons: Its emergence and transmission. *PLoS Biology* 2(4): e106. Retrieved on June 16, 2011, doi:10.1371/journal.pbio.0020106.

Sayre, Lewis A. 1872. Partial paralysis from reflex irritation, caused by congenital phimosis and adherent prepuce. *American Journal of the Medical Sciences* 60(125): 220–221.

Schaffner, C. M., and J. A. French. 2004. Behavioral and endocrine responses in male marmosets to the establishment of multimale breeding groups: Evidence for non-monopolizing facultative polyandry. *International Journal of Primatology* 25(3): 709–732.

Schlafly, Phyliss. 2004. Another CBS travesty. *Eagle Forum.* Retrieved on June 7, 2011, from http://www.eagleforum.org.

Schmandt-Besserat, Denise. 2007. *When Writing Met Art: From Symbol to Story.* Austin: University of Texas Press.

Schneider, William M., and Mary Jo Schneider. 1991. Selako male initiation. *Ethnology* 30(3): 279–291.

Schoröder, Inge. 1993. Concealed ovulation and clandestine copulation: A female contribution to human evolution. *Ethology and Sociobiology* 14(6): 381–389.

Schroeter, Careet Angela, Jan Stephen Gorenewegen, Thorsten Reineke, and Hendrik Arend Martino Neuman. 2003. Ninety percent permanent hair reduction in transsexual patients. *Annals of Plastic Surgery* 51(3): 243–248.

Schultz, A. H. 1942. Growth and development of the proboscis monkey. *Bulletin of the Museum of Comparative Zoology* 89: 279–314.

Schweitzer, Isaac. 1990.Genital self-amputation and the Klingsor syndrome. *Australian and New Zealand Journal of Psychiatry* 24(4): 566–569.

Seeger, Anthony. 1975. The meaning of body ornaments: A Suya example. *Ethnology* 14(3): 211–244.

Selden, Daniel L. 1998. Alibis. *Classical Antiquity* 17(2): 289–412.

Shaikh, A. A., C. L. Celaya, I. Gomex, and S. A. Shaikh. 1982. Temporal relationship of hormonal peaks to ovulation and sex skin deturgescence in the baboon. *Primates* 23: 444–452.

Shapiro, Warren. 2009. *Partible Paternity and Anthropological Theory: The Construction of an Ethnographic Fantasy.* Lanham, MD: University Press of America.

Sharma, Pradeep, G. D. Koolwal, Sanjay Gehlot, Surender Kumar, and Ankit Awasthi. 2010. *Journal of Mental Health and Human Behavior* 15(2): 116–118.

Sharpe, Richard M., and Niels E. Shakkebaek. 1993. Are oestrogens involved in falling sperm counts and disorders of the male reproductive tract? *The Lancet* 341(8857): 1392–1395.

Shaw, Melanie, and Jochen F. Müller. 2005. Preliminary evaluation of the occurrence of herbicides and PAHs in the wet tropics region of the Great Barrier Reef, Australia, using passive samplers. *Marine Pollution Bulletin* 51: 876–881.

Sheets-Johnstone, Maxine. 1992. Corporal archetypes and power: Preliminary clarifications and considerations of sex. *Hypatia* 7(3): 39–76.

Shennan, Stephen, and Kevan Edinborough. 2007. Prehistoric population history: From the Late Glacial to the Late Neolithic in Central and Northern Europe. *Journal of Archaeological Science* 34(8): 1339–1345.

Shepard, Glen H. Jr. 2002. Three days for weeping: Dreams, emotions, and death in the Peruvian Amazon. *Medical Anthropology Quarterly* 16(2): 200–209.

Shields, Charles J. 2006. *Mockingbird: A Portrait of Harper Lee*. New York: Owl Books.

Shimizu, Akira, and Ichiro Mizuta. 1995. Male genital self-mutilation: A case report. *British Journal of Medical Psychology* 68(2): 187–189.

Shokeir, A. A., and M. I. Hussein. 1999. The urology of Pharaonic Egypt. *British Journal of Urology International* 84: 755–761.

Short, J. W., S. D. Rice, C. C. Bordersen, and W. B. Stickle. 1989. Occurrence of tri-n-butyltin-caused imposex in the North Pacific marine snail *Nucella lima* in Auke Bay, Alaska. *Marine Biology* 102(3): 291–297.

Siddiquee, Rehan Ahmed, and Sandip Deshpande. 2007. A-case of genital self-mutilation in a patient with psychosis. *German Journal of Psychiatry* 10: 25–28.

Silverman, Eric K. 2004. Anthropology and circumcision. *Annual Review of Anthropology* 33: 419–445.

Simmer-Brown, Judith. 2001. *Dakini's Warm Breath: The Feminine Principle in Tibetan Buddhism*. Boston: Shambhala.

Singer, Philip, and Daniel E. Desole. 1967. The Australian subincision ceremony reconsidered: Vaginal envy or kangaroo bifid penis envy. *American Anthropologist* 69: 355–358.

Skakkebæk, E., Rajpert-De Meyts, and K. M. Main. 2001. Testicular dysgenesis syndrome: An increasingly common developmental disorder with environmental aspects. *Human Reproduction* 16(5): 972–978.

Skoglund, Pontus, Helena Malmström, Maanasa Raghavan, Jan Storå, Per Hall, Eske Willerslev, M. Thomas P. Gilbert, Anders Götherström, and Mattias Jakobsson. 2012. Origins and genetic legacy of Neolithic farmers and hunter-gatherers in Europe. *Science* 336(6080): 466–469.

Skougard, Erika. 2011. The best interests of transgendered children. *Utah Law Review* 3: 1161–1201.

Slattery, Dennis Patrick. 2005. Review of J. Campbell, "Pathways to Bliss: Mythology and Personal Transformation," 2004. *Psychological Perspectives: A Quarterly Journal of Jungian Thought* 48(2): 331–332.

Slijper, E. J. 1966. Functional morphology of the reproductive system in Cetacea. In *Whales, Dolphins, and Porpoises*, ed. Kenneth Stafford Norris, 278–319. Berkeley and Los Angeles: University of California Press.

Slocum, Sally. 1975. Woman the gatherer: Male bias in anthropology. In *Towards an Anthropology of Women*, ed. R. R. Reiter, 36–50. New York: Monthly Review Press.

Smith, B. A. 1971. Sexuality in the American mud snail, *Nassarius obsoletus* (Say). *Proceedings of the Malacological Society of London* 39: 377–381.

Smith, Bruce D. 1997. The initial domestication of Curcurbita pepo in the Americas 10,000 years ago. *Science* 276(5314): 932–934.

Smith, M. G. 1953. Secondary marriage in Northern Nigeria. *Africa: Journal of the International African Institute* 23(4): 298–323.

Smith, Moira. 2002. The flying phallus and the laughing inquisitor: Penis theft in the "Malleus Maleficarum." *Journal of Folklore Research* 39(1): 85–117.

Smuts, Barbara. 2006. Between species: Science and subjectivity. *Configurations* 14(1): 115–126.

Smuts, Barbara B. 1985. *Sex and Friendship in Baboons*. New York: Aldine.

Snellgrove, David L. 2002. *Indo-Tibetan Buddhism: Indian Buddhists and Their Tibetan Successors*. Boston: Shambhala.

Söderberg, Bertil. 1953. Musical instruments used by the Babembe. *The African Music Society Newsletter* 1(6): 46–56.

Sodhi, Navjot S., David Bickford, Arvin C. Diesmos, Tien Ming Lee, Lian Pin Koh, Barry W. Brook, Cagan H. Sekercioglu, and Corey J. A. Bradshaw. 2008. Measuring the meltdown: Drivers of global amphibian extinction and decline. *PloS ONE* 3(2): e1636. Retrieved on September 16, 2012, from http://www.plosone.org.

Soffer, O., J. M. Adovasio, J. S. Illingworth, H. A. Amirkhanov, N. D. Praslov, and M. Street. 2000. Paleolithic perishables made permanent. *Antiquity* 74(286): 812–821.

Solé, M., D. Raldua, F. Piferrer, D. Barceló, and C. Porte. 2003. Feminization of wild carp, *Cyprinus carpio*, in a polluted environment: Plasma steroid hormones, gonadal moprhology, and xenobiotic metabolizing system. *Comparative Biochemistry and Physiology Part C: Toxicology and Pharmacology* 136(2): 145–156.

Solomon, Keith R., James A. Carr, Louis H. Du Preez, Joh P. Giesy, Ronald J. Kendall, Ernest E. Smith, and Glen J. Van Der Kraak. 2008. Effects of atrazine on fish, amphibians, and aquatic reptiles: A critical review. *Critical Reviews in Toxicology* 38: 721–772.

Speck, Frank G. 1944. Catabwa games and amusements. *Primitive Man* 17: 19–28.

Speert, Harold. 1953. Circumcision of the newborn: An appraisal of its present status. *Obstetrics and Gynecology* 2(2): 164–172.

Spencer, Herbert. 1860. The social organism. *The Westminster Review* 79: 90–121.

Springer, Carolyn. 2010. *Armour and Masculinity in the Italian Renaissance*. Toronto, Canada: University of Toronto Press.

Stanner, W. E. H. 1963. On Aboriginal religion VI: Cosmos and society made correlative. *Oceania* 33(4): 239–273.

Stevenson, Walter. 1995. The rise of eunuchs in Greco-Roman antiquity. *Journal of the History of Sexuality* 5(4): 495–511.

Stoddart, D. Michael. 1990. *The Scented Ape: The Biology and Culture of Human Odour.* Cambridge: Cambridge University Press.

Stoler, Ann. 1989. Making the empire respectable: The politics of race and sexual morality in twentieth-century colonial cultures. *American Ethnologist* 16(4): 634–660.

St. Peter, Matthew, Anton Trinidad, and Michael S. Irwig. 2012. Self-castration by a transsexual woman: Financial and psychological costs; A case report. *The Journal of Sexual Medicine* 9(4): 1216–1219.

Stranne, Johan, Ulf G. H. Malmsten, Björn Areskoug, Ian Milson, Ulla Molander, and Ralph Peeker. 2012. Influence of age and changes over time on erectile dysfunction: Results from two large cross-sectional surveys 11 years apart. *Scandinavian Journal of Urology and Nephrology* 10(2012): 1–8.

Strier, Karen B. 2011. *Primate Behavioral Ecology.* Saddle River, NJ: Prentice Hall.

Stuart, Anthony John. 1999. Late Pleistocene megafaunal extinctions. In *Extinctions in Near Time.* Eds. Ross D.E. McPhee and Hans-Dieter Sues, 257–269. New York: Springer.

Stunell, Helen, Richard E. Power, Michael Floyd Jr., and David M. Quinlin. 2006. Genital self-mutiliation. *International Journal of Urology* 13(10): 1358–1360.

Sudarshan, C. Y., K. Hagaraja Rao, and S. V. Santosh. 2006. Genital self-mutilation in erectile disorder. *Indian Journal of Psychiatry* 48(1): 64–65.

Swanson, W. F., W. E. Johnson, R. C. Cambre, S. B. Citano, K. B. Quigley, D. M. Brousset, R. N. Morais, N. Moreira, S. J. O'Brien, and D. E. Wildt. 2003. Reproductive status of endemic felid species in Latin American zoos and implications for ex situ conservation. *Zoological Biology* 22: 421–441.

Symons, Donald. 1979. *The Evolution of Human Sexuality.* Oxford: Oxford University Press.

Tallmon, David A., and Lisa Hoferkamp. 2009. Long-term changes in imposex frequency in file dogwinkles, *Nucella lima G.*, and tributyltin concentrations in bay mussels. *Mytilus trossulus G. Bulletin of Environmental Contamination and Toxicology* 83(2): 235–238.

Tamaro, Janet. 2005. *So That's What They're For!: The Definitive Guide to Breastfeeding.* 3rd ed. Avon, MA: Adams Media.

Taube, Karl. 1993. *Aztec & Maya Myths.* Austin: University of Texas Press.

Tavera-Mendoza, Luz, Sylvia Ruby, Pauline Brousseau, Michel Fournier, Daniel Cyr, and David Marcogliese. 2002. Response of the amphibian tadpole (*Xenopus laevis*) to atrazine during sexual differentiation of the testis. *Environmental Toxicology and Chemistry* 21(3): 527–531.

Terborgh, John, and Ann Wilson Goldizen. 1985. On the mating system of the cooperatively breeding saddle-backed tamarin (*Saguinus fuscicollis*). *Behavioral Ecology and Sociobiology* 16: 285–299.

Tharoor, Hema. 2007. A case of genital self-mutilation in an elderly man. *Primary Care Companion to the Journal of Clinical Psychiatry* 9(5): 396–397.

Thierry, B., M. Heistermann, F. Aujard, and J. Hodges. 1996. Long-term data on basic reproductive parameters and evaluation of endocrine, morphological, and behavioral measures for monitoring reproductive status in a group of semifreeranging Tonkean macaques (*Macaca tonkeana*). *American Journal of Primatology* 39: 47–62.

Thomas, Calvin. 1996. *Male Matters: Masculinity, Anxiety, and the Male Body on the Line.* Chicago: University of Illinois Press.

Thomson, J. A., D. L. Hess, K. D. Dahl, S. A. Iliff-Sizemore, R. L. Stouffer, and D. P. Wolf. 1992. The Sulawesi crested black macaque (*Macaca nigra*) menstrual cycle: Changes in perineal tumescence and serum estradiol, progesterone, follicle-stimulating hormone, and luteinizing hormone levels. *Biological Reproduction* 46: 879–884.

Thorén, Sandra, Patrik Lindenfors, and Peter M. Kappeler. 2006. Phylogenetic analyses of dimorphism in primates: Evidence for stronger selection on canine size than body size. *American Journal of Physical Anthropology* 130: 50–59.

Thornhill, Randy, and Steven W. Gangestad. 2008. *The Evolutionary Biology of Human Female Sexuality.* New York: Oxford University Press.

Thornhill, Randy, and Craig T. Palmer. 2000. *A Natural History of Rape: Biological Bases of Sexual Coercion.* Cambridge: MIT Press.

Toledano, Ehud R. 1984. The imperial eunuchs of Istanbul: From Africa to the heart of Islam. *Middle Eastern Studies* 20(3): 379–390.

Torrentera, Laura, and Denton Belk. 2002. New penis characters to distinguish between two American *Artemia* species. *Hydobiologia* 470: 149–156.

Træen, Bente, Kristin Spitznogle, and Alexandra Beverfjord. 2004. Attitudes and use of pornography in the Norweigian population. *Journal of Sex Research* 41(2): 193–200.

Trivers, Robert L. 1972. Parental investment and sexual selection. In *Sexual Selection and the Descent of Man: 1871–1971*, ed. Bernard G. Campbell, 136–179. Chicago: Aldine.

Tsai, Shih-Shan Henry. 1996. *The Eunuchs in the Ming Dynasty.* Albany: State University of New York Press.

Tseng, Wen-Shing, Mo Kan-Ming, Jing Hsu, Li Li-Shuen, Ou Li-Wah, Chen Guo-Qian, and Jiang Da-Wei. 1988. A sociocultural study of koro epidemics in Guangdong, China. *The American Journal of Psychiatry* 145(12): 1538–1543.

Tuana, Nancy. 2004. Coming to understand: Orgasm and the epistemology of ignorance. *Hypatia* 19(1): 194–232.

Tulpe, Irina A., and Evgeny A. Torchinov. 2000. The Castrati ("Skoptsy") sect in Russia: History, teaching, and religious practice. *The International Journal of Transpersonal Studies* 19: 77–87.

Turnbull, Colin M. 1957. Initiation among the BaMbuti pygmies of the Central Ituri. *The Journal of the Royal Institute of Great Britain and Ireland* 87(2): 191–216.

Turner, Terence. 1991. Representing, resisting, rethinking: Historical transformations of Kayapo culture and anthropological consciousness. In *Colonial Situations: Essays on the Contextualization of Ethnographic Knowledge*, ed. George W. Stocking Jr., 285–312. Madison: University of Wisconsin Press.

Turner, Terence S. 1971. Cosmetics: The language of bodily adornment. In *Conformity and Conflict: Readings in Cultural Anthropology*, ed. J. P. Spradley and D. W. McCurdy, 96–105. Boston: Little Brown.

Tüttelmann, F., and J. Gromoll. 2010. Novel genetic aspects of Klinefelter's syndrome. *Molecular and Human Reproduction* 16(6): 386–395.

Tuzin, Donald. 1984. Miraculous voices: The auditory experience of numinous objects. *Current Anthropology* 25(5): 579–596.

Tyldesley, Joyce. 1995. *Daughters of Isis: Women of Ancient Egypt*. London: Penguin Books.

Tyler, Hamilton A. 1964. *Pueblo Gods and Myths*. Norman: University of Oklahoma Press.

Ucko, Peter J. 1969. Penis sheaths: A comparative study. *Royal Institute of Great Britain and Ireland* 1969: 27–67.

Urbach, Achia, and Nissam Benvenisty. 2009. Studying early lethality of 45, X0 (Turner's Syndrome) using human embryonic stem cells. *PLoS One* 4(1):34175. Retrieved on December 7, 2012, from http://www.plosone.org.

Urban Dictionary. 2012. Retrieved on September 9, 2012, from http://www.urbandictionary.com.

Utami, Sri Suci, Benoît Goossens, Michael W. Bruford, Jan R. de Ruiter, and Jan A.R.A.M. van Hoof. 2002. Male bimaturism and reproductive success in Sumatran orangutans. *Behavioral Ecology* 13(5): 643–652.

Vale, Kayla, Thomas W. Johnson, Maren S. Jansen, B. Keith Lawson, Tucker Lieberman, K. H. Willette, and Richard J. Wassersug. 2010. The development of standards of care for individiuals with a male-to-eunuch gender identity disorder. *International Journal of Transgenderism* 12(1): 40–51.

Valeri, Valerio. 1985. *Kingship and Sacrifice: Ritual and Society in Ancient Hawaii*. Chicago: Chicago University Press.

Van Aerle, Ronny, Monique Nolanusan, Susan Jobling, Lisette B. Christiansen, John P. Sumpter, and Charles R. Tyler. 2001. Sexual disruption in a second species of wild cyprinid fish (the gudgeon *Gobio gobio*) in United Kingdom Freshwaters. *Environmental Toxicology and Chemistry* 20(12): 2841–2847.

Van Baal, J. 1963. The cult of the bull-roarer in Australia and Southern New Guinea. *Bijdragen tot de Taal-, Land-en Volkendunde* 119: 201–214.

Vance, Carole S. 2007. Anthropology Rediscovers Sexuality: A Theoretical Comment. In *Culture, Society, and Sexuality: A Reader*, ed. Richard Parker and Peter Aggleton, 41–57. New York: Routledge.

Van der Dennen, J. M. G. 2007. The origins of war. *Mankind Quarterly* 47(4): 61–104.

Vanpé, Cécile, Jean-Michel Gaillard, Peter Kellander, Atle Mysterud, Pauline

Magnien, Daniel Delorme, Guy Van Laere, François Klein, Olof Liberg, and A. J. Mark Hewison. 2007. Antler size provides an honest signal of male phenotypic quality in roe deer. *The American Naturalist* 169(4): 481–493.

Varone, Antonio. 2001. *Eroticism in Pompeii*. Los Angeles, CA: J. Paul Getty Museum.

Vicary, Grace Q. 1989. Visual art as social data: The Renaissance codpiece. *Cultural Anthropology* 4(1): 3–25.

Viganò, L., A. Arillo, S. Bottero, A. Massari, and A. Mandich. 2001. First observation of intersex cyprinids in the Po River (Italy). *Science of the Total Environment* 269: 189–194.

Volkmer, B. G., and S. Maier. 2002. Successful penile reimplantation following autoamputation: Twice! *International Journal of Impotence Research* 14: 197–198.

Von Hornbostel, E. M. 1933. The ethnology of African sound-instruments. Comments on "Geist und Werden der Musikinstrumente" by C. Sachs. *Africa: Journal of the International African Institute* 6(2): 129–157.

Wagner, Martin, and Jörg Oehlmann. 2009. Endocrine disruptors in bottled mineral water: Total estrogenic burden and migration from plastic bottles. *Environmental Science Pollution Research* 16: 278–286.

Wake, David B., and Vance T. Vredenburg. 2008. Are we in the midst of the sixth mass extinction? A view from the world of amphibians. *Proceedings of the National Academy of Sciences of the United States of America* 105(S1): S11466–S11473.

Wallis, Simon J. 1981. The behavioral repertoire of the grey-cheeked mangabey, *Cercocebus albigena johnstoni*. *Primates* 22(4): 523–532.

Ward, Captain F. Kingdon. 1921. *In Farthest Burma: The Record of an Arduous Journey of Exploration and Research Through the Unknown Frontier Territory of Burma and Tibet*. Philadelphia: J. B. Lippincott.

Washington-Williams, Essie Mae, and William Stadiem. 2005. *Dear Senator: A Memoir by the Daughter of Strom Thurmond*. New York: HarperCollins.

Wassersug, Richard, J. Sari A. Zelenietz, and G. Farrell Squire. 2004. New age eunuchs: Motivation and rationale for voluntary castration. *Archives of Sexual Behavior* 33(5): 433–442.

Waszak, Stephen J. 1978. The historic significance of circumcision. *Obstetrics and Gynecology* 51(4): 499–501.

Weatherall, D. J., and J. B. Clegg. 2001. Inherited haemoglobin disorders: An increasing global health problem. *Bulletin of the World Health Organization* 79(8): 704–712.

Weaver, Sonja. 2005. From bracelets to blowjobs: The ideological representation of childhood sexuality in the media. *McMaster Journal of Communication* 2(1): 35–49.

Weeks, John H. 1914. *Among the Primitive Bakongo: A Record of Thirty Years' Close Intercourse with the Bakongo and other Tribes of Equatorial Africa with a Description of Their Habits, Customs, and Religious Beliefs*. Philadelphia: J. B. Lippincott.

Weigel, Ronald M. 1979. The facial expressions of the brown capuchin monkey (*Cebus apella*). *Behaviour* 68(3/4): 250–276.

Weiss, Shari. 2010. Kanye West nude photos hit the web: Rapper exposes himself in leaked self-taken pictures. *New York Daily News*. Retrieved on December 1, 2012, from http://articles.nydailynews.com.

Wentz, Elisabet, I. Carina Gillberg, Henrick Anckarsater, Christopher Gillberg, and Maria Råstam. 2009. Adolescent-onset anorxia nervosa: 18-year outcome. *British Journal of Psychiatry* 194: 168–174.

Werner, Dennis. 1984. Paid sex specialists among the Mekranoti. *Journal of Anthropological Research* 40(3): 394–405.

Whistler, W. Arthur. 1984. Annotated list of Samoan plant names. *Economic Botany* 38(4): 464–489.

Whiting, John W. M., and Stephen W. Reed. 1938. Kwoma culture: Report on field work in the mandated territory of New Guinea. *Oceania* 9(2): 170–216.

Whitridge, Peter. 2004. Landscapes, houses, bodies, things: "Place" and the archaeology of Inuit imaginaries. *Journal of Archaeological Method and Theory* 11(2): 213–250.

Whitsett, J. M., Patricia F. Noden, J. Cherry, and A. D. Lawton. 1984. Effect of transitional photoperiods on testicular development and puberty in male deer mice (*Peromyscus maniculatus*). *Journal of Reproduction and Fertility* 72: 277–286.

Wiber, Melanie G. 1997. *Erect Men/Undulating Women: The Visual Imagery of Gender, Race, and Progress in Reconstructive Illustrations of Human Evolution*. Waterloo, Ont: Wilfrid Laurier University Press.

Wikipedia contributors. 2014. Ashvamedha. *Wikipedia, The Free Encyclopedia*. Retrieved on December 26, 2014, from http://en.wikipedia.org.

———. 2012. Kanamara Matsuri. *Wikipedia, The Free Encyclopedia*. Retrieved on October 25, 2012, from http://en.wikipedia.org.

Wild, Stephen A. 1977. Men as women: Female dance symbolism in Walbiri men's rituals. *Dance Research Journal* 10(1): 14–22.

Williams, George C. 1957. Pleiotropy, natural selection, and the evolution of senescence. *Evolution* 11(4): 398–411.

Wilson, Edward O. 1992. *The Diversity of Life*. Cambridge, MA: : Harvard University Press.

———. 2000. *Sociobiology: The New Synthesis*. Cambridge, MA: Harvard University Press.

Wilson, Edward O., and Robert H. MacArthur. 1967. *The Theory of Island Biogeography*. Princeton, NJ: Princeton University Press.

Wilson, Peter J. 1975. The promising primate. *Man* 10(1): 5–20.

Wilson-Haffenden, J. R. 1930. Initiation ceremonies in Northern Nigeria. *Journal of the Royal African Society* 29(116): 370–375.

———. 1927. Ethnological notes on the Kwottos of Toto (Panda) District, Keffi Division, Benue Province, Northern Nigeria: Part II. *Journal of the Royal African Society* 27(105): 24–46.

Winston, George T. 1901. The relation of the whites to the negroes. *Annals of the American Academy of Political and Social Science* 18: 105–118.

Wise, Jacqui. 2010. UK supermarket is granted license to sell Viagra to reduce Internet sales. *British Medical Journal* 341: c5294.

Wong, Gane Ka-Shu, Bin Liu, Jun Wang, Xu Yang, Zengjin Zhang, Qingshun Meng, Jun Zhou, Dawei Li, Jingjing Zhang, Peixiang Ni, Songgang Li, Longhua Ran, Heng Li, Jianguo Zhang, Ruiqiang Li, Shengting Li, Hongkun Zheng, Wei Lin, and Guangyuang Li. 2004. A genetic variation map for chicken with 2.8 million single-nucleotide polymorphisms. *Nature* 432(7018): 717–722.

Woodling, John D., Elena M. Lopez, Tammy A. Maldonado, David O. Norris, and Alan M. Vajda. 2006. Intersex and other reproductive disruption of fish in wastewater effluent dominated Colorado streams. *Comparative Biochemistry and Physiology Part C: Toxicology and Pharmacology* 144(1): 10–15.

World Penis Average Size Database. 2012. Retrieved on October 15, 2012, from http://www.everyoneweb.com

Worms, Ernest Ailred. 1950. Djamar, the Creator: A myth of the Bād. *Anthropos* 45: 641–658.

Wrangham, Richard W. 1993. The evolution of sexuality in chimpanzees and bonobos. *Human Nature* 4(1): 47–79.

Wrangham, Richard W., and Luke Glowaki. 2012. Intergroup aggression in chimpanzees and war in nomadic hunter-gatherers: Evaluating the chimpanzee model. *Human Nature* 23(1): 5–29.

Wrangham, Richard W., and Dale Peterson. 1996. *Demonic Males: Apes and the Origin of Human Violence.* Boston: Houghton Mifflin.

Wright, Rita P. 2009. *The Ancient Indus: Urbanism, Economy, and Society.* Cambridge: Cambridge University Press.

Wright, Robin M., and Jonathan D. Hill. 1986. History, ritual, and myth: Nineteenth-century millenarian movements in the Northwest Amazon. *Ethnohistory* 33(1): 31–54.

Wu, Jing-Ying, Pei-Jie Meng, Ming-Yie Liu, Yuh-Wen Chiu, and Li-Lian Liu. 2010. A high incidence of imposex in *Pomacea* apple snails in Taiwan: A decade after triphenyltin was banned. *Zoological Studies* 49(1): 85–93.

Wysowski, Diane K., and Joslyn Swann. 2003. Use of medications for erectile dysfunction in the United States, 1996–2001. *The Journal of Urology* 169(3): 1040–1042.

Wylie, Kevan R., and Ian Eardley. 2007. Penile size and the 'small penis syndrome.' *British Journal of Urology International* 99(6): 1449–1455.

Yamane, Takashi, and Takahisa Miyatake. 2010. Inhibition of female mating receptivity by male-derived extracts in two *Callosobruchus* species: Consequences for interspecific mating. *Journal of Insect Physiology* 56(11): 1565–1571.

Yap, P. M. 1965. Koro: A culture-bound depersonalization syndrome. *British Journal of Psychiatry* 111: 43–49.

Yeager, Carey P. 2005. Proboscis monkey (*Nasalis larvatus*) social organization: Nature and possible functions of intergroup patterns of association. *American Journal of Primatology* 26(2): 133–137.

———. 1992. Probocis monkey (*Nasalis larvatus*) social organization: Nature and possible functions of intergroup patterns of association. *American Journal of Primatology* 26(2): 133–137.

Yuan, J., A. N. Hoang, C. A. Romero, Y. Dai, and R. Wang. 2010. Vacuum therapy in erectile dysfunction: Science and clinical evidence. *International Journal of Impotence Research* 22: 211–219.

Yusuf, A. J., A. Bello, M. L. Abubakar, and N. H. Mbibu. 2009. Genital self-mutiliation in schizophrenic patients: A report of two patients. *African Journal of Urology* 15(3): 189–191.

Zahavi, Amotz. 1975. Mate selection: A selection for handicap. *Journal of Theoretical Biology* 53: 205–214.

Zamma, Koichiro, and Shiho Fujita. 2004. Genito-genital rubbing among the chimpanzees of Mahale and Bossou. *Pan African News* 11: 5–8.

Zastrow, Charles. 2010. *Introduction to Social Work and Social Welfare: Empowering People*. 10th ed. Bedmont, CA: Brooks/Cole, Cengage Learning.

Zaviačic, M., V. Jakubovská, M. Belošovič, and J. Breza. 2000. Ultrastructure of the normal adult human female prostate gland (Skene's gland). *Anatomy and Embryology* 201(1): 51–61.

Zias, Nikolaos, Vishnu Bezwada, Sean Gilman, and Alexandra Chroneou. 2009. Obstructive sleep apnea and erectile dysfunction: Still a neglected risk factor? *Sleep Breath* 13:3–10.

Zihlman, Adrienne L. 1981. Woman as shapers of the human adaptation. In *Woman the Gatherer*, ed. Frances Dalhberg, 75–120. New Haven, CT: Yale University Press.

Zucker, Kenneth J. 2005. Gender identity disorder in children and adolescents. *Annual Review of Clinical Psychology* 1: 467–492.

Index

o sheathing

Holloway, Natalee, 128

Holmes, John, 133

homosexuality, 4, 93, 104, 113, 120, 121, 138. *See also* same-sex relations

Hopi people, 97, 120

hormone therapy, 140

Hornbostel, Reich von, 92

horse, 11, 70, 110, 160n122

Horus, 57

horticulture, 80, 88. *See also* agriculture

House of Phalli, Uxmal, 84

HRAF (Human Relations Area Files), 28, 113

Huangdi Neiching (medical text), 106

hunter-gatherers/hunting and gathering, 4, 5, 8, 26, 28, 37, 38, 45, 46, 49, 52, 91, 96, 147, 151n16

hunting hypothesis, 37–38, 40

Hurricane Katrina, 4

Hurston, Zora Neale, 119

Hutton, Ronald, 110

hydraulic hypothesis, 22

Hylobatidae. See gibbon; siamang

hypermasculinity, 60, 66, 86

hypersexuality, 107, 122, 127, 129, 131

Icarus, 59

Idoma people, 96

Ifill, Gwen, 128

ijara. See hijra

Ilahita Arapesh people, 94

Ilechukwu, Sunny, 106

imposex, 146

impotence, 75, 123, 138

Inca people, ancient, 53

increase ceremony, 98

India, 14, 67, 68–71, 73, 76, 78,
79, 106, 138, 139, 159n93

Indus Valley, 47, 67–73, 86, 159n84

Inis Beag people, 122

Inquisition, 106

insect, 3, 11, 13, 19. *See also* beetle; mosquito; praying mantis

insulin resistence, 144

internet, 136

intersexuality, 143

Introduction to Social Work and Social Welfare, 122

Inuit people, 97, 129, 142

Iraq, 128

Irigaray, Luce, 14–15, 22

Iron Age, 58, 109, 110

Isis, 57, 58, 158n52

Island of Menstruating Men, 105

Is There Anything Good About Men?, 32

Italy, 56, 58, 64–66, 108, 138, 143, 157n25. *See also* Roman people, ancient

Ivory Coast, 106, 121

Izanagi, 74

Izanami, 74

Jackson, Janet, 114

Jackson, Michael, 145

James, E. L., 133

Japan, 73, 74–76

Japanese people, ancient, 74–76

jaqui flute dance, 98

Jefferson, Thomas, 127

Johnson, Shoshona, 128

Johnson, Virginia, 14, 125, 126

Judaism, 103, 104

Jung, Carl, 91

Ju/'hoan people, 96

Kadera people, 96

Kagwihiv people, 101

Kalahari Desert, southern Africa, 97

Kaliai people, 94, 95, 104

polyandry: human, 25–29, 35; non-human primate, 24–26
polygyny: human, 25–29, 31, 38, 39; nonhuman primate, 24, 25
Polynesia, 80, 81, 104, 161n162
Pomo people, 97
Pompeii site, Italy, 59, 61–63, 159n79
Ponape people. *See* Pohnpei people
Pongo spp. *See* orangutan
pornography, 120, 133; mommy porn, 133
Powell, Michael, 115
praying mantis, 11
Priapus divinity, 58, 59
Primate Sexuality, 24
proboscis monkey, 11
prolactin, 144
prosimian, 19, 24
prostitution, 3, 124
protofarming, 49
psychic unity, 90–91, 92
psychosis, 139, 145
Ptolemy II Philadelphus, 60
Pueblo people, 97
Pulitzer Prize, 124
Puma spp. *See* feline

Quaternary period, 50
Quetzalcoatl, 82–83

Race, Evolution, and Behavior, 125
raitsui stone phalluses, 75
Ramadan, 106
Rana spp. *See* frog: green, leopard
rape, 3, 35, 40–42, 43, 94, 98, 116, 127, 128
Rappahannock people, 97
Rattus spp. *See* rodent
Ratzel, Frienrich, 96
Ray J. (William Ray Norwood Jr.), 117
Reagan, Ronald, 135
referential modeling, 37
Reign of the Phallus, 124

Reisman, Judith, 119–120
Renaissance, 64, 66, 101–103
reproductive crypsis. *See* concealed ovulation
reptile: alligator, 142; turtle, 85, 95, 105
Rigveda, 70
rite of passage, 104, 138
ritual penis modification complex, 89, 102–105. *See also* castration; circumcision; subincision
Rivers, Joan, 145
Robertson, Pat, 4
rock art, 90, 100, 110
rodent, 19, 21; mouse, 139; rat, 144
Romano-British Age, 109
Roman people, ancient, 47, 58, 61–62, 64, 103, 109, 137
Rourke, Mickey, 145
Rushton, J. Philippe, 125–126, 129, 170n57
Russia, 138, 139
Rutilus rutilus. *See* fish: roach fish

Saimiri spp. *See* squirrel monkey
Saint Peter's Square, Vatican City, 65
Saguinus spp. *See* tamarin
same-sex relations, 3, 10. *See also* homosexuality
Samoan people, 104
Sanskrit, 70
Sapajus spp. *See* capuchin
Saqqara site, Egypt, 103
Satan, 115. *See also* Devil's penis
Saturday Night Live, 1, 116
satyr, 59, 60, 108
Sayre, Lewis A., 104
schizophrenogenic mother, 122
Schlafly, Phyllis, 114–115
segregation, racial, 127
Selako people, 104
selection, 19, 24, 36, 147, 149; agonistic

sexual selection, 12; artificial
selection, 50, 141; cryptic, 9, 36;
intersexual, 10, 11, 17, 20; intrasexual, 10, 11, 17; natural, 10–13,
50; runaway, 152n8; sexual, 8,
10–13, 18, 21, 40; "unnatural"
141–144. *See also* female choice
semen, 23, 26–27, 55, 56, 144; semen displacement device, 23. *See also* sperm
Senegal, 106
Seri people, 97
Serrano people, 97
Seth, 57
Sex and Friendship in Baboons, 33
sex change, 132, 140. *See also* sexual reassignment surgery
sex offender, 138
sex reversal in fish, 132
sexual cannibalism, 11
sexual dimorphism, 11
sexual dysfunction, 135–137
Sexual Practices, 123
sexual reassignment surgery, 7, 8,
139–141; female to male (ftm),
140; male to eunuch (mte), 141;
male to female (mtf), 140
sexual swellings, 9, 36–38, 39,
155n122. *See also* estrus/estrous
sex versus gender, 139–140
Shakti, 68
shaman, 97–99; *ruwang* shaman, 98
Shavante people, 101
sheep, 3, 5, 55, 57, 61, 67, 160n122
Sheets-Johnson, Maxine, 21
Sherente people, 98
Shintoism, 72–75
Shiva, 68–73; Shiva Pasupati, 67
siamang, 25, 26
sickle-cell trait, 13
sigi ceremony, 96
Sinkyone people, 97

Skene's paraurethral glands, 14
Skoptsky Christian sect. *See* Christianity
slavery, 5, 52, 127, 138
Slocum, Sally, 38
small penis syndrome, 134–135
Smith, Grafton Elliot, 103
Smith, Moira, 107
Smith, Susan, 124
Smuts, Barbara, 33–34, 37; 155n122
snail, 7, 142–143
sorcery, 80, 106
Sosum, supernatural being, 95
South Africa, 42, 101, 143
Southeast Asia, 67–73, 104, 106, 127,
160n106. *See also individual countries*
sperm, 12, 17, 23, 40, 81, 117, 130; sperm
competition, 36; sperm count, 7,
132; sperm quality, 142, 144
spider, 11
spider monkey, 22
squirrel monkey, 21, 34, 35, 154n72
Sterger, Jenn, 117
sterility, 50, 143
Stoler, Ann, 127–128
Stone Age, 110, 118. *See also*
Paleolithic period
stone tool, 49
subincision, 81, 88, 93, 105, 112, 132
suicide, 139
Super Bowl, 114–115
Sumatra, 99
Sumba, Indonesia, 104
Sumeria, 53–54
syncretism, 104
syphilis, 102
Syrian people, ancient, 103
Switzerland, 90

taboo, 1, 17, 18, 89, 90, 92, 93, 98,
112, 114–117, 121, 130, 131
Tahitian people, 104